MOVING TOWARDS PRODUCTIVITY AND QUALITY EXCELLENCE

MOVING TOWARDS PRODUCTIVITY AND QUALITY EXCELLENCE

FONG Ho-Keng
MBA(IS), MSc(IE), BE(HONS)

PARTRIDGE

ISBN:	Softcover	978-1-5437-4773-7
	eBook	978-1-5437-4778-2

Print information available on the last page.

To order additional copies of this book, contact
Toll Free 800 101 2657 (Singapore)
Toll Free 1 800 81 7340 (Malaysia)
orders.singapore@partridgepublishing.com

www.partridgepublishing.com/singapore

Dedicated to:

My wife Khoo Sou Hoo, my daughter Sau Wei and my son Sau Shung for their patience, understanding, support and encouragement in my pursuit towards personal excellence.

My grandmother Cheong Kwai Chee, my father Fong Kee Fatt and my mother Chan Ngan Yin for their selfless love, and for inculcating in me the life-long passion for learning, innovating and sharing.

PREFACE

Several reasons have prompted me to write this fifth book 'Moving Towards Productivity and Quality Excellence'. Firstly, there has been increasing emphasis on productivity to help transform an organization to better compete in a more globalized market. Secondly, the market is more receptive to my concept on 'The Trilogy of Productivity Gains'. In view of this, in this new book, I have enhanced the concept of productivity and its application to the organization and the society as a whole.

In Oct 2010, I was interviewed by the "Management World" magazine of the Chinese State Council Development Research Center. One question being asked was: 'While there has not been much problems in understanding and promoting productivity, why is it so difficult to achieve productivity gains?'. My answer was: 'It's easy to understand the concept of Productivity and Quality, but very often, they are also easily misunderstood when applied in practice. One needs to look at them from a holistic perspective in order to appreciate and harness the tremendous beneficial impact on the effectiveness of the organization and the efficiency of their processes'.

In April 2014, I was invited to give a talk in Shanghai China on "How to Move ahead of Competitors and Achieve Business Excellence". Having just successfully completed a HIMS (Holistic and Integrated Management System) consultancy project, I took the opportunity to share with the participants the concept of 'The Trilogy of Productivity Gains'.

In September 2014, The Straits Times of Singapore published my article on 'The Trilogy of Productivity Gains' with the title 'Productivity Goals for Organizations'. And in July 2015, my follow-up article with the title 'Better to be Effective than Efficient' was published.

To assist the reader to understand the productivity concept better, 'The Trilogy of Productivity Gains' was explained in the Productivity chapter. I have also included a few case studies to illustrate the beneficial impact of the Total Factor Productivity to an organization through the implementation of HIMS®, SDMS®, HOCI®, KOFK®, and HIMS-IRS™. The concepts of my proprietary management systems HIMS® and SDMS® were briefly explained in the Introduction chapter.

The chapters on ISO9000 Quality Management System and ISO14000 Environmental Management System were brought up to date to their 2015 versions.

In the World Class Organization Standards chapter, the Singapore Quality Award model, its criteria and excellence indicators were also updated to the latest 2017 version. A case study on 'The practical approach to moving towards Organizational Excellence' was included.

ABOUT THE AUTHOR

Mr Fong Ho Keng graduated in 1971 from the University of Malaya with a Bachelor Degree (Honours) in Mechanical Engineering. He also holds a Master of Science Degree (Industrial Engineering) from the University of Singapore, a Master in Business Administration (Information System) with Distinction, and a Diploma in Management Consultancy.

Mr. Fong Ho Keng is the Founder and CEO of the FHK Group of Companies that is in the business of management consultancy, software solutions, and property investments. He is also the principal consultant of HIMS Management & IT Consultants PL, and the developer of the proprietary pace-setting management systems of HIMS®, SDMS®, and HOCI®.

Prior to this, Mr Fong has worked in the industry for many years holding various engineering and senior management positions. He was the Managing Director of an engineering company. And concurrently, as Executive Director, he was also involved in the management of its associated companies that were in the business of property development, housing construction, trading and export. He has also worked in a tertiary institution as Principal Lecturer and the Director of Organisational Excellence Office.

Mr. Fong has been actively involved in the Productivity and Quality movement since 1985. And since then, he has facilitated a few hundred quality improvement projects, including more than a hundred projects with Motorola Singapore, saving the company millions of dollars in operational costs. His contributions have won him the "Outstanding QC Facilitator of the year" in 1995 and the "Outstanding WITS Facilitator of the Year" in 1996 and 1998. In 1998, he was invited by Prentice Hall to author his first book entitled "Productivity and Quality Studies – House of Continuous Improvement (HOCI®)".

From January 1999 to December 2003, as Director of Organisational Excellence (OE) in a tertiary institution, Mr Fong was responsible for spearheading his organization's journey towards organizational excellence. Under his stewardship, the OE Office initiated and successfully implemented some pace-setting management systems, which included the Strategic Deployment Management System, Integrated Balanced Scorecard, Best Practices Management System, Customer Satisfaction Value Chain, and a Totally Integrated Management System. The organization was awarded Singapore Quality Class in June 1999, ISO9001:2000 certification in March 2001 and the Public Service Award for Organisational Excellence in July 2001. In 2001, Mr Fong was awarded the "Outstanding QC Manager of the Year", and in 2003, he was appointed by PSCOE (The Public Service Centre for Organizational Excellence) as the subject matter expert in "Strategy Formulation and Implementation".

In 2000, Mr Fong authored his second book "Moving towards Quality Excellence". The second edition with the incorporation of the Strategic Deployment Management System (SDMS®) was published in January 2002, and the third edition with the incorporation of Holistic and Integrated Management System (HIMS®) was published in January 2010. His latest book "Moving towards Productivity and Quality Excellence", with more emphasis on total factor productivity and case studies, was published in 2017 in Chinese version and in 2018 in English version.

Since 2001, Mr Fong has been sharing his experiences in organizational excellence and his pace-setting management systems with thousands of participants in Singapore, and overseas, through talks, training and consultancy services. His training and consultancy clients include Asian Productivity Organization, Best Practices Search Pte Ltd, Castrol (Far East) Ltd, CitiBank Singapore, Civil Service College (Singapore), Colombo Plan Bureau, DHL International (S) Pte Ltd, Evergreen Group, Government Ministries and Agencies, Innox Asia, Lasalle-SIA College of the Arts, Lucent Technologies Pte Ltd, Merchant Court Hotel, Motorola (Tianjing, China), National Productivity Centre (Malaysia), Raffles Hotel, Sakti Suria Group, Singapore Health Services Pte Ltd, Singapore Productivity Association, Singapore Productivity and Standard Board, SI Management Consultants (Thailand), UNI-LINK Smart Venture Sdn Bhd and Wonton Food Inc (USA). Recently, he has successfully penetrated the tough China market.

In 2001, Mr Fong initiated and successfully implemented his pilot SDMS Software Solutions. In 2011, Mr Fong developed the first version of HIMS® software solutions, and in March 2013, the second version of the HIMS® Software Solutions was successfully completed. In October 2014, the latest "HIMS-BEST Business Excellence Software Solutions" was introduced at the

Asia Cloud Expo. In October 2017, the web based HIMS-BEST Business Excellence Software Solutions version 2 was successfully implemented and put into the cloud.

In view of his contribution in the quality and productivity movement and the development of some proprietary pace-setting management systems, Mr Fong was awarded the "World Outstanding Chinese Innovative Person (世界杰出华人创新人物)" in 2010 in Beijing, China, and the "World Top Ten Outstanding Enterprise Leader (全球杰出领军人物奖)" in 2011 again in Beijing, China. In 2012, he was recognized as "Leading Asia's Think Tanks (引领亚洲智库)" in the interview by the "Management World Press" of the China State Council Development Research Centre. His recognition was confirmed through the interview by the Hong Kong TV (HKS) in the program on "Revelation of Business Roadmap - Leading Asia's Think Tanks (商道启示录 - 引领亚洲智库)" in 2013.

On 9th of September 2013 at the 8th Asia Brand Award Ceremony in Hong Kong, Mr Fong and his companies were honoured with three awards: "Top 500 Asia Brand Award (亚洲品牌500强)" for FHK Group of Companies, "Asia Famous Brand Award (亚洲名优品牌奖)" for HIMS Management Consultants LLP, and "Asia Brand Excellent Manager Award (亚洲品牌管理优秀人物奖)" for Fong Ho Keng.

In 2014, Mr Fong was invited by the China State Council Development Research Centre to be included in the "World Chinese Entrepreneur Hall of Fame (全球华商名人堂)".

CONTENTS

Preface vii

About The Author ix

Introduction 1

1.1 World Class Organization Standards 1
1.2 Approaches to Achieving World Class Organization Standards 2
1.3 House of Continuous Improvement (HOCI®) 3
1.4 Moving towards Productivity and Quality Excellence 8
1.5 Strategic Deployment Management System (SDMS®) 10
1.6 Holistic and Integrated Management System (HIMS®) 12
1.7 Business Excellence Software Solutions (HIMS-BEST™) 13
1.8 The Trilogy of Moving Towards Business Excellence 14

Productivity 15

2.1 Definition of Productivity 15
2.2 Productivity and Production 17
2.3 Examples of Productivity of the Various Resources 18
2.4 Measurement of Productivity 19
2.5 Total Factor Productivity (TFP) 21
2.6 Value Added and Productivity 23
2.7 Productivity and Quality 30
2.8 The Trilogy of Productivity Gains 32
2.9 Case Study on Productivity Gains 33

Quality 36

3.1 The Evolution of Quality Concepts 36
3.2 Some Fundamental Quality Concepts 38
3.3 Quality Principles and Philosophy 40

3.4 The Eight Dimensions of Quality 41
3.5 Cost of Quality 43
3.6 Service Quality 48

The 5S Housekeeping And 8 Wastes 57

4.1 5S Housekeeping 57
4.2 SEIRI (Organization) 57
4.3 SEITON (Neatness) 58
4.4 SEISO (Cleaning) 59
4.5 SEIKETSU (Standardization) 59
4.6 SHISUKE (Discipline) 60
4.7 8 Wastes 61

Quality Circles 63

5.1. Introduction 63
5.2. Plan-Do-Check-Action (PDCA) Cycle 66
5.3. Theme Selection 69
5.4. Plan Schedule 74
5.5. Establish Present Status 76
5.6. Set Target 88
5.7. Analyze and Determine Problem 90
5.8. Plan Solution 100
5.9. Implement Plan and Evaluate Results 106
5.10. Standardization and Review 109
5.11. Self-Evaluation 110
5.12. Future Project Selection 113
5.13. Conclusion 113

Six Sigma 115

6.1 Background of Six Sigma (6σ) 115
6.2 What is Six Sigma? 115
6.3 Sigma and PPM (Parts per Million) 116
6.4 μ with 1.5σ Shift 119
6.5 Why Embark on Six Sigma? 120
6.6 Six Sigma Strategy 120
6.7 Six Sigma Organisation 121
6.8 The DMAIC Implementation Process 123
6.9 Process Design / Redesign 132

Benchmarking....134

7.1 Introduction....134
7.2 Definition....135
7.3 Types of Benchmarking....135
7.4 Benchmarking Process....137
7.5 The Benchmarking Code of Conduct....141

Total Quality Management (TQM)....144

8.1 Evolution of Quality System....144
8.2 Background Knowledge....145
8.3 Introduction to Total Quality Management....147
8.4 Four Key Elements of Total Quality Management....148
8.5 TQM Implementation....149
8.6 TQM Implementation Model....153

Total Productive Maintenance (TPM)....154

9.1 Introduction....154
9.2 Definition....154
9.3 Six Aims of TPM....155
9.4 Scope of TPM Activities....155
9.5 Eliminating Equipment Losses....156
9.6 Measurement of Equipment Effectiveness....157
9.7 Case Study for Discussion....159

ISO 9000 Quality Management System....161

10.1 Introduction....161
10.2 ISO 9000:1994 Quality Management System....162
10.3 ISO 9000:2000 Quality Management System....163
10.4 ISO 9001:2000/08 Quality Management System Model....168
10.5 ISO 9001:2000/08 Quality Management System Structure....168
10.6 Changes in ISO 9001:2008 Quality Management System....169
10.7 ISO9001:2008 Quality Management System....170
10.8 From ISO9001:2008 to ISO9001:2015....188
10.9 ISO9001:2015 Quality Management System....191

ISO 14000 Environmental Management System....200

11.1 Introduction....200

11.2 Overview of ISO 14000 Standards 200
11.3 Environmental Risk and Sustainable Development 201
11.4 Development of ISO 14000 Standards 202
11.5 ISO 14000 Series 203
11.6 ISO 14000 EMS Principles 203
11.7 ISO 14001 Environmental Management System (EMS) 204
11.8 Benefits of an Effective ISO 14001 EMS 211
11.9 Relationship between ISO 14000 and ISO 9000 211
11.10 ISO 14001:2015 Environmental Management System 212

World-Class Organization Standards 229

12.1 USA National Quality Award Model 229
12.2 European EFQM Excellence Model 230
12.3 Japanese Deming Prize Model 230
12.4 Singapore Quality Award Model 231
12.5 Comparison of World-Class Organization Standards 232
12.6 Singapore Quality Award (SQA) 233
12.7 The SQA Criteria: Excellence Indicators 239
12.8 The SQA Scoring System 245
12.9 The 2017 Business Excellence Framework 249
12.10 Case Study 265

Acknowledgement 269

1

INTRODUCTION

1.1 World Class Organization Standards

i) The USA Malcolm Baldridge National Quality Award

The Malcolm Baldrige National Quality Award was created by Public Law 100-107, and signed into law on August 20, 1987. The Award Program, responsive to the purposes of Public Law 100-107, led to the creation of a new public-private partnership. Principal support for the program comes from the Foundation for the Malcolm Baldrige National Quality Award, established in 1988.

One of the purposes in establishing this national quality award program is to help improve quality and productivity by:

a) helping to stimulate American companies to improve quality and productivity for the pride of recognition while obtaining a competitive edge through increased profits;
b) recognizing the achievements of those companies that improve the quality of their goods and services and providing an example to others;
c) establishing guidelines and criteria that can be used by business, industrial, governmental, and other organizations in evaluating their own quality improvement efforts; and
d) providing specific guidance for other American organizations that wish to learn how to manage for high quality by making available detailed information on how winning organizations were able to change their cultures and achieve eminence.

ii) The European EFQM Excellence Model

The EFQM (European Foundation of Quality Management) Excellence Model was introduced at the beginning of 1992 as the framework for assessing organizations for the European Quality Award. It is now the most widely used organizational framework in Europe and it has become the basis for the majority of national and regional Quality Awards.

iii) The Japanese Deming Prize

The Deming Prize is one of the highest awards in TQM (Total Quality Management) in the world. It was established in 1951 in commemoration of the late Dr W E Deming who contributed greatly to Japan's proliferation of statistical quality control after the World War II. His teachings helped Japan product quality build its function by which the level of Japanese product quality has been recognized as the highest in the world.

iv) Singapore Quality Award (SQA)

SQA signifies the pinnacle of Quality Excellence in the Singapore context. It also embraces the world-class status as it is developed basing primarily on the American, Japanese and European Quality Award criteria. The aim of SQA is to establish Singapore as a country totally committed to Quality Excellence.

1.2 Approaches to Achieving World Class Organization Standards

i) Holistic Approach

This approach provides management with a bird's eye view of the planning, operation and performance of the whole organization. It will ensure effective implementation of the organization corporate goals and strategic thrusts.

ii) Integrated Approach

Organization implements various systems to facilitate implementation of different initiatives and processes. This approach will encourage implementation and management synergy of the various systems. It will also ensure minimum duplications and wastes in the implementation and execution of the systems, initiatives and processes.

iii) Systemic Approach

Management strategies, systems, initiatives and processes run across the whole organization vertically and horizontally. This approach will ensure organization mission, vision, corporate goals and strategic thrusts are deployed to all functions and all staff of the organization. Conversely, all initiatives and processes of all functions are aligned to the strategic goals and thrusts of the organization.

1.3 House of Continuous Improvement (HOCI®)

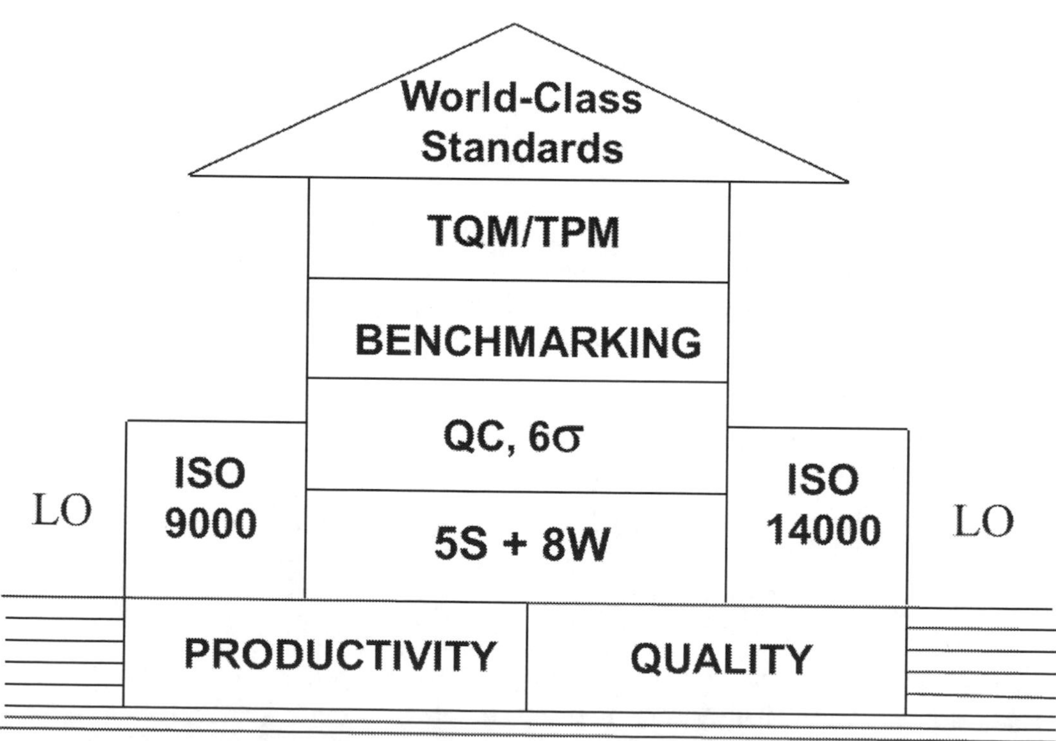

House of Continuous Improvement (HOCI®) is a continuous improvement management system that could be used by an organization in their pursuit towards productivity and quality excellence based on world-class organization standards.

HOCI® has been integrated into HIMS® (Holistic Integrated Management System) and become one of its key pillars. HIMS® is a holistic and integrated management system that could be used in assisting organization achieve organizational goals, mission and vision. HIMS® and HOCI® are trademarks registered and owned by HIMS Management Consultants LLP.

i) World Class Organization Standards

Generally, World Class Organization Standards can be classified under seven categories; i.e., Leadership, Planning, Information, People, Process, Customer, and Results. An organization can use the criteria under each of the seven categories to assess and identify its strengths and areas for improvement. Scores or points can be allotted to each criterion to identify its achievement in the level of excellence. The aggregate of the scores of all the seven criteria will give an indication of the status of the organization in the organizational excellence yardstick. For example, in the case of SQA standard, if an organization scores 700 points and above, it will be awarded a SQA (Singapore Quality Award); and if the score is above 400, it will be awarded a SQC (Singapore Quality Class).

ii) Total Quality Management (TQM)

TQM is a management approach to long-term success through customer satisfaction. It is based on the participation of all members of an organization to excel in all dimensions of products and services that are important to the customer. The four key elements of TQM are:

- o Total Quality is Customer Driven,
- o Total Quality is Continuous Improvement,
- o Total Quality is Total Involvement, and
- o Total Quality is Societal Networking.

iii) Total Productive Maintenance (TPM)

TPM is designed to maximize equipment effectiveness (improving overall efficiency) by establishing a comprehensive Productive Maintenance System covering the entire life of the equipment, spanning all equipment-related fields (planning, use, maintenance, and disposal) and with the participation of all employees from top management down to shop-floor workers, to promote Productive Maintenance through voluntary small-group activities.

iv) Benchmarking

Benchmarking is an improvement process in which a company measures its performance against that of best-in-class companies, determines how those companies achieved their performance levels, and uses the information to improve its own performance. The subjects that can be benchmarked include strategies, operations, processes, and procedures.

v) Quality Circles (QC), Six Sigma (6σ), Staff Suggestion Scheme (SSS), and other problem-solving techniques

a) Quality Circles (QC)

A Quality Circle is a small group of employees that meet regularly on a voluntary basis to solve problems concerning their work and workplace. Members of the circle normally come from the same section and perform similar or related tasks.

The concept of QC has now expanded to include Quality Improvement Team (QIT), and Cross-functional Team (CFT). Quality Improvement Team is a form of QC that will dissolve after completion of the project, and Cross-functional Team is one that comprises members coming from different functional areas.

b) Six Sigma (6σ)

Six Sigma is a management philosophy that attempts to improve customer satisfaction to near perfection. It is a measure of quality and efficiency, but furthermore, it is a measure of excellence. For an organisation to embark on a 6σ program means delivering top quality service and product, while at the same time virtually eliminating all internal inefficiencies. It means having a common focus on excellence throughout the whole organisation.

c) Staff Suggestion Scheme (SSS)

Staff Suggestion Scheme is a formalized system through which employees can channel their ideas for workplace improvement. The improvement ideas can come from an individual, or the outcome of a team brainstorming session. No systematic and elaborate analysis, like QC, is required to substantiate the improvement ideas.

d) Other Problem-Solving Techniques

Other problem-solving techniques include quality function deployment (QFD), task force, focus group, etc.

vi) 5S Housekeeping and 8 Wastes (5S + 8W)

a) 5S Housekeeping

The 5S refer to the five Japanese words of seiri, seiton, seiso, seiketsu and shitsuke. They are the five keys to a Total Quality Environment.

If every worker practices the 5S, the result is a disciplined workplace that could be used as a platform for elimination of wastes and continuous improvement.

b) 8 Wastes

Waste is defined as any activity that does not add value. Toyota Motors has classified waste into seven (7) categories, i.e., over-production, defects, waiting/delay, inventory/work-in-process, transport, process, and motion.

The author suggests that "inspection" can be considered the eight-waste, as it also does not add any value to the process/product.

vii) Productivity

Productivity is measured as the ratio of output to input. Measures can be characterized as Partial Productivity and Total Productivity measures. The ultimate indicator of an organization's effectiveness in addressing productivity is Total Productivity measure. In terms of national measurement, while GDP per employee, which is a Partial Productivity measure, is more popularly used, Total Factor Productivity (TFP) Growth is a more comprehensive measure, as it captures all the qualitative improvements after accounting for the contributions of labor and capital growth. At the factory level, value added concept is frequently used to measure its productivity.

viii) Quality

The concept of Quality has been evolving since it was defined as "conformance to specification" in the 50s. The concept of "customer satisfaction" came in the 60s; and in the 70s, "fitness to cost" was introduced. Since then, "fitness to latent requirement or customer delight" is commonly used to define quality. While the concept of Quality began with product quality, it has since been expanded to include service quality. Today, organization focuses on customer loyalty and customer retention, in addition to delighting the customer.

ix) ISO9000 Quality Management System

ISO 9000 standards set the basic rules for a Quality Management System (QMS), from conception to implementation. They provide guidelines and spell out the requirements of a QMS, and determine the key elements of such a system.

ISO 9000 standards are not product standards but QMS standards. They are generic in applications. Besides manufacturing, they have been applied to service industries such as banks, transport, construction, information technology companies and educational institutions.

x) ISO14000 Environment Management System

ISO 14000 is an Environmental Management System (EMS) standard. The overall aim of the ISO 1400 standard is to support environmental protection and prevention of pollution in balance with socio-economic needs.

An EMS provides the framework for an organization to examine issues such as the allocation of resources, assignment of responsibilities and on-going evaluation of practices, procedures and processes systematically, and to achieve continuous improvement in environmental performance through effective management of their environmental impacts.

xi) Learning Organization (LO)

Knowledge is fast being recognized as the primary resource for many of today's organizations. Increasingly, organization success depends on the capacity to acquire, extend, apply and exploit knowledge.

1.4 Moving towards Productivity and Quality Excellence

HOCI® is a continuous improvement management system that can be used for continuous improvement and moving an organization towards productivity and quality excellence. To ensure effective implementation of the system, organizations need to adopt a two-pronged approach – a top-down commitment and a bottom-up involvement approach.

The top-down approach requires the management to commit and drive the organization with World Class Organization Standards. The standards will provide the organization with a holistic and long-range direction, and supporting corporate guidelines and yardstick. Total Quality Management and Total Productive Maintenance can then be used to reinforce its management philosophies, corporate values and implementation policies. Once the organization systems, initiatives and processes are optimized, the management can use the ISO Quality and Environmental Management Systems to standardize their procedures. The outcome is the organization will be provided with a platform and direction for moving towards productivity and quality excellence.

Employees must respond bottom-up through involving in continuous improvement programs using the various problem-solving tools and techniques, such as Benchmarking, Quality Circles, and Six Sigma. To ensure effective implementation of these continuous improvement programs, a good understanding of the concepts of productivity and quality and 5S&8W is imperative. Continuous improvement will include continuous learning. Management must build a learning environment in the organization to encourage employees in taking up training and development programs.

Management can adopt the following steps in moving its organization towards productivity and quality excellence.

i) Use World Class Organization Standards to determine its present status, identify its strengths and areas for improvement, and chart its direction in moving towards productivity and quality excellence. The most critical task here is for the management to deploy the organizational mission, vision, corporate goals and strategic thrusts to all functions and all levels of its employees. One proven and effective system is the Strategic Deployment Management System (SDMS®). SDMS® is a trademark registered and owned by HIMS Management Consultants LLP.

ii) Use TQM/TPM as a change force for attaining its competitive advantages and a strategy in achieving productivity and quality excellence. This provides the top-down total-approach policies and methodologies for all employees to move towards productivity and quality excellence.

iii) Understand the concepts of productivity and quality, which form the foundation of the House of Continuous Improvement (HOCI®). Select the appropriate concepts, methodologies, and formulae and apply them to improve productivity and quality.

iv) Use the 5S Housekeeping concept to improve the working environment. Identify the eight Wastes and use them as a basis for continuous improvement. Set a timeframe to reduce or eliminate them.

v) Form Quality Circles to identify the areas for improvement, analyze them and solve the problems using PDCA Cycle methodology. Use other problem solving techniques such as 6s, SSS, Benchmarking, QFD, focus group, etc to supplement and enhance your continuous improvement programs.

vi) Step (iii), (iv) and (v) provide the organization a solid foundation and bottom-up approach to identifying and solving critical problems. The outcome will have significant positive impact on its journey towards productivity and quality excellence.

vii) Expand the scope of areas for improvement to all equipments, and across their whole life span through Total Productive Maintenance.

viii) Use ISO9000 Quality Management System and ISO14000 Environment Management System to standardize the procedures of the optimized systems and processes and comply with them for continuous improvement.

ix) To add value, all employees, through effective learning, should utilize the new information and knowledge acquired to better plan and predict, and to improve the problem analysis and solving processes for continuous improvement.

1.5 Strategic Deployment Management System (SDMS®)

i) SDMS® Analytical Model

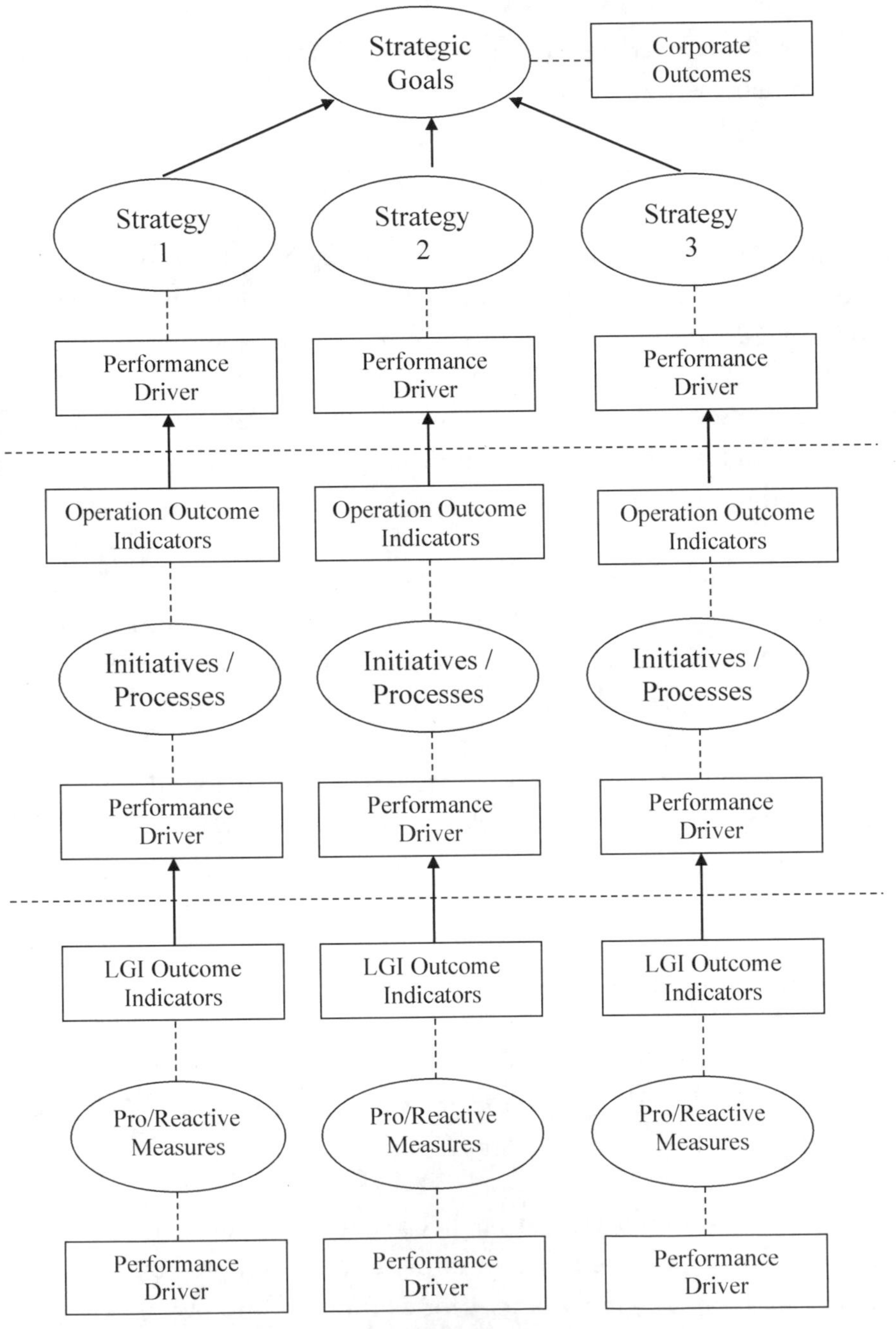

ii) Strategic Deployment Management System (SDMS®)

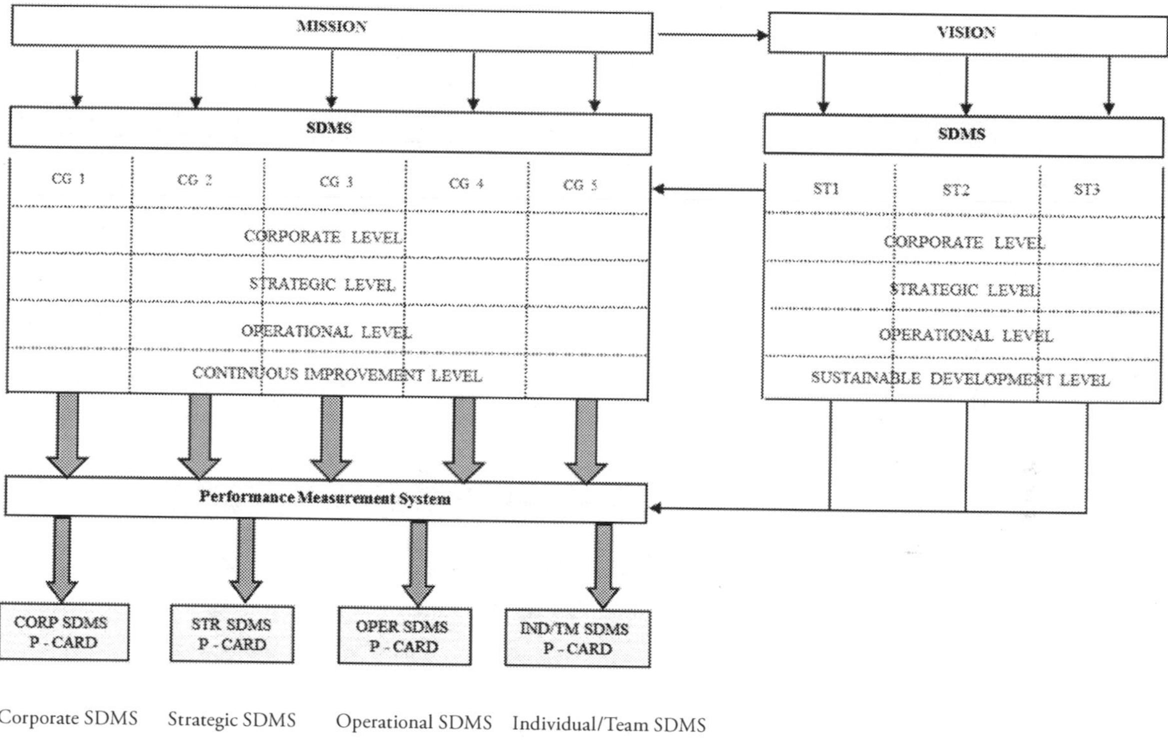

Corporate SDMS Performance Card	Strategic SDMS Performance Card	Operational SDMS Performance Card	Individual/Team SDMS Performance Cards

Strategic Deployment Management System (SDMS®) is a holistic management system that could be used to assist organization in first translating its mission into organizational goals at the corporate level, and then cascading them into strategic goals at the strategic level and key processes at the operational level. Similarly, its vision is first translated into strategic thrusts which are then cascaded into strategic goals and key initiatives at their respective levels. SDMS Performance Cards (SDMS-PC®) are established for all goals at all levels for continuous improvement and sustainable development.

SDMS® has been integrated into HIMS® (Holistic Integrated Management System) and become one of its key pillars. HIMS® is a holistic and integrated management system that could be used in assisting organization achieve organizational goals, mission and vision. HIMS®, SDMS® and SDMS-PC® are trademarks registered and owned by HIMS Management Consultants LLP.

1.6 Holistic and Integrated Management System (HIMS®)

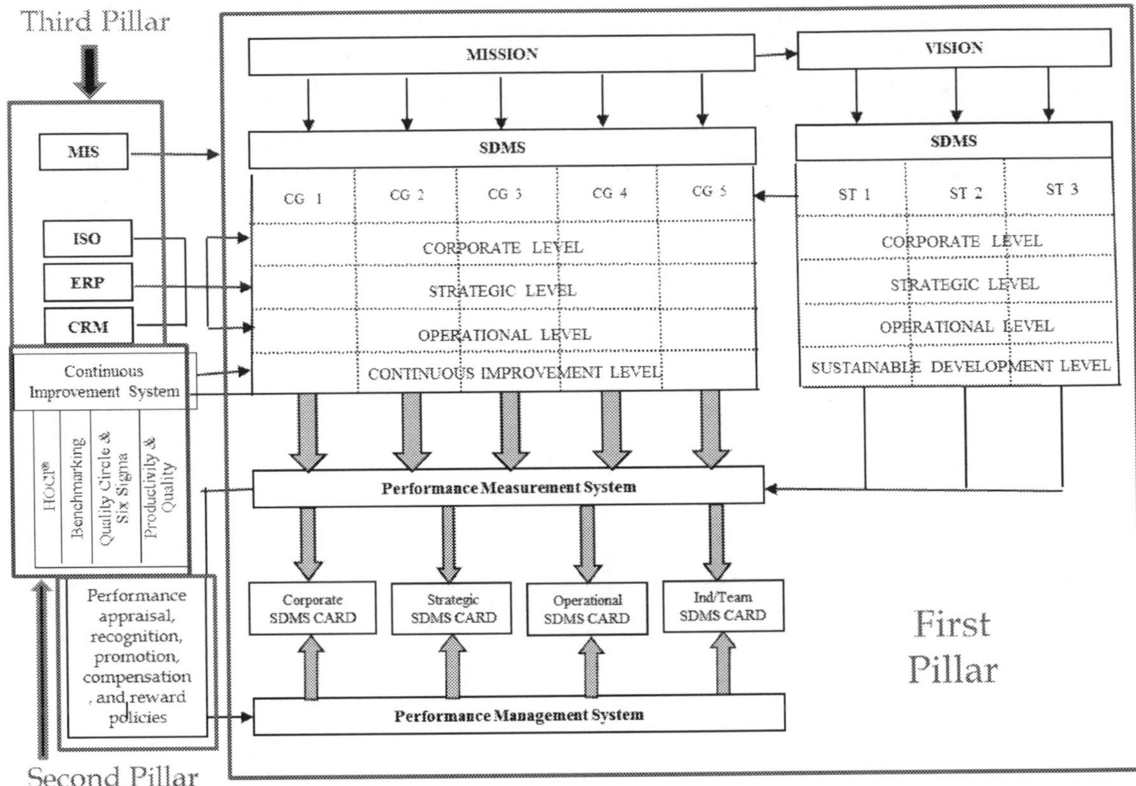

Holistic and Integrated Management System (HIMS®) is a management system that helps organizations implement their strategic plans effectively, and achieve organizational goals, mission and vision effectively through harnessing the total factor productivity of the organizations. HIMS® is a trademark registered and owned by HIMS Management Consultants LLP.

HIMS® is an overarching management system that encompasses three pillar management systems, i.e.,

i) Strategic Deployment Management System (SDMS®),
ii) Continuous Improvement Management System (HOCI®), and
iii) Integration with other Operations Management Systems, such as ISO series, ERP, CRM, BD, ECOM, FINTECH, AI, IOT, etc.

1.7 Business Excellence Software Solutions (HIMS-BEST™)

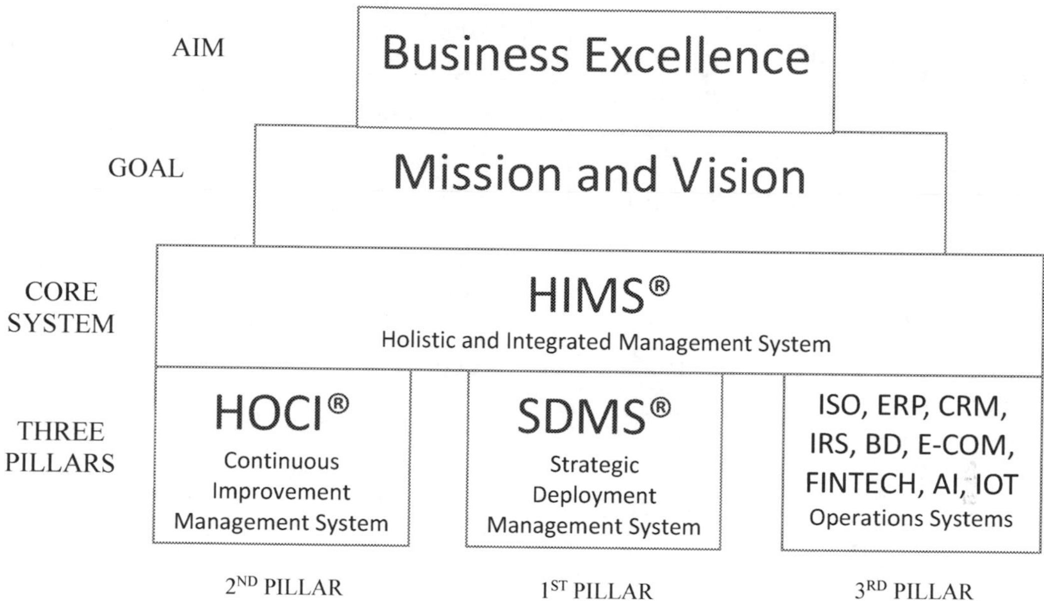

HIMS® is the core management system that encompasses three pillar management systems.

SDMS® ensures all employees of all functions align their goals to the organizational goals.

HOCI® provides a prevention based continuous improvement system that helps identify, prioritize and eliminate the root cause of the problems. Its Key of the Keys module (KOFK®) helps prevent possible disastrous problems from happening.

The 3rd pillar consists of other operations management systems, such as ISO series, ERP, CRM, IRS, BD, E-COM, FINTECH, AI, IOT, etc.

HIMS® integrates all pillar management systems to achieve the organizational goals, mission, vision and core values of the organization.

Through customized consultancy services and harnessing Total Factor Productivity, HIMS Management and IT Consultants PL help the organization move towards business excellence.

The overall management system is named HIMS-BEST™ Business Excellence Software Solutions.

1.8 The Trilogy of Moving Towards Business Excellence

Aim / Objective	Moving Towards Quality Excellence	Moving Towards Productivity Excellence	Moving Towards Business Excellence
Strategy	Digitalization of ISO Quality Management Systems	Harnessing Total Factor Productivity	Adoption of World Class Standards
Effective Tools	SDMS® HIMS-ISO™ HOCI® SDMS-PC®	HIMS® HIMS-OPS™ HIMS-IRS™ KOFK®	HIMS-BEST™
Key Techniques	• Process Optimization • Continuous Improvement	• System Integration • Sustainable Development	• Inculcate Core Values • Build Business Excellence Culture
Duration	½ - 1 Year	1 – 2 Year	≥ 3 Year

Moving towards business excellence could be implemented in 3 phases.

The first phase, moving towards quality excellence, adopts ISO standards as its benchmark to achieve quality excellence. Its strategy is to digitalize the ISO9001:2015 Quality Management System. Key techniques used are process optimization and HOCI® continuous improvement management system. The project will take 6 to 12 months, depending on the size and complexity of the organization.

The strategy to achieve productivity excellence is to harness the Total Factor Productivity of the organization. The key technique is system integration – some case studies are illustrated in chapter 2.9. Sustainable development is paramount to ensure you are always moving ahead of your competitors. The project will take 1 to 2 years.

After successful completion of phase 1 and 2 projects, moving towards business excellence is a matter of changing the mindset of the employees. HIMS-IRS™ Incentive and Rewarding System helps in inculcating the core values of the organization to all employees (please see case study 2.9.iii). The whole HIMS-BEST™ Business Excellence Software Solutions are developed based on the concepts of business excellence on all its modules. Successful implementation of HIMS-BEST™ will help build business excellence culture to all employees of the organization. Paradigm shift needs times to realize. It will take at least 3 years to achieve the goal of business excellence.

2

PRODUCTIVITY

2.1 Definition of Productivity

i) Generic

$$\text{Productivity} = \frac{\text{Output}}{\text{Input}}$$

ii) International Labour Organization (ILO)

Productivity is the ratio of output to input.

iii) Organization for Economic Cooperation & Development (OECD)

Productivity is equal to output divided by one of its production elements.

iv) European Productivity Agency (EPA)

Productivity is the degree of the effective utilization of each productivity element.

Above all else, productivity is an attitude of mind. It is the mentality of progress, of the constant improvement of that which exists. It is the certainty of being able to do better today than yesterday, and less well than tomorrow. It is the will to improve on the present situation, no matter how good it may seem, no matter how good it may really be. It is the constant adaptation of economic and social life to changing conditions; it is the continual effort to apply new techniques and new methods; it is the faith in human progress.

v) Productivity and Standard Board, Singapore (PSB)

Productivity is an attitude of mind that strives for and achieves the habit for improvements, the systems and the set of practices that translates that attitude into action:

a) in and by ourselves through constantly upgrading our knowledge, skills, discipline, individual efforts and teamwork.

b) in our work through better management and work methods, cost reduction, timeliness, better systems and better technology so as to achieve high quality products and services, a better market share and a higher standard of living.

This definition emphasizes the interaction of man, machine and systems – a total approach to produce higher value added to achieve customer satisfaction. In essence, productivity is about people adding value to a work process by their skills, team spirit, efficiency, pride in work and customer orientation.

vi) The Basic Concept

Quantitatively, productivity is the relationship between the quantity of output and the quantity of input used to produce that output. The numerator of the productivity ratio is the output generated, and the denominator is the input used.

Although productivity is an input-output relationship, it is not just about getting maximum efficiency by "doing things right", but also achieving maximum effectiveness by "doing the right things". Even if a company does things in the best possible way to maximize output from a given amount of inputs, its efforts will be negated if the outputs produced are unable to satisfy customers' needs. Thus, productivity encompasses both efficiency and effectiveness.

Productivity = Efficiency + Effectiveness

= Doing things right + Doing the right things

2.2 Productivity and Production

i) Example 1

Ten clerks process an average of 1,000 invoices per day. As a result of expansion within the company, it is now necessary to process an average of 1,540 invoices per day. This is achieved by employing four more clerks. What is the present and new production and productivity? What is the change in production and productivity?

Present Production = 1,000 invoices per day

Present Productivity = 1,000/10 = 100 invoices per clerk per day

New Production = 1,540 invoices per day

New Productivity = 1,540/14 = 110 invoices per clerk per day

Change in Production = 1,540 – 1,000 = 540 (Increase)

Change in Production (%) = (540/1,000) x 100% = 54% (Increase)

Change in Productivity = 110 – 100 = 10 (Increase)

Change in Productivity (%) = (10/100) x 100% = 10% (Increase)

ii) Example 2

The business of the company expands further and the number of invoices that need to be processed per day now has increased to 1,995. The company employs seven more clerks. What is the new production and productivity? What is the change in production and productivity as compared to the original figures?

New Production = 1,995 invoices per day

New Productivity = 1,995/21 = 95 invoices per clerk per day

Change in Production = 1,995 – 1,000 = 995 (Increase)

Change in Production (%) = 995/1,000 = 99.5% (Increase)

Change in Productivity = 95 – 100 = -5 (Decrease)

Change in Productivity (%) = (-5/100) x 100% = -5% (Decrease)

2.3 Examples of Productivity of the Various Resources

i) Productivity of Land

As a result of a 5S+8W project, XYZ Pte Ltd saves 200 square feet of storage space in its factory in Jurong. The size of the factory is 2,000 square feet. The present cost of lease of industrial land around XYZ is $10.00 per square foot per month. The company now operates his business with 10% less space and a monthly saving of $2,000. We say that the improvement has resulted in more productive use of the factory space (land), other conditions being the same.

ii) Productivity of Materials

A tailor may be able to make a shirt out of 3 meters of material whereas another tailor may require 4 meters to make the same shirt of the same size and pattern. This may be due to experience, better method, or better planning. We say that the first tailor is able to make more productive use of the material.

iii) Productivity of Machine

If machine X can be made to produce 100 parts per hour; and a similar machine Y, 80 parts per hour; and other conditions being the same, we say that the productivity of machine X is higher than that of machine Y.

iv) Productivity of Man

If operator A can assemble 50 computers per day, and operator B perhaps with better work attitudes, skills, and experience, can assemble 60 computers per day, then other conditions remaining the same, we say that operator B is more productive.

2.4 Measurement of Productivity

i) Introduction

Productivity is measured as the ratio of total output to total input, i.e.,

$$\text{Productivity} = \frac{\text{Output}}{\text{Input}}$$

It has been said that, "if you can't measure it, you can't manage it." This is particularly true for productivity.

The existence of productivity measurement tends to heighten the awareness of productivity; people tend to pay more attention to things that are being measured.

Productivity measurement is also useful as a diagnostic tool, in the sense that it identifies which organizational units and which inputs are productivity problems.

ii) Partial Productivity Measurement

Measures can be characterized as either Partial Productivity or Total Productivity measures. Partial measures are derived by dividing the total output of a unit/section/department/ organization by a single input; e.g.

$$\text{Partial Productivity} = \frac{\text{Output}}{\text{Labour}} \text{ or } \frac{\text{Output}}{\text{Capital}} \text{ or } \frac{\text{Output}}{\text{Materials}} \text{ or } \frac{\text{Output}}{\text{Energy}}$$

Partial productivity measures are useful but have a shortcoming; one partial measure can be improved at the expense of another (the substitution effect). A common example is the installation of labour-saving capital equipment; labour productivity should improve as a result, but capital productivity may decline.

Some examples:

$$a)\quad \frac{\text{Sales Revenue}}{\text{Sales Personnel Expenditure}}$$

$$b)\quad \frac{\text{Number of Engineering Drawings}}{\text{Number of Draftsmen}}$$

$$c)\quad \frac{\text{Value Added}}{\text{Number of Employees}}$$

iii) Total Productivity Measurement

The ultimate indicator of an organization's effectiveness in addressing productivity is a Total Productivity measure. Total Productivity is defined as total output divided by the sum of all the inputs.

$$\text{Total Productivity} = \frac{\text{Output}}{\text{Labour + Materials + Capital + Energy}}$$

Example:

$$a)\quad \frac{\text{Total Production}}{\text{Direct Labour + Indirect Labour + Materials + Overheads}}$$

iv) Measurement of Productivity at the National Level

$$\text{Productivity} = \frac{\text{Real GDP}}{\text{Employed Manpower}}$$

Gross Domestic Product (GDP) is the market value of all the final output of goods and services generated by a nation's economy, excluding its import. Real GDP is used to take into consideration the effect of price changes.

For the input measure, the manpower refers to the members of the population who are involved in the activity, which generates that national output. That is, only employed persons are included. Those who are not part of the labour force are excluded, and so are those in the labour force but unemployed.

It is basically a measurement of Labour Productivity (Real GDP per employee); in other words, it is a Partial Productivity indicator. It takes into account not only the efficiency of employees, their attitudes, their level of skills, etc. but also investments in machine and equipment, level of technology, effectiveness of systems and other factors not directly related to the labour input.

The labour productivity definition provides a good indication of the productivity of the economy, but it must also be examined in the context of other productivity ratios which take into consideration non-labour resources. Capital productivity and total factor productivity measures are other common indicators of productivity.

2.5 Total Factor Productivity (TFP)

i) Introduction

TFP is defined as the output generated per unit of combined inputs of labour and capital (including land), which are the two basic factors of production. Conceptually, TFP can be expressed as follows:

$$\text{TFP} = \frac{\text{Output}}{\text{Labour + Capital}}$$

As opposed to quantitative increases in inputs, the growth in TFP reflects the effects of qualitative improvements that allow output to increase without any use of additional inputs. That is, output growth results either from (a) employing more resources (quantitative increases) or (b) using existing resources more efficiently and effectively (qualitative improvements or TFP growth). Simply put:

Output Growth = Labour Growth + Capital Growth + TFP Growth

or,

TFP Growth = Output Growth - Labour Growth - Capital Growth

TFP growth is therefore the "residual" – the X-factor capturing all the qualitative improvements – after accounting for the contributions of labour and capital in the growth equation.

TFP captures the effects of the qualitative or intangible factors that contribute towards productive effort.

TFP represents the amount of extra output created solely through higher efficiency, and without the use of any additional inputs; it represents real saving in resources. This makes available extra money for distribution to both providers of capital (as profit) and labour (as wages). When TFP is growing rapidly, both workers and entrepreneurs can expect higher returns on the inputs.

ii) Sources of TFP Growth

TFP growth is generally the result of:

a) Investment in human capital (education, training, etc)
b) Technological progress
c) Better management systems
d) More efficient resource allocation
e) Economies of scale
f) Improved labour-management relations

iii) Importance of TFP Growth

Once an economy is close to capacity limits, it cannot grow faster than productivity rises. The attempt to do so produces inflation, not real growth.

For example, Singapore's labour supply growth is reaching the upper limit of its capacity. If producers continue to depend on this diminishing labour supply in order to increase output, they would have to increase salaries and wages. The resultant higher labour costs would in turn be passed on to customers in the form of higher price of goods and services. Carrying this a step further, the price competitiveness of Singapore manufactured goods and services in export markets would be eroded. The consequence fall in demand for exports would hurt the Singapore economy, as was the case in 1985.

When TFP growth rises, it enables the supply potential of the economy to expand. This in turn leads to higher investment, as well as higher wages and living standards, but without the side effect of a wage-price spiral.

2.6 Value Added and Productivity

i) Introduction

In order to produce goods or services, a company has to purchase the necessary raw materials and other inputs, which would fuel its activities. The difference between the total value of outputs (turnover) and total cost of inputs (bought-in materials and services) is called Valued Added.

Thus, value added denotes the net wealth created by a company. When we compare value added against the amount of labour and capital required to generate it, we are in effect measuring the productivity of the organization.

Since value added is a measure of the wealth generated by the collective effort of those who work in a business enterprise (i.e., employees) and those who provide the capital (namely, the employers and investors), it must therefore be used to pay those who have contributed to its creation. One part of the wealth is distributed as wages, salaries, pensions, interest on loans, taxes and dividends. The remaining portion is retained as reserves, or for investment and depreciation.

It is important to note that the value added generated by a business measures the difference between what the customer pays and what the manufacturer or supplier has to pay for the raw materials and other intermediate inputs. In other words, value added does not only measure the effort which has gone into the activity, but also measures the customer's satisfaction in terms of what he is prepared to pay. To illustrate, consider a product whose manufacture calls for much effort; if nobody wants this product, then no value added has been generated.

ii) Value Added Calculation

a) Subtraction Method

Valued Added = Total Sales – Bought-In Materials and Services

b) Addition Method

Value Added = Labour Cost + Interest + Taxation + Depreciation + Profit

iii) Importance of Value Added Analysis

An analysis of the production of value added can be used to assess the efficiency of the enterprise. Such analysis enables management to make decisions on issues such as cost reduction and capital intensity. It short, it indicates how productivity can be increased, thereby leading to higher profits. On the other hand, an analysis of the distribution of value added is useful because it shows the link between employees' rewards and the success of the enterprise. This helps to encourage employees' participation in improving the performance of the enterprise.

The importance of value added analysis lies therefore in it being a basis for measuring productivity. An understanding of value added provides evidence of how all parties stand to gain by being more productive, thus motivating them to give of their best.

iv) Value Added Productivity Analysis

Value added ratios and other ratios related to them collectively form the basis of value added productivity analysis. The measurement of these ratios allows productivity comparisons to be made between similar businesses in common industries. In addition, these ratios can be used to measure the progress achieved in the area of productivity for individual enterprises over time.

a) Value Added per Employee (Labour Productivity Ratio)

$$\text{Value Added per Employee} = \frac{\text{Value Added}}{\text{Number of Employees}}$$

The increase in the value added per employee may not only reflect the efficiency with which labour produces output, but may also be due to other factors such as technology improvement and better management systems.

For a better understanding of the factors which affect the value added per employee, the ratio may be decomposed into its components as follows:

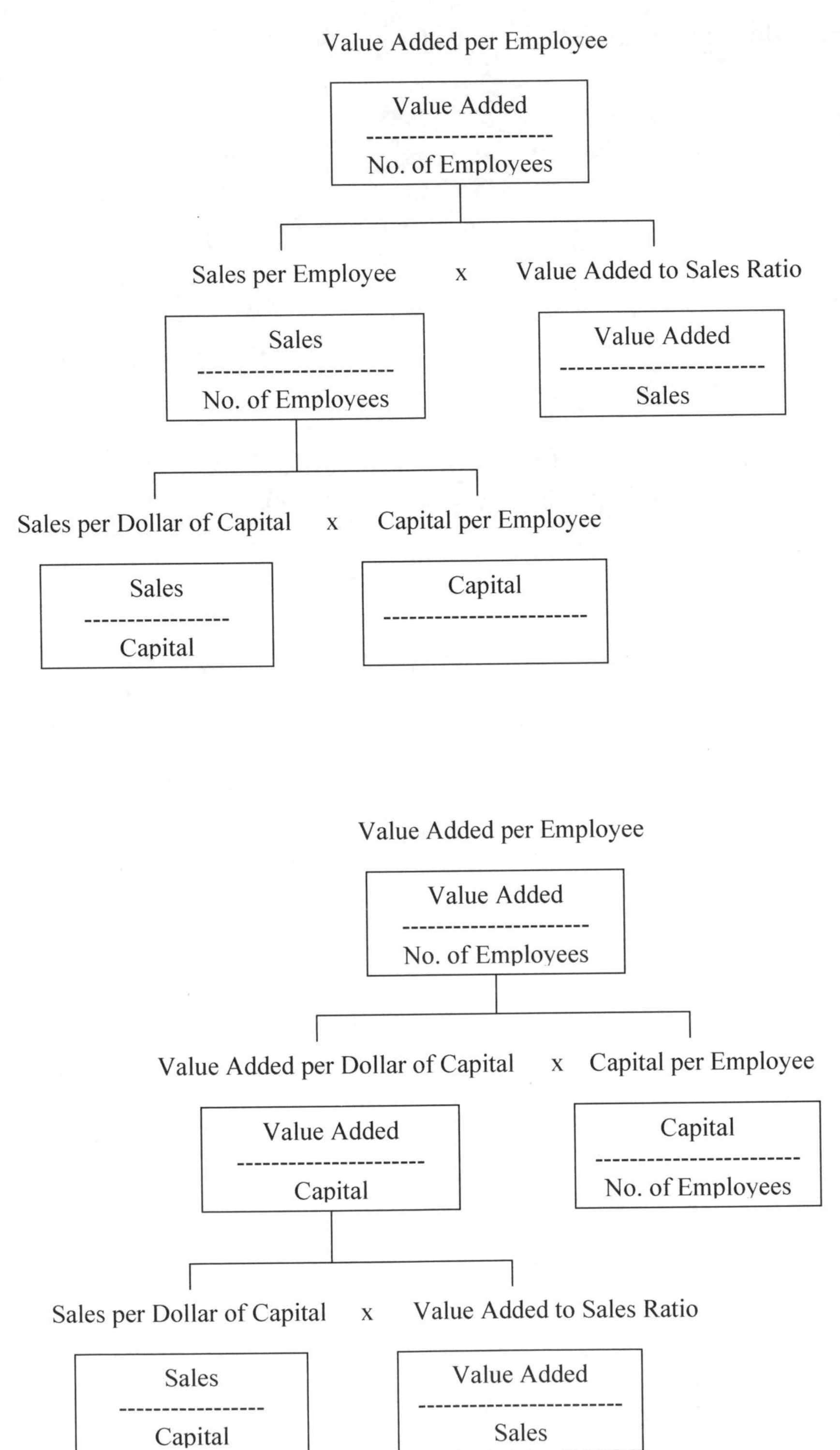
Value Added per Employee
Value Added
No. of Employees
Sales per Employee
x
Value Added to Sales Ratio
Sales
No. of Employees
Value Added
Sales
Sales per Dollar of Capital
x
Capital per Employee
Sales
Capital
Capital
Value Added per Employee
Value Added
No. of Employees
Value Added per Dollar of Capital
x
Capital per Employee
Value Added
Capital
Capital
No. of Employees
Sales per Dollar of Capital
x
Value Added to Sales Ratio
Sales
Capital
Value Added
Sales

b) Labour Cost Competitiveness

Labour Cost Competitiveness is measured by the ratio of value added to labour cost, indicating the value added that is generated by the company for each dollar paid to the employees. The relationships among labour cost competitiveness, the value added per employee and the labour cost per employee are illustrated below:

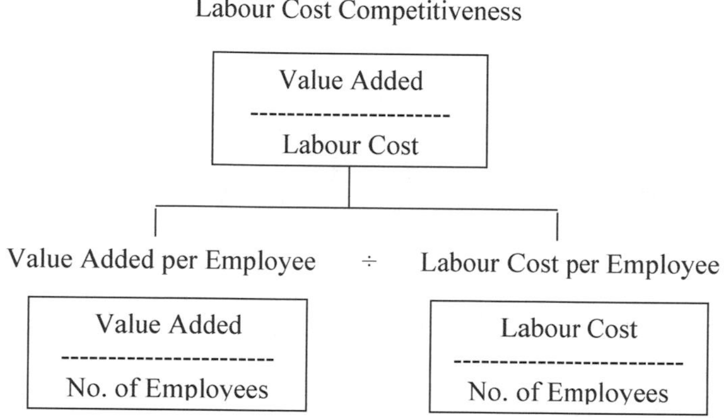

Labour Cost Competitiveness can be maintained by ensuring that increases in the labour cost per employee are matched by proportionate increases in the value added per employee.

c) Profitability

The most commonly used measure of a company's performance is its profitability. This is popularly analysed using the ratio of profit to capital employed, which indicates the return to the capital invested in the business or how well the capital is being used. Profitability can be expressed as:

$$\text{Profitability} = \frac{\text{Operating Profit (Before Interest)}}{\text{Operating Capital}}$$

The profitability ratio can be decomposed as follows:

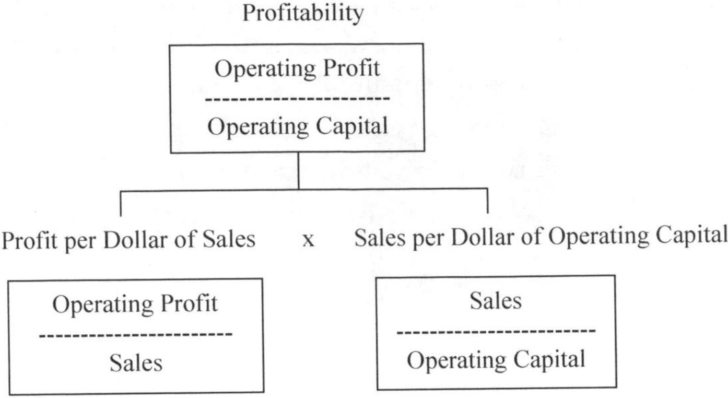

Alternatively, profitability may also be decomposed as follows:

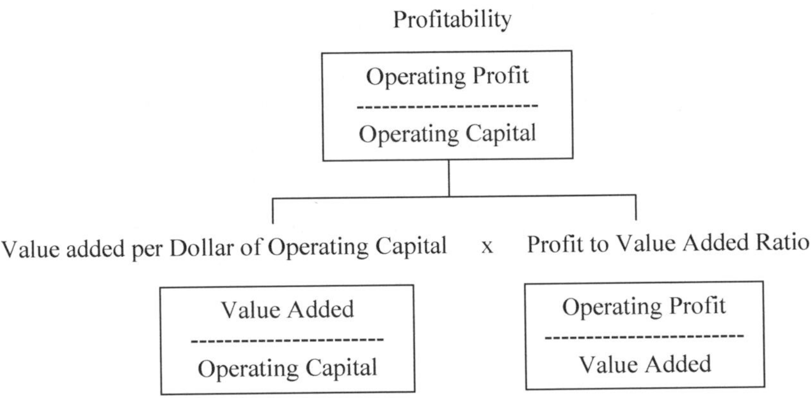

This decomposition indicates that profitability is determined not only by the proportion of value added which goes to the company and the providers of capital in the form of profit, but by how well capital is used to generate value added. In other words, securing a higher value added with the available capital is a means of obtaining improved profitability, as profits are a component of value added.

v) Case Study

a) Value Added Statement

The following diagram shows an example on how information from a Profit and Loss Statement can easily be obtained to develop a Value Added Statement.

Profit and Loss Statement	$	Value Added Statement	$
Sales	500,000	Sales	500,000
Less: Cost of sales		Less: change in inventory level	
Opening stock	230,000	Operating stock	(230,000)
Purchases	300,000	Closing stock	150,000
Less: Closing stock	(150,000)	Gross output	420,000
	380,000		
		Less: Purchase of goods and services	
Gross Profit	120,000		
Non-operating income	8,000	Purchases of stock	(300,000)
		Services & administration expenses	(27,200)
Less: Operating expenses			
Director fees	5,000		
Staff costs	35,000	Value added	92,800
Staff welfare & development	5,000		=====
Depreciation	2,000		
Interest	3,000	Distribution of value added	
Foreign worker levy	500		
Advertising & marketing	5,000	Staff cost and other benefits	45,000
Audit fees	6,000	Depreciation	2,000
Rental	10,000	Interest	3,000
Repairs & maintenance	500	Tax	4,800
Office & other supplies	500	Profit after tax	45,000
Utilities	3,000	Less: Non-operating income	(8,000)
Transport & communications	2,000		
Other operating expenses	200	Add: Non-operating expenses	1,000
Total operating expenses	77,700		
			92,800
Non-operating expenses	1,000	Value Added	=====
Profit before tax	49,300		
Income tax expenses	(4,300)		
Profit after tax	45,000		

2.7 Productivity and Quality

Productivity and quality are sometimes perceived to be trade-off. For example, a production line may assemble more disk drives per hour (which means higher productivity), but more parts are assembled wrongly (which means poorer quality). However, this is not necessarily the case. In fact, quality and productivity often move in the same direction.

The positive relationship between productivity and quality becomes clearer when we examine the components of the productivity ratio as follows:

$$\text{Labour Productivity} = \frac{\text{Value Added}}{\text{Number of Employees}}$$

where

Value Added = Sales/Production - Cost of Purchased Goods and Services

Based on this equation, productivity can be improved by increasing value added while maintaining employment. To increase value added, we can increase sales, and at the same time, reduce the cost of purchased goods and services.

How do these relate to quality? When the process quality is good, there are less rework, wastage and reject, which lead to lower costs. At the same time, better product and service quality are achieved. Both ultimately result in higher sales. Therefore, the pursuit of quality is an integral part of productivity movement. (See Figure in the next page).

Productivity and Quality Linkage

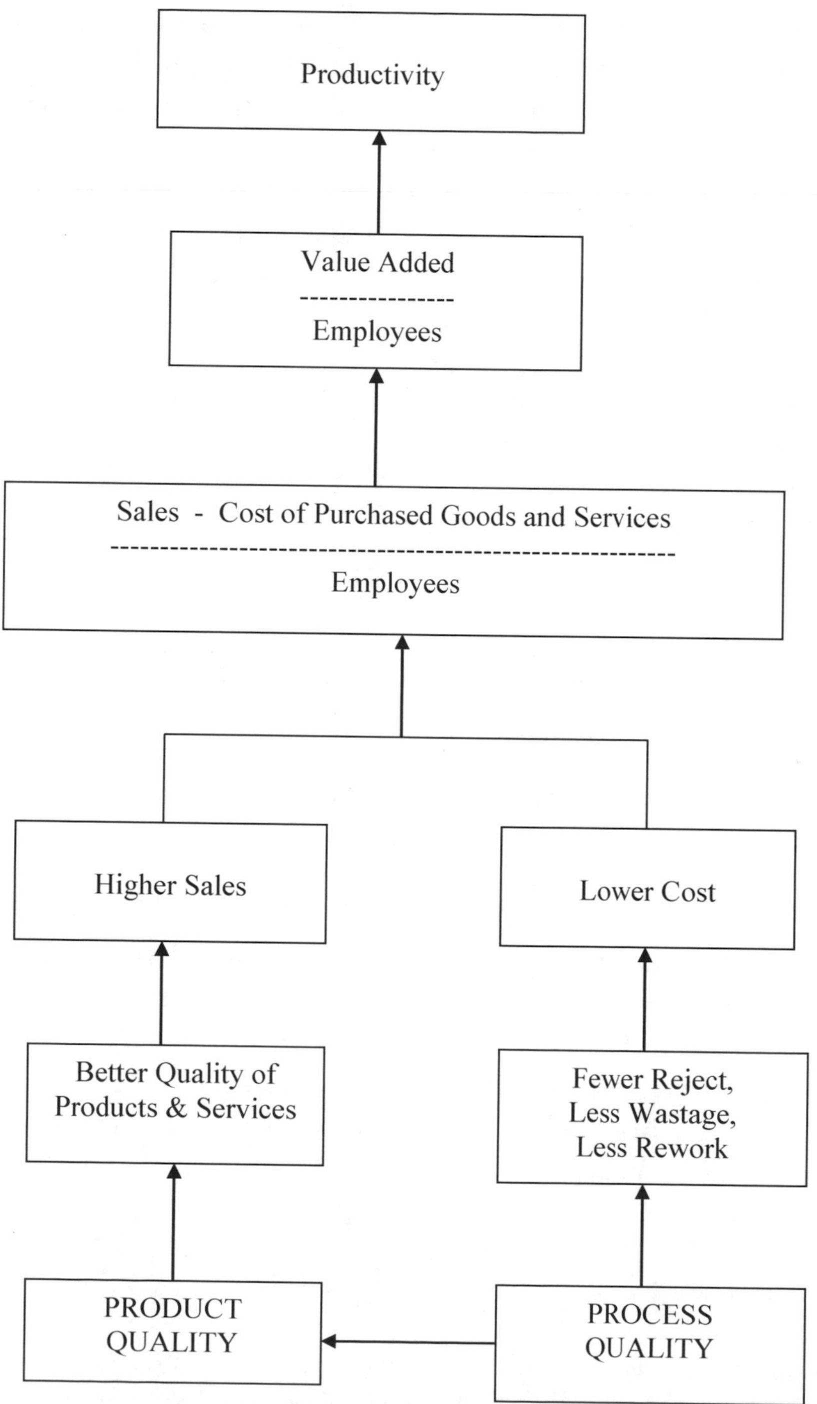

2.8 The Trilogy of Productivity Gains

In Oct 2010, the author was interviewed by the "Management World" magazine of the Chinese State Council Development Research Center. One question being asked was: 'While there has not been much problems in understanding and promoting productivity, why is it so difficult to achieve productivity gains?'. The author replied: 'It's easy to understand the concept of Productivity and Quality, but very often, they are also easily misunderstood when applied in practice. One needs to look at them from a holistic perspective in order to appreciate and harness the tremendous beneficial impact on the effectiveness of the organization and the efficiency of their processes'.

In April 2014, the author was invited to give a talk in Shanghai China on "How to Move ahead of Competitors and Achieve Business Excellence". Having just successfully completed a HIMS (Holistic and Integrated Management System) consultancy project, the author took the opportunity to share with the participants the concept of 'The Trilogy of Productivity Gains'.

1. Improve Operational Efficiency

   First, the organization has to improve the efficiency of the operational processes. This could be achieved through computerization of the operational processes with computer software such as ERP, CRM, etc., and automation of the labour intensive operational processes through installation of conveyor, AGV, robot, etc.

2. Enhance Organizational Effectiveness

   Next, the organization has to strive for organizational effectiveness. This means achieving the organizational goals, mission and vision of the organization. Practically, this has proven to be very difficult as it needs to first execute its strategic plans effectively. A survey conducted by Fortune Magazine reported that "Less than 10% of strategies effectively formulated are effectively executed". Furthermore, to ensure their sustainability, they need to be achieved through harnessing the total factor productivity of the organization.

3. Achieve Business Excellence

   However, if the above phases 1 and 2 have been successfully achieved, then moving towards business excellence is made much easier through filling the gaps in the world class organization standards. The key challenges in this phase are mainly qualitative in nature, such as inculcating the organizational core values to all employees, and building the business excellence culture throughout the whole organization.

2.9 Case Study on Productivity Gains

i) Raise Organization Productivity

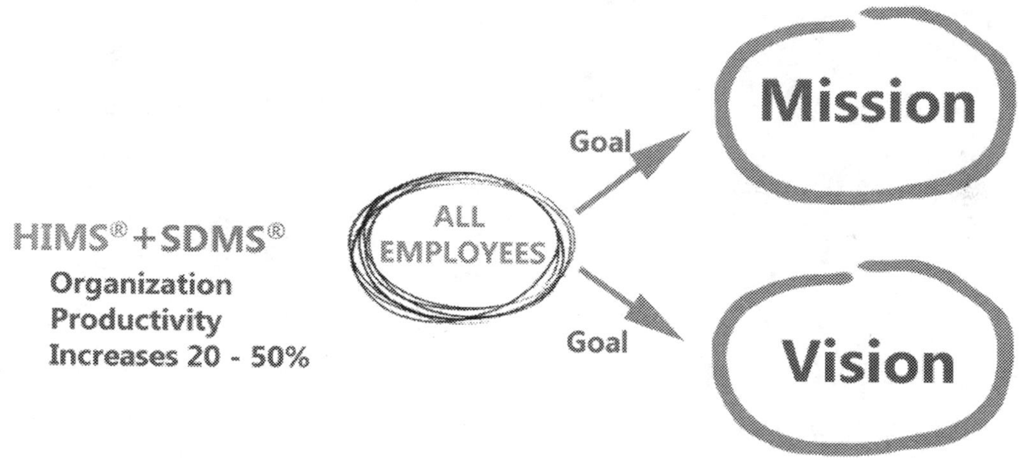

HIMS® (Holistic and Integrated Management System) and SDMS® (Strategic Deployment Management System) ensure all employees of all functions move in the same direction focusing on achieving the organization goals, mission and vision. All non-value added processes are optimized or eliminated in the process of implementing these initiatives.

Our consultancy experience shows that this enabling alone will help raise the organizational productivity by at least 20-50%.

ii) Reduce Operational Cost

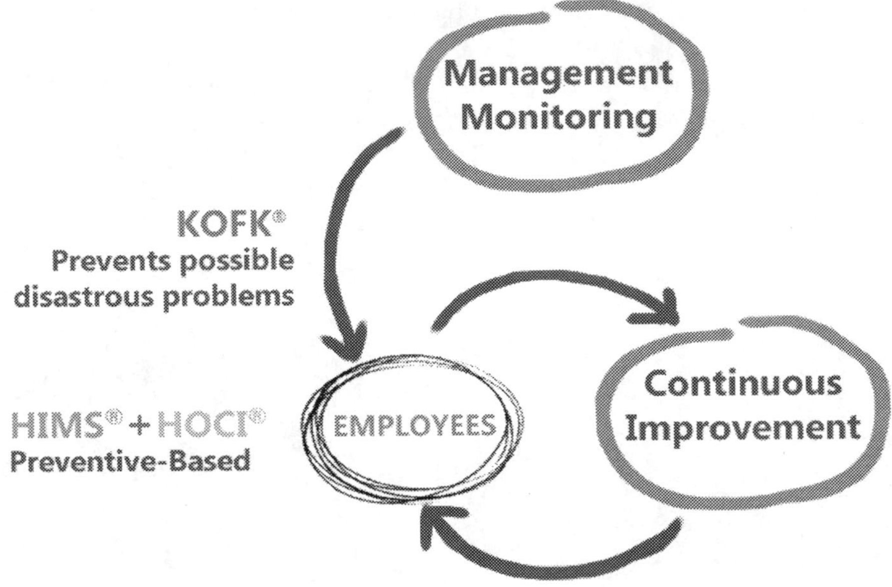

HIMS® (Holistic and Integrated Management System) and HOCI® (Continuous Improvement Management System) provide a preventive-based continuous improvement system for all employees. Top management can monitor the key of the keys (KOFK®) goals and operations to prevent any possible disastrous problems from happening.

Our hands-on experience in facilitating hundreds of preventive-based improvement projects, including more than a hundred with Motorola in the 1990s, showed that millions of dollars in operating costs can easily be saved.

iii) Harness Synergic Benefits

Do you wish to add value to your existing operations system? HIMS® provides synergic benefits through integration with other operations systems such as ISO series, ERP, CRM, IRS, etc. It's a 1+1=3 benefit.

For example, when we integrate our incentive and rewarding system IRS with HIMS® (HIMS-IRS™), we found that employees are motivated to achieving the organizational goals, as HIMS® provides a more transparent and equitable rewarding system. So, it's a win-win situation; both employees and the organization benefit from HIMS®.

3

QUALITY

3.1 The Evolution of Quality Concepts

i) Fitness to Standard

This is a concept of the 50s. It defines Quality as the product that does what the designer intends it to do. The quality of the product is determined by inspection. If the product complies with the standard established, it is a quality product; irrespective of whether the customer feels otherwise. In the 50s, where demand mostly exceeded supply and competition was scarce, the concept was generally acceptable to the public.

To ensure quality, organizations established procedures for workers to follow. First, each task of production was defined. It was then recorded as standard practices in manuals. Finally, inspection procedures were established to enforce the standard.

The shortcoming of this concept of ensuring quality is that product/service produced/offered might not meet customers' requirements.

ii) Fitness to Use

In the 60s, the concept of "Fitness to Use" became more popular, as the voices of customer were becoming louder and the suppliers were facing more competition. That means suppliers had to assure satisfaction of market needs. In other words, their products had to satisfy the customers' requirements.

To ensure quality, a more stringent procedure was established. However, it was only achieved by inspection after the product was made. In other words, the procedure ensured "inspecting Quality in".

The shortcoming of this concept of ensuring quality is that it incurs high costs due to the stringent procedures of inspecting the quality in.

iii) Fitness to Cost

In the 70s, suppliers found that the high cost of inspecting the quality-in was eroding their market shares when some enlightened organizations were able to produce similar quality products with less cost. They realized that "high quality and low cost" are the two most universal requirements for virtually all customers, products, and services. They started to shift their focus from controlling the output through inspection to controlling the process. In other words, they learnt to "build quality in". The approach is multi-dimensional in terms of people, process, and structure.

The shortcoming of this concept of ensuring quality is that competitors can catch up quickly in creating similarly reliable and inexpensive products.

iv) Fitness to Latent Requirement (Delighting the Customer)

In the 80s and 90s, competitions became fiercer as manufacturers from the emerging markets were also joining the bandwagon. This was the time when "quality circles", "benchmarking", "quality function deployment" techniques and "total customer satisfaction", "total quality management" concepts were prolific. They suddenly realized that customer satisfaction was not enough. They had to forecast customer needs; in other words, they had to ensure that their products met their customer needs before customers were aware of those needs. They delight the customers.

The advantage of this concept of ensuring quality is that it is proactive. However, it may only achieve monopoly for a little while.

Some industrial examples are: Polaroid instant photography, Sony Walkman, and Swatch Watch. Other examples in Education are Smart Lecture Theatre, Virtual Laboratory, and Flexible supplementary examination system. Examples in Public Services are Singapore

HDB (Housing Development Board) Upgrading Program, Singapore LRT (Light Rail Transport) to Housing Estate.

v) Important Timeless Quality Concepts

As we enter the 2000s, while many ideas of the above concepts are still relevant, product manufacturers and service providers are invariably concerned if they still have the customers and their businesses still survive. "Customer Loyalty" and "Customer Retention" are their key concerns now.

Organizations now focus more of their resources in ensuring their customers keep on coming back, recommend their products to their friend, and never buy their competitors products/ services. This is "Customer Loyalty". In addition, organizations need to continuously innovate, benchmark and improve their products / services, policies, systems and processes to ensure their customers will not go away. This is "Customer Retention".

3.2 Some Fundamental Quality Concepts

i) Who decides on quality?

The customer decides on quality.

Sam Walton, founder of Wal-Mart said: "There is only one boss – the customer. And he can fire everybody in the company, from the chairman on down, simply by spending his money somewhere else."

ii) External Customer

The external customer is the end-user.

They will buy a product that is:

- o Desirable to own and meets intended purposes
- o Functional and robust against environment, deterioration and variation
- o Better than competitive products for features and style, and value for money

iii) Internal Customers

Your next-in-line is your internal customer.

They are the ones who receive our work, process it and pass it on to the next process. In a sense, they are "buying" our piece of work. Hence, we have to ensure that our work meets their requirements and does not contain errors.

iv) Do it Right the First Time

You must know exactly what is considered right. Without knowing the specifications and requirements of your job as well as the products, we can never do our jobs right.

It implies that you are capable of producing the targeted quality and doing it right the first time every time. As a result, the next station or process is not required to check your quality.

Similarly, you should not rely on screening and inspection by another party to produce quality products.

v) The Impact of Not Doing It Right the First Time

- Impact on Cost
    - We will have to incur additional cost to remedy the fault.
    - Additional manpower and material are required to make it right again.
    - Cost of rectifying the fault will even be higher if the product has been shipped out to the customer – we might even lose this customer.

- Impact on Schedule
    - We need additional time to put it right the second time.
    - We may have to scrap the rejected part and start to fabricate another part and all these remedial activities take time and will definitely delay the schedule.
    - It will definitely affect the confidence our clients have in us.

- Impact on Morale

- o It will be frustrating and demoralizing if you need to rework, repair or reject a piece of work due to wrong information, material, or component given by your "suppliers" or misleading requirements given by your "internal customers" – it affects your relationship with your fellow colleagues.
- o It also affects the profitability and productivity of your company and even your job

3.3 Quality Principles and Philosophy

i) Philip Crosby

- ♦ All work is a process.
- ♦ Quality is meeting requirements.
- ♦ We focus on processes by measuring.
- ♦ Our quality standard is 100% right.
- ♦ The system for quality is prevention.

ii) Edward Deming

- ♦ Create constancy of purpose for continual improvement of product and service.
- ♦ Adopt the new philosophy for economic stability.
- ♦ Cease dependence on inspection to achieve quality.
- ♦ End the practice of awarding business on price tag alone.
- ♦ Improve constantly and for ever the system of production and service.
- ♦ Institute training on the job.
- ♦ Adopt and institute modern methods of supervision and leadership.
- ♦ Drive out fear.
- ♦ Break down barriers between departments and individuals.
- ♦ Eliminate the use of slogans, posters and exhortations.
- ♦ Eliminate work standards and numerical quotas.
- ♦ Institute a vigorous program of education and retraining.
- ♦ Remove barriers that rob the hourly worker of the right to pride in workmanship.
- ♦ Define top management's permanent commitment to ever-improving quality and productivity.

iii) Joseph Juran

- Quality is defined as fitness for use.
- Survival and growth are dependent on "breakthrough" to new levels of performance.
- Customer needs are translated into product and process features.
- Cost of poor quality is the attention-getting detail.
- Chronic waste must be identified and eliminated.
- Prime improvement opportunities should be targeted by separating the "vital few" from the "trivial many".
- The Quality Trilogy: Planning, Control and Improvement.

iv) Genichi Taguchi

- The quality of a product is the (minimum) loss imparted by the product to the society from the time the product is shipped.
- This view extends from the manufacturer at the time of production to the consumer and to society as a whole

3.4 The Eight Dimensions of Quality

i) Performance

- Refers to a product's primary operating characteristics.
- Example: ease of use, speed, practicality and ability to interface for a micro-computer software program.

ii) Features

- Refers to a product's secondary product characteristics – supplement the product's basic functioning.
- Example: colour graphics, on-line help screens, for a micro-computer software program.

iii) Conformance to Specifications

- Refers to the degree to which a product's design and operating characteristics meet prior established standards.
- Focus on the internal and operations view of quality. Basic subject matter of statistical quality control (SQC).

iv) Reliability

- Refer to the likelihood of a product failure (malfunctioning) within a specific time period.
- Must be "designed" into a product.
- SQC ensures that the end result of the manufacturing process is that the product turn out as design.
- Reliability engineering distinguishes three types of failures or malfunctions: early failures, wear-out failures and random failures or failures caused by sudden stress accumulations on equipment.
- Everything else being equal, the fewer the parts, the higher the reliability (or the lower the failure rate).

v) Durability

- Refers to the length of life of a product.
- Example: the filament of a light bulb burns up after 1,000 hours. In this case, the bulb must be replaced. Repair is impossible.
- There is a high correlation between reliability and durability when products can be repaired. A product with a high failure rate (lack of reliability) is scrapped earlier than more reliable products.

vi) Serviceability

- Refers to speed, courtesy and competence of repair.
- Examples: the elapsed time before service is restored, the timeliness with which service appointments are kept, the nature of their dealings with service personnel, the frequency with which service calls or repairs fail to correct outstanding problems.

vii) Perceived Quality

- Refers to what customers "perceive" they are buying rather than what they are actually buying.
- Example: A $10,000. Rolax watch does not belong to and will not sell in a discount store. It must be sold through up-scale department stores and appointed agents.
- Put it differently, a Rolax watch is more than the physical product itself. It extends beyond what is put into the package. Packaging, distribution channels, pricing, advertising themes and the like create what is called the perceived quality.

viii) Aesthetics

- Refers to "how a product looks, feels, tastes, or smells".
- Example: the condition of the carpet, lavatory, linens, windows, ashtrays, etc collectively constitutes the "Hotel Appearance".

3.5 Cost of Quality

3.5.1 Cost of Conformance (COC)

COC is the cost that is associated with making certain the product meets the requirements. Examples of Cost of Conformance:

- Applicant screening
- Audits
- Controlled storage
- Design reviews
- Document reviews
- Drawing checking
- Equipment calibration
- Equipment maintenance and repair
- Field testing
- Fixture design and fabrication
- Housekeeping
- Job description

- Market analysis
- Prototype construction
- Training
- Survey

3.5.2 Cost of Non-Conformance (CON)

CON is the cost that is associated with failure to meet the requirements. Examples of Cost of Non-Conformance:

- Accidents
- Bad debts
- Customer dissatisfaction
- Employee turnover
- Equipment downtime
- Excess installation costs
- Excess interest expense
- Excess inventory
- Excess material handling
- Excess travel expense
- Excess telephone expense
- Failure reviews
- Liability
- Loss of market share
- Obsolescence due to design change
- Overpayments
- Penalties
- Premium freight
- Rework
- Scrap
- Warranty expense

3.5.3 Direct Costs of Quality (DCOQ)

i) Prevention Cost

ii) Appraisal Cost

iii) Internal Failure Cost

iv) External Failure Cost

i) Prevention Cost

Any cost incurred in an effort to prevent a failure in meeting requirements. It is a Cost of Conformance (COC). Examples of Prevention Cost:

- Application screening
- Controlled storage
- Design reviews
- Document reviews
- Equipment maintenance
- Field testing
- Fixture design and fabrication
- Housekeeping
- Job description
- Market analysis
- Prototype construction
- Survey
- Training

ii) Appraisal Cost

Any cost incurred in an effort to detect a failure in meeting requirements. It is a Cost of Conformance (COC). Examples of Appraisal Cost:

- Audit
- Document checking
- Drawing checking
- Equipment calibration
- Final inspection
- In-process inspection
- Laboratory inspection
- Personnel testing

- Procedure checking
- Prototype inspection
- Receiving inspection
- Shipping inspection

iii) Internal Failure Cost

Any cost incurred for products that do not meet requirements and have not been transferred to the customer. It is a Cost of Non-Conformance (CON). Examples of Internal Failure Cost:

- Accidents
- Employee turnover
- Engineering change notices
- Equipment downtime
- Excess interest expense
- Excess inventory
- Excess material handling
- Excess travel expense
- Failure reviews
- Obsolescence due to design changes
- Overpayments
- Premium freight
- Redesign
- Repair costs
- Re-testing
- Rework
- Scrap
- Sorting

iv) External Failure Cost

Any cost incurred for products that do not meet requirements and have been transferred to the customer. It is a Cost of Non-Conformance (CON). Examples of External Failure Cost:

- Bad debts
- Customer dissatisfaction
- Equipment downtime

- Excess installation costs
- Excess interest expense
- Excess inventory
- Excess handling
- Failure review
- Loss of market share
- Overpayments
- Penalties
- Premium freight
- Price concessions
- Recalls
- Repair costs
- Rework
- Scrap
- Warranty expense

3.5.4 Indirect Costs of Quality (ICOQ)

ICOQ are usually difficult, if not impossible, to identify and track. They are associated with non-conformance and related to the direct quality cost categories of internal and external failure. They are separated into the following categories:

- Loss of opportunity costs
- Customer goodwill
- Erosion of market share
- Liability
- Penalty

3.5.5 Total Cost of Quality (TCOQ)

- Total Cost of Quality = Direct Cost of Quality + Indirect Cost of Quality

  TCOQ = DCOQ + ICOQ

- As ICOQ are difficult to identify and measure,

  TCOQ = DCOQ

- COQ is often expressed as % of gross sales
- Not uncommon for COQ to amount to 20 – 25% of gross sales
- As high as 40% of gross sales for service industry
- Rule of Thumb

  - Correcting an error found in a part drawing that has not yet been released to manufacturing may cost $10.
  - Correcting the error may cost $100. once the part is made.
  - If the part is used in an assembly, and the error is found before shipment to the customer, the error may cause $1,000. to correct.
  - Once assembled and shipped to customers, correcting the error may cost $10,000.
  - If the error is serious enough to require a product recall, the error may cause $100,000.
  - If a death results from the error, the error may cause $1,000,000.

3.6 Service Quality

i) Introduction

Service Quality is a global judgment or attitude relating to a particular service - the customers' overall expression of the relative inferiority or superiority of the organization and its services. Service quality is a cognitive judgment.

Customer Services are transactions aimed at meeting the needs and expectations of the customers, as defined by the customers. It is the service encounter or series of encounters.

Customer Expectations are what a customer wants before a transaction. A customer forms expectations from several different sources: advertising, previous experience, word of mouth, the competition.

Customer Perceptions are created during and after a transaction. A customer's perception is based on how your service measured up against her or his expectations.

Exceptional Customer Service = Perception – Expectation.

Customer Satisfaction is the overall evaluation of an organization's products and services versus the customer's expectation. Customer satisfaction includes but is not limited to service quality. Customer satisfaction is an attitude.

Customer Loyalty is the preference of an organization or its brands over other acceptable products or services, conveniently available. Customer loyalty includes but is not limited to evaluations of service quality and customer satisfaction. Customer loyalty is behavior.

[Service Quality] → [Customer Satisfaction] → [Customer Loyalty] → [Profit]

ii) Importance of Service Quality

Customers have become increasingly demanding in their service requirements. More and more markets are becoming "commodity" markets. Companies are beginning to realize that increases in customer satisfaction and customer retention can have a significant impact on company profitability and corporate success.

A survey conducted by The Forum Corporation indicates that: "70% of the identifiable reasons why customers stop doing business with an organization has nothing to do with product. Customers surveyed reported that they left because they received a lack of personal attention, were treated rudely, or found an employee unhelpful."

"68% of customers who quit doing business with an organization do so because of perceived indifference on the part of employees." This is the result of the survey conducted by the US White House Office of Consumer Affairs and the Technical Assistance Research Program.

iii) Customer Satisfaction

Researchers have found that firms that create superior customer satisfaction enjoy superior profit.

Researcher from the University of Michigan found that "On average, every 1% increase in customer satisfaction is associated with a 2.37% increase in a firm's Return on Investment (ROI)."

Merely satisfying one's customers is a low hurdle – you should aim for delight. "Satisfaction guaranteed" simply commits the firm to preventing dissatisfaction.

"Delight", on the other hand, commits a firm to attaining the very highest level of customer satisfaction

Understanding how customer satisfaction translates into retention, increased market share, and enhanced profitability is the key. Satisfaction isn't an end in itself – it triggers a chain of results. Astute managers will strive to better understand that chain before investing in it.

iv) Level of Customer Satisfaction

The impact of an increase in customer satisfaction levels is almost never as substantial as an equivalent decrease in satisfaction. The relationship between satisfaction and customer behavior is not linear. At some points the relationship shows diminishing returns. Likewise, at other points there are increasing returns.

There are three levels of customer satisfaction (See diagram below):

Zone of Pain – a company cannot survive in this region, unless its strategy is pure price leadership and customers are willing to trade off satisfaction for a low price.

Zone of Mere Satisfaction – for most companies, this is not a winning situation – mere satisfaction seldom drives profits. Slight differences in mere satisfaction levels are unlikely to engender loyalty.

Zone of Delight – success comes when customers are moved out of the Zone of Mere Satisfaction and into the Zone of Delight. Customers need to be able to describe their experience as delightful

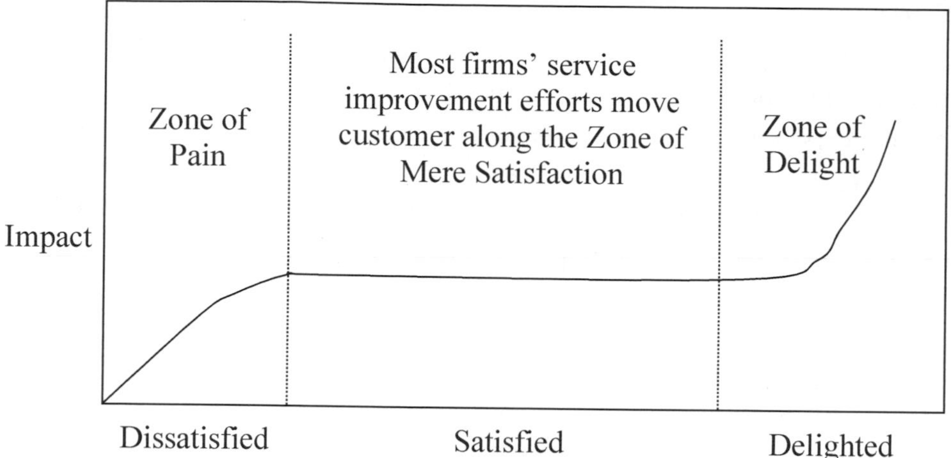

v) Kano Analysis of Customer Satisfaction

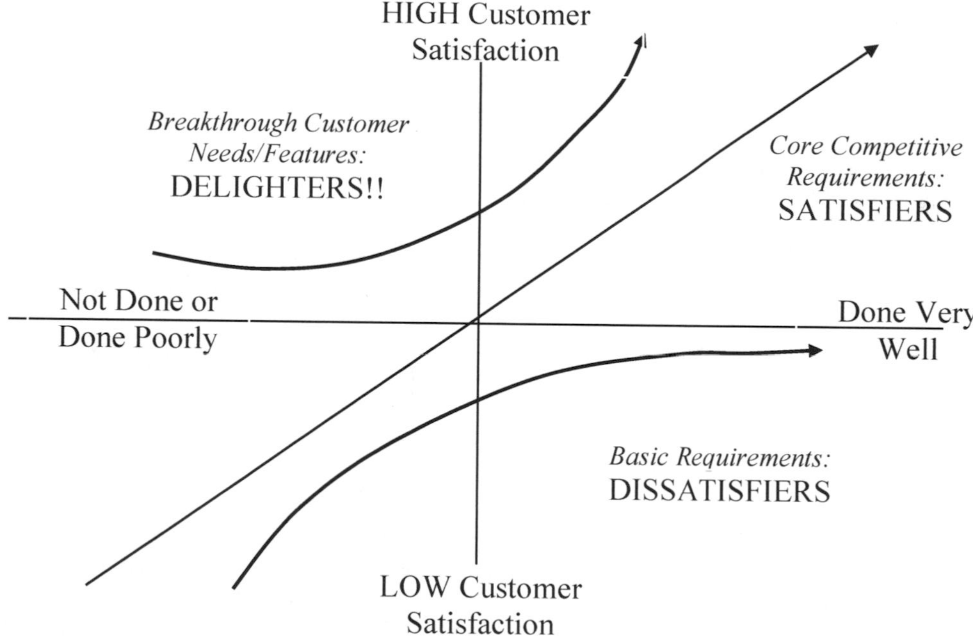

vi) Customer Satisfaction and Expectation/Perception

Satisfaction and delight are strongly influenced by customers' expectations in regard to how the experience could, should, will, and better not occur.

The difference between what customers expect to receive and what customers actually experience according to their perception is a very strong predictor of satisfaction. Exceeding expectations corresponds with Delight, meeting expectation with Mere Satisfaction, and not meeting expectations with Dissatisfaction.

If perceived quality is higher than expected, customers' subsequent expectations will generally be raised. Expectations will change over time and usually increase.

Perceptions tend to generate emotional response from customers. So managers must be concerned not only with how customer perceives service but how they feel about it.

vii) Customer Loyalty

Loyalty involves more than just making a purchase, or even repeat purchases. Loyalty represents a positive level of commitment by the customer to the supplier and it is the degree of positive commitment, which distinguishes truly loyal customers.

When seeking to maximize customer retention, businesses should focus on commitment and not loyalty. Customer commitment will often be reflected in customers' behavior. They may choose to recommend a favored supplier. They might demonstrate commitment by traveling further than necessary or paying a higher price if they believe a supplier provides a superior total value package. Commitment might also be reflected in their attitudes. Committed customers will believe that their chosen supplier is the best in its field.

viii) Quality-Satisfaction-Loyalty/Retention-Profitability Model

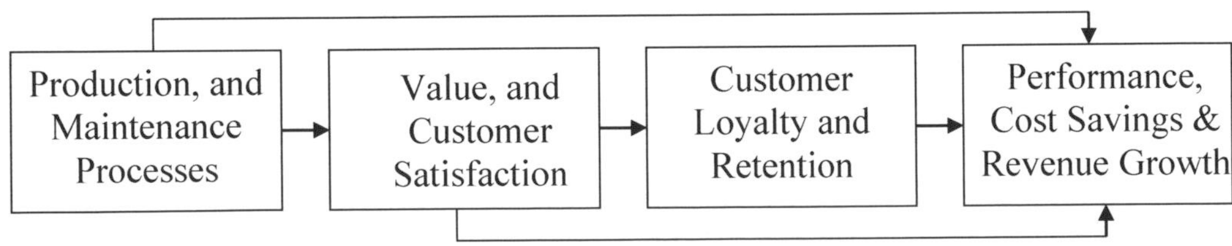

Internal Quality

Internal Quality encompasses various production and maintenance processes, which have direct effect on costs and revenue.

External Quality and Satisfaction

External Quality and Satisfaction encompasses what customers see in the purchase and consumption experience – the attributes and benefits that products and services provide and the costs they impose, and the conclusions the customers draw about the company. They have both direct and indirect effects on costs and revenues

Customer Loyalty and Retention

Loyalty is the customer's intention or predisposition to buy; Retention is the behavior – as when a customer returns to a restaurant, comes back to buy the same brand of car, etc.

They have direct effects, which include revenues from repeat purchases, reduction in costs of finding new customers, and revenues generated through cross-selling. Another direct effect is the price premium that loyal customers often pay.

ix) Service Quality Measurement

If you are not measuring it, you are not managing it.

The average company loses 10-30% of its customers each year. But few know: which, When, why, or Lost Sales Revenue?

a) Service Quality Gaps

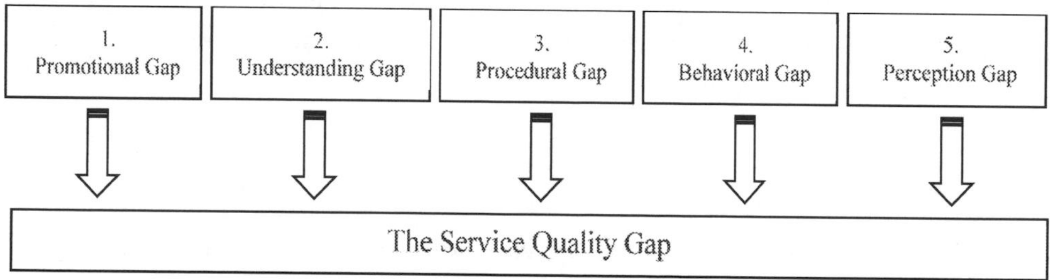

The Service Quality gap is the difference between customers' expectation of a service and their expectations of the actual service delivered by an organization.

Gap 1: The Promotional gap – What is said about the service differs from the standards actually delivered.

Gap 2: The Understanding gap – Managers' perceptions of customers' expectations are inaccurate.

Gap 3: The Procedural gap – Customers' expectations are not translated into appropriated operating procedures/systems.

Gap 4: The Behavioral gap – The service that is delivered is different from the specification for the service.

Gap 5: The Perception gap – The level of service perceived by customers differs from the service actually provided.

b) The Concept of Lifetime Customer Values

The lifetime value of a customer is a function of the customer's average spent with the business, multiplied by the length of time the business will retain the customer.

For example, if the average supermarket customer spends around $100 per week, or $5,000 per annum, and remains loyal for ten years, the lifetime value to the business is $50,000.

The power of the concept is demonstrated by what can be achieved through very small increases in customer retention. Indeed, with a very small incremental improvement in customer loyalty, turnover can be increased quite dramatically and with relatively little associated cost. Thus much of the gross profit from that additional turnover would find its way onto the bottom line.

c) Customer Value package

To satisfy customers you must meet their needs. You must "do best what matters most to customers". The customer value package is the combined set of benefits provided by the supplier to customers. If your customer value package meets customers' needs they will be satisfied and are much more likely to be committed.

The customer value package must therefore form the basis of your customer satisfaction survey.

Employees deliver the customer value package. Internal quality is measured by the feelings that employees have towards their jobs, colleagues and employers.

If employees feel that the company, through its strategies, procedures or lack of efficiency is constraining their ability to deliver the customer value package, employee satisfaction will be reduced.

Equally, if they feel that the customer value package is reduced by the other colleagues or departments they will be demotivated.

d) Kano's Three Level of Satisfaction

Expected Quality

Expected Quality measures can make or break decisions in buying. If you meet the standard, doing a better job at that feature doesn't buy more business. Example: the size of the blanket.

Desired Quality

However, the time spent waiting to check in may fall under the desired quality category. The shorter the wait, the greater will be the satisfaction. The better you are at providing desired features, the greater the satisfaction.

Excited Quality

The third level is excited quality. Customers aren't expecting these features of your product or service. They are "wowed" or pleasantly surprised. Receiving champagne while you wait to check in to the hotel may be a wow experience. Note that it doesn't take long for wows to turn into expected quality.

Expected quality gives a base threshold of satisfaction. Desired quality improves satisfaction as you improve that feature. Excited quality delights.

e) SERVQUAL

SERVQUAL is a model designed to measure customers' perception of service quality. It was developed by Parasuraman, Zeithaml and Berry.

SERVQUAL Questionnaire comprises 5 service quality dimensions and 22 criteria. The 5 dimensions are:

1. Tangibles – the physical facilities, equipment and appearance of personnel.
2. Reliability – the ability to perform the promised service dependably and accurately.
3. Responsiveness – willingness to help customers and provide prompt service.
4. Assurance – knowledge and courtesy of employees and their ability to inspire trust and confidence.
5. Empathy – caring, individualized attention that the firm provides in customers.

4

THE 5S HOUSEKEEPING AND 8 WASTES

4.1 5S Housekeeping

5S stands for the five Japanese words starting with the alphabet S as shown below. They are the five Keys to a Total Quality Environment in an organization.

1. SEIRI : Organization
2. SEITON : Neatness
3. SEISO : Cleaning
4. SEIKETSU : Standardization
5. SHITSUKE : Discipline

4.2 SEIRI (Organization)

i) Meaning

Distinguish between the necessary and the unnecessary and getting rid of what you do not need.

ii) Aims

- Establish criteria and stick to them in eliminating the unnecessary

- Practice stratification management to set priorities
- Be able to deal with the causes of filth

iii) Activities

- Eliminate the unnecessary
- Deal with the causes of filth
- Continuous improvement and standardization based on fundamentals

iv) Principles

Stratification management and dealing with the causes

4.3 SEITON (Neatness)

i) Meaning

Establish a neat layout so you can always get just as much of what you need when you need it

ii) Aims

- A neat looking work-place
- Efficient (including quality and safety) layout and placement
- Raise productivity by eliminating the waste of looking for things

iii) Activities

- Functional storage based on the 5W's and 1H
- Practice and competition in putting things away and getting them out
- Neater work-place and equipment
- Eliminate the waste of looking for things

iv) Principles

Functional storage and eliminate the need to look for things

4.4 SEISO (Cleaning)

v) Meaning

Eliminate trash, filth, and foreign matter for a cleaner work place. Cleaning as a form of inspection.

vi) Aims

- A degree of cleanliness commensurate to your needs. Achieve zero grime and zero dirt.
- Find minor problems with cleaning inspections
- Understand that cleaning is inspecting

vii) Activities

- 5S's where it counts
- More efficient cleaning
- Clean and inspect equipment and tools

viii) Principles

Cleaning as inspection

4.5 SEIKETSU (Standardization)

i) Meaning

Keeping things organized, neat, and clean, even in personal and pollution-related aspects

ii) Aims

- Management standards for maintaining the 5S's
- Innovative visible management so that abnormalities show up

iii) Activities

- Innovative visible management
- Early detection and early action
- Tools (e.g. manuals) for maintaining standardization
- Colour coding

iv) Principles

Visual management and 5S standardization

4.6 SHISUKE (Discipline)

i) Meaning

Do the right thing as a matter of course

ii) Aims

- Full participation in developing good habits
- Workshops that follow the rules
- Communication and feedback as daily routine

iii) Activities

- One-minute 5S
- Communication and feedback
- Individual responsibility
- Practice good habits

iv) Principles

Habit formation and a disciplined work place

4.7 8 Wastes

i) Definition

Waste is defined as any activity that does not add value to a process/product.

ii) Classification of Waste

Toyota Motors has classified waste into 7 categories:

1. Overproduction
2. Defects
3. Waiting/Delay
4. Inventory/Work-in-process
5. Transport
6. Process
7. Motion

Inspection can also be considered as waste, as it does not add any value to the process/product. Together with inspection, there are 8 wastes.

iii) Examples of Waste Items

a) Overproduction

Production of excessively large lots or production and far ahead of schedule, which can result in:

- Obsolescence
- Handling charges
- Storage space

b) Defects

- Spoiled items
- Returned goods
- Warranty claims
- Liability costs
- Recall costs

- Concession costs e.g. discount

c) Waiting/Delay

- Downtime
- Set-up time for machines
- Imbalance in line loading
- Late delivery of parts
- Supplier rejects

d) Inventory/Work-in-progress

- Handling charges
- Storage space
- Interest charges
- Obsolescence

e) Transport

- Parts transported from a central warehouse to a sub-warehouse before they actually reach the factory
- Parts stored at one end of the building and transported to the work station when needed
- Parts transported from large pallets to small pallets before reaching the machines

f) Process

- Ill-maintained machines
- Unnecessary steps

g) Motion

- Unnecessary actions e.g. searching, selecting, positioning, inspection, planning, holding, etc.

h) Inspection

- Incoming inspection
- WIP inspection
- Finished product inspection

5

QUALITY CIRCLES

5.1 Introduction

5.1.1 Different Approaches to Problem Solving

i) Quality Circle

A Quality Circle is a group of employees that meets regularly for the purpose of identifying, recommending, and making workplace improvements.

ii) Quality Improvement Team

A Quality Improvement Team is a form of Quality Circle that will dissolve after completion of the project.

iii) Cross-Functional Team

A Cross-Functional Team is a form of Quality Circle that comprises members of different functional areas.

iv) Suggestion System

Staff Suggestion Scheme is a formalized system through which employees can channel their ideas for workplace improvement. The improvement ideas can come from an individual, or the outcome of a team brainstorming session. No systematic and elaborated analysis, like QC, is required to substantiate the improvement ideas.

v) Quality Function Deployment

Quality Function Deployment is an integrated approach to product development and quality in all pre-production activities. It ensures that products entering production would fully satisfy the needs of their customers by building in the necessary quality levels as well as maximum suitability at every stage of product development.

5.1.2 Background Knowledge of Quality Circle

i) Quality Circle

A Quality Circle (QC) is a small group of employees which meet regularly on a voluntary basis to solve problems concerning their work and workplace. Members of the circle are normally from the same section and perform similar or related tasks.

Part of the philosophy of the QC is that if employees are given the opportunity for decision making at work, or if they have a say in how work should be conducted, then nearly everybody will take more interest and pride in his work.

ii) Objectives of Quality Circles

a) To promote job involvement and employee motivation.
b) To enhance the quality of an organization's products or service.
c) To promote more effective teamwork.
d) To promote employee decision-making through participation.
e) To improve communication within an organization.
f) To improve the management/employee relationship.
g) To improve leadership qualities.
h) To provide training in defining and solving problems.

iii) Organization Structure of Quality Circles

a) A **Steering Committee** overseas the entire QC development within a company, setting guidelines, policies and procedures;
b) A **Secretariat** maintains QC records, organizes promotional activities and handles all the paper work generated by QC programs;
c) A **Facilitator** is a senior member of management or executive who motivates, trains and guides QC leaders;
d) A **QC Leader** guides and trains his members who form the QC.

iv) Benefits of QC to Circle Members

a) Each individual is encouraged to develop to the best of his ability.
b) QC promotes self-education & self-confidence.
c) QC satisfies the individual's ego.
d) Closer relationship with colleagues through better communication.
e) Opportunity to participate and feel important.
f) Career advancement.

v) Fundamentals of QC Activities

a) Voluntary
b) Group based
c) Participation by every member
d) Continuous process
e) Application of problem-solving tools
f) Projects/themes to be related to the work or workplace

5.1.3 Quality Circles Organization Structure

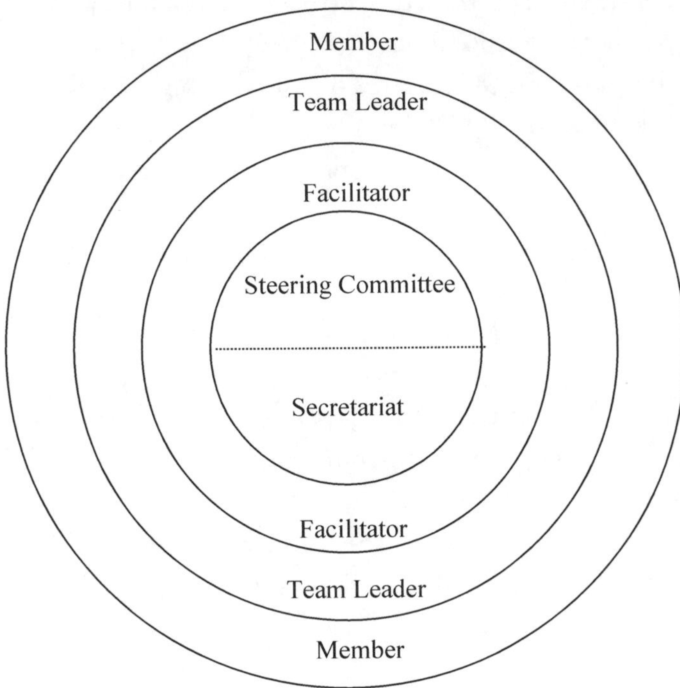

5.2 Plan-Do-Check-Action (PDCA) Cycle

5.2.1 Purpose of PDCA Cycle

The PDCA cycle is a systematic approach to work improvement. It provides the framework that enables the QC to use the various tools to:

a) identify and analyze areas for improvement
b) develop workable solutions
c) check if the selected solution works and
d) ensure that the solution is properly applied and the problem does not recur.

5.2.2 Eight (8) Steps in PDCA

i)	PLAN	Step 1:	Select Theme
		Step 2:	Plan Schedule
		Step 3:	Grasp Present Situation
		Step 4:	Set Target
		Step 5:	Analyze and Determine Problem and Plan Corrective Action
ii)	DO	Step 6:	Implement Plan
iii)	CHECK	Step 7:	Evaluate Results
iv)	ACTION	Step 8:	Standardize Action Taken / Review

The 8 steps in the PDCA cycle are commonly used by Quality Circles. You follow the steps one at a time and check your results at step 7. If your results do not meet your target, go back to step 5 in the PLAN stage to find out why the target is not met.

5.2.3 Twelve (12) Steps PDCA

i)	PLAN	Step 1:	Select Theme
		Step 2:	Plan Schedule
		Step 3:	Grasp Present Situation
		Step 4:	Set Target
		Step 5:	Identify Causes

		Step 6:	Check Causes
		Step 7:	Propose Solutions
ii)	DO	Step 8:	Try Solution
iii)	CHECK	Step 9:	Check Solution
iv)	ACTION	Step 10:	Obtain Management Approval
		Step 11:	Implement Solution (Standardization)
		Step 12:	Review

5.2.4 Other Type of Problem Solving Cycle

Motorola 6-Step Problem Solving Cycle

Step 1: Identify and Define the Problems

Step 2: Analyze the Facts

Step 3: Generate Alternative Solutions

Step 4: Make Decisions

Step 5: Take the Actions

Step 6: Evaluate the Results

5.2.5 PDCA – Continuous Cycle of Improvement

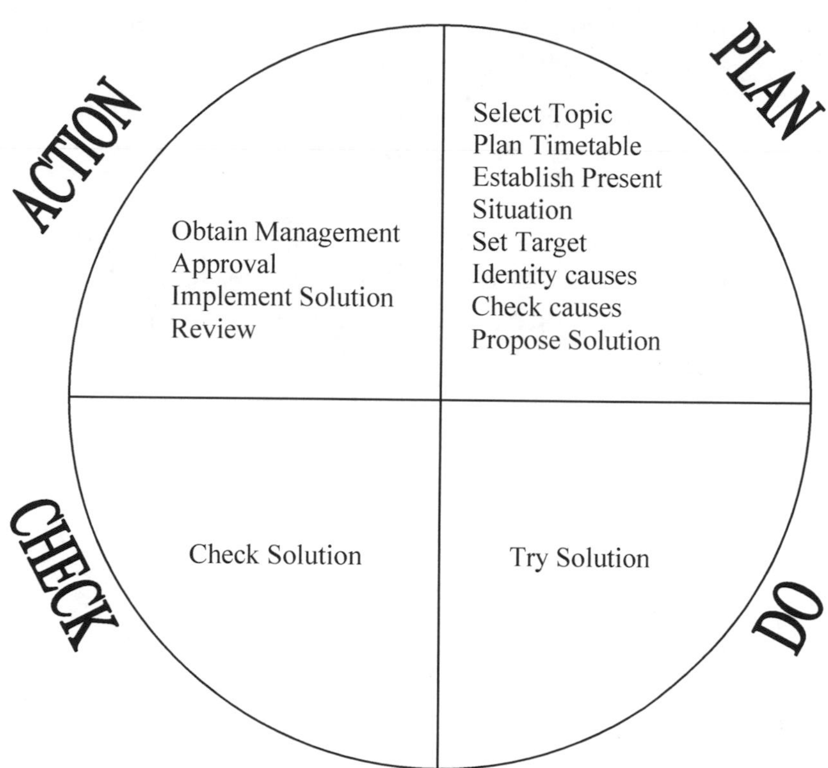

5.3 Theme Selection

5.3.1 Different Approaches to Theme Selection

When a QC starts a project, a project theme is required. The theme is generally quite broad. It is usually a statement of a problem area. For a new circle, you may choose a theme that you and your fellow members are familiar with.

There are several approaches in selecting a project theme. However, to ensure organizational effectiveness, the project should invariably solve a problem that is aligned to the organization objectives. The following are some approaches:

a) Bottom up approach – Based on the key processes that are cascaded from the strategic goals of the organization through the Strategic Deployment Management System (SDMS®), members can brainstorm to select a theme related to these key processes.
b) Top down approach – Members can select one of the problems identified by the management through the SDMS® as their theme.
c) Horizontal approach – This approach is more commonly used in a cross-functional team. The theme selected is more likely related to systemic problems identified through the SDMS®.
d) Suggestion Scheme – Some ideas suggested through the suggestion scheme can not be solved with common sense. The root cause of the problem is not obvious. A QC or QIT team can be form to formulate a project theme based on the ideas and resolve the problem systematically.

5.3.2 Common Tools Used in Theme Selection

a) Brainstorming
b) Decision Matrix
c) Affinity Diagram

5.3.3 Brainstorming

Brainstorming is an idea-generating technique aimed at getting the ideas of each member out in the open. A group can generate many ideas. Brainstorming is thus a group approach to creative thinking.

i) Rules for a Brainstorming Session

a) Define exactly the topic that will be brainstormed
b) Each member, in turn, is asked for ideas
c) A member can offer only one idea each time
d) When the member has no idea, he simply says, "PASS"
e) Criticisms are not allowed
f) Free-wheeling is welcome
g) A large number of ideas is desirable
h) Combination of ideas for improvement

i) Make sure that all members, no matter how shy and reluctant they are, contribute ideas
j) Record all ideas

ii) Methods used in Brainstorming

a) The "5W+1H" method

Why	Why solve this problem?
What	What purpose does it serve?
Where	Where is it accomplished and why?
When	When is it accomplished and why?
Who	Who is involved and why?
How	How is it accomplished and why?

b) Exaggeration
c) Building on Other's Ideas

5.3.4 Decision Matrix

It is a graphical method of showing relationships between a number of choices and criteria. It facilitates you to select important issues from a number of perspectives: a multi-dimensional approach to analysis.

i) Drawing the Matrix

The following steps are used to draw a decision matrix diagram:

a) Set up graphic format: Vertical columns: choices; Horizontal columns: criteria
b) Enter choices in vertical columns
c) List criteria in horizontal columns
d) Add weightages to criteria to reflect degree of importance, if necessary
e) Mark relationships between items with a scale from 0 to 5
f) Score relationships
g) Select most important relationships for analysis

ii) Decision Matrix Table (Individual Member)

Criteria / Choices	Control 0 – 5 (W =)	Ability 0 – 5 (W =)	Urgency 0 – 5 (W =)	Cost 0 – 5 (W =)	Total

iii) Decision Form (Team)

Choice	Individual Member's Score						Total

5.3.5 Affinity Diagram

i) What is an Affinity Diagram

An Affinity Diagram is the organized output from a team brainstorming session. The purpose of an Affinity Diagram is to generate, organize, and consolidate information concerning a product, process, or complex issue or problem.

ii) When is it Used?

Use an Affinity Diagram when you can answer "yes" to these questions:

a) Is the problem complex and hard to understand?
b) Is the problem uncertain, disorganized, or overwhelming?
c) Does the problem require the involvement and support of a group?

iii) How is it made?

a) State the problem
b) Brainstorm and record ideas on index cards
c) Move the cards into like piles
d) Name each pile with a header card
e) Draw the Affinity Diagram

iv) Example of an Affinity Diagram

Affinity Diagram

Respect for elders

a) Improper time management
b) Being rude or impolite to lecturers

Diligence

a) Sleeping during lessons
b) Studying in the wrong method

Self - discipline

a) Smoking and drinking
b) vandalism or graffiti
c) Gambling or playing card
d) Vulgar language
e) Taking attendance on behalf of friends
f) Fighting
g) Eating at restricted place
h) Inappropriate appearance
i) Skipping lessons without valid reasons
j) Spitting

Social responsibilities

a) Dangerous motorcycle riding
b) Making unnecessary noise during lecture or along corridors
c) Littering

Personal integrity

a) Cheating during tests or examination
b) Shoplifting

5.4 Plan Schedule

5.4.1 Different Approaches to Schedule Planning

i) Forward Planning

This approach is suitable when resources are constrained while completion date is not critical.

ii) Backward Planning

This approach is suitable when resources are flexible while completion date is critical.

5.4.2 Gantt Chart

Gantt Chart is a graphic method of showing sequence of project tasks. It is often used as a project planning tool for scheduling project activities.

Steps involved in drawing the Gantt Chart are:

a) Define project tasks and/or steps

b) Estimate time needed for each task, and start and finish dates

c) Create Gantt Chart: Horizontal axis: time
Vertical axis: tasks

d) Chart non-dependent tasks in parallel; contingent tasks in sequence

e) Monitor actual progress against chart

5.4.3 Other Tools and Techniques

Critical Path Analysis (CPA), Performance Evaluation Review Technique (PERT)

5.4.4 Example of Gantt Chart

GANTT CHART

	No	STEPS / Month	JUL	AUG	SEP	OCT	NOV
P	1	SELECT TOPIC					
	2	PLAN TIMETABLE					
	3	ESTAB. PRESENT SITUATION					
	4	IDENTIFY PRODLEM					
	5	IDENTIFY CAUSES					
	6	PROPOSE SOLUTION					
D	7	IMPLEMENTATION					
C	8	REVIEW					
	9	FOLLOW-UP					
A	10	STANDARDIZATION					

5.5 Establish Present Status

5.5.1 Purpose of Establishing Present Status

After identifying the project theme, you need to know what the present situation is. That is, how bad or big the problem is. You do so by:

- Identifying the present status of the problem
- Collecting data to confirm the situation

5.5.2 Tools and Techniques used in identifying Present Status

- Flowchart
- Activity Analysis
- Block Diagram

5.5.3 Flowchart

A flowchart is a tool for recording an operation or process in a logical and condensed form. It shows clearly all the activities in that process or operation. This includes time spent in waiting or in storage as well. Steps used in drawing a flowchart are:

- Decide on start and end points of the process
- List all key activities in sequence
- Using flowcharting symbols, create a flowchart

  O Operation
  ☐ Inspection
  ⇒ Transport
  Δ Delay
  ∇ Storage

- Check validity by tracing different scenarios through the chart; add links as necessary
- Draw up final version

5.5.4 Tools and techniques used in Collecting Data

i) Checksheet

Checksheet is used for collecting data over time to show trends and recurring patterns which need to be understood and controlled. The steps involved are:

- Define what to observe, measure and record
- Set observation intervals
- Make checksheet with things to measure down the left, and measurement intervals along the top
- Collect data
- Present results in an appropriate format

ii) Checklist

Checklist is a list of things to be routinely done, remembered or checked. Steps involved in drawing up a checklist are:

- Identify points in processes or procedures where checklists are needed
- List all the things that have to be checked
- Construct checklist – a tickbox followed by things which need to be checked
- Make copies of checklists and have them available at the point of use
- Tick off points as they are dealt with, and sign completed set

iii) Survey

Survey can come in the form of Questionnaire, Attitude Survey, Customer Needs Analysis, Customer Satisfaction Assessment, Supplier Survey, etc.

- Questionnaire – used for gathering information from a number of people.
- Attitude Survey – used for sampling opinion about changes or particular initiatives.
- Customer Needs Analysis – a structured approach for ensuring customer needs are met.
- Customer Satisfaction Assessment – used for monitoring levels of customer satisfaction.
- Supplier Survey – used for gathering information about suppliers to predict quality of suppliers

iv) Stratification

Stratification is a way of sorting out or arranging the data to be collected. The purpose of stratification is to aid in problem-solving by breaking down the causes of the problem into parts to examine each cause better. Usually, when you plan to collect data, you will need to stratify the data to be collected. With proper stratification, you are less likely to collect the wrong data. Also, if your analysis shows the result is not what you expected, it means you need to re-stratify and collect data again. Stratification can be classified into different types, i.e., by material, machine, operator, inspection, method, time, and others.

5.5.5 Tools and Techniques for Data Analysis

After you have collected the data, you have to sort, group and analyze the data. Data analysis is a process where raw data is organized using charts and diagrams. This allows the patterns and trends to be seen more clearly. This helps you to analyze the situation. Some of the data analysis tools used are: Pareto Diagram, graphs, scatter diagram, control chart and histogram.

i) Graphs

a) Line Graphs

Are the most common of all graphs. They are used to plot things as they happen.

b) Column Graphs (Bar Charts)

Are just what the name implies. Vertical columns show the information desired. They are drawn with spacing between adjacent bars and without any regards to its height.

c) Bar Graphs

Are just like column graphs, except that they run horizontally.

d) Pie Graphs

Are commonly used to show, e.g., how much money is spent and where or what percentage of sales they represent

ii) Histograms

Histogram shows the frequency distribution of a variable. It can be recognized by its characteristic bell-shape. No spacing is drawn by adjacent bars.

5.5.6 Examples

i) Flow Chart (a)

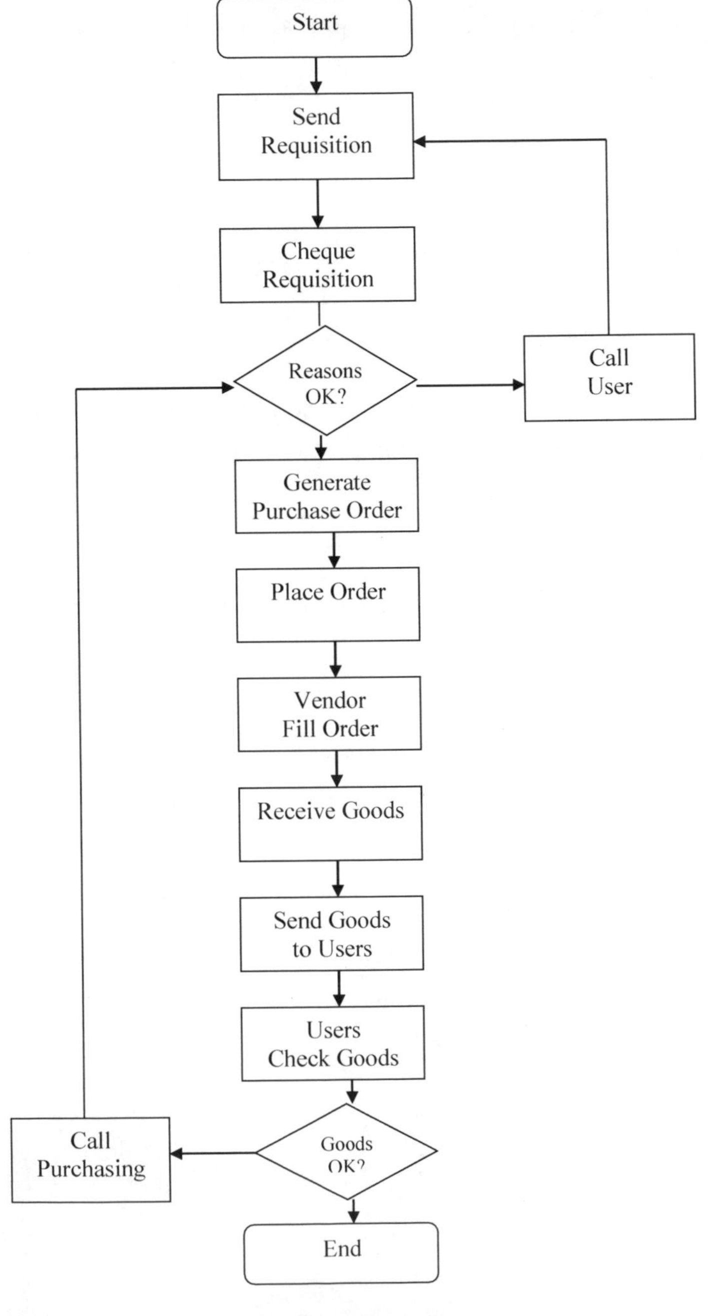

Flow Chart (b)

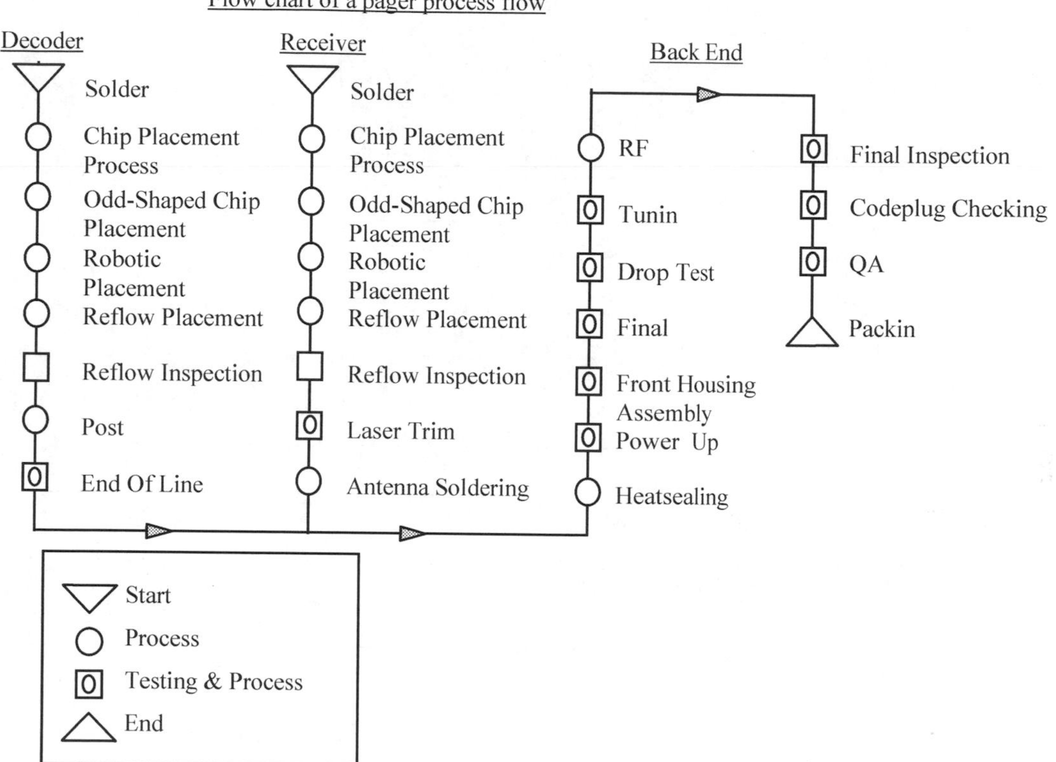
Flow chart of a pager process flow
Decoder
Solder
Chip Placement Process
Odd-Shaped Chip Placement
Robotic Placement
Reflow Placement
Reflow Inspection
Post
End Of Line
Receiver
Solder
Chip Placement Process
Odd-Shaped Chip Placement
Robotic Placement
Reflow Placement
Reflow Inspection
Laser Trim
Antenna Soldering
Back End
RF
Tunin
Drop Test
Final
Front Housing Assembly
Power Up
Heatsealing
Final Inspection
Codeplug Checking
QA
Packin
Start
Process
Testing & Process
End

ii) Checksheet

FREQUENCY CHECK SHEET

SCRATCHES ON TV CASINGS

Situation	TV sets with scratches on casing
Name of Checker	Samy
Start Date	2 November
End Date	7 November

TIME	CHECK MARKS	TOTAL
2 Nov	𝍸 𝍸 𝍸 III	18
3 Nov	𝍸 𝍸	10
4 Nov	𝍸 𝍸 II	12
5 Nov	𝍸 𝍸 𝍸 𝍸	20
6 Nov	𝍸 𝍸 IIII	14
7 Nov	𝍸 𝍸 𝍸 I	16

ITEM CHECK SHEET

TYPES OF REJECTS

Situation	Types of rejects in the colour TV Department
Name of Checker	Mohamed
Start Date	3 March
End Date	9 March

TIME	CHECK MARKS	TOTAL
PCB Lead Trimming	𝍸 𝍸 𝍸 IIII	19
Breakdown of transistor forming machine	III	3
Cabinet scratshes	𝍸 𝍸 𝍸	15
Dry joints	𝍸 𝍸 III	13
Solder shorts	𝍸 III	8

iii) Check List

Print Specification Checklist

- ❐ Printing Process specified
- ❐ Printer capability checked
- ❐ Delivery cost included
- ❐ Level of quality specified
- ❐ Film supplied
- ❐ Any part of job subcontracted
- ❐ Specification agreed
- ❐ Time to pass proofs agreed
- ❐ Proof type specified
- ❐ Appropriate binding system specified
- ❐ Imposition follows binding method
- ❐ Best following method agreed
- ❐ Ink colours agreed
- ❐ Dummies wanted
- ❐ Number in print run specified
- ❐ Delivery dates agreed
- ❐ Out-of-hours contact agreed
- ❐ Person to sign off print specified
- ❐ Date:
- ❐ Signed by:

iv) Customer Needs Analysis Questionnaire

Accounts Department
Customer Needs Analysis Questionnaire

Please fill in this questionnaire to give us a clearer understanding of the services you need from us.
Answers will be treated with complete confidentially.

1. What financial information do you need from us?
   ....
   ....
2. What other services do you need from us?
   ....
   ....
3. What response time to you queries would you find acceptable?
   ....
   ....
4. Do we provide information you do not use?
   ☐ Yes ☐ No
5. Do our staff understand their roles?
   ☐ Yes ☐ No
6. Do our staff need any basic training in accountancy?
   ☐ Yes ☐ No
7. What gaps are there in the service we offer?
   ....
   ....
8. Do we present information in the most readable way?
   ☐ Yes ☐ No
9. Are there any ways in which we could improve?
   ☐ Yes ☐ No

   If Yes, say how
   ....
   ....
10. How could we improve to meet your needs more exactly?
    ....
    ....

v) Line Graph

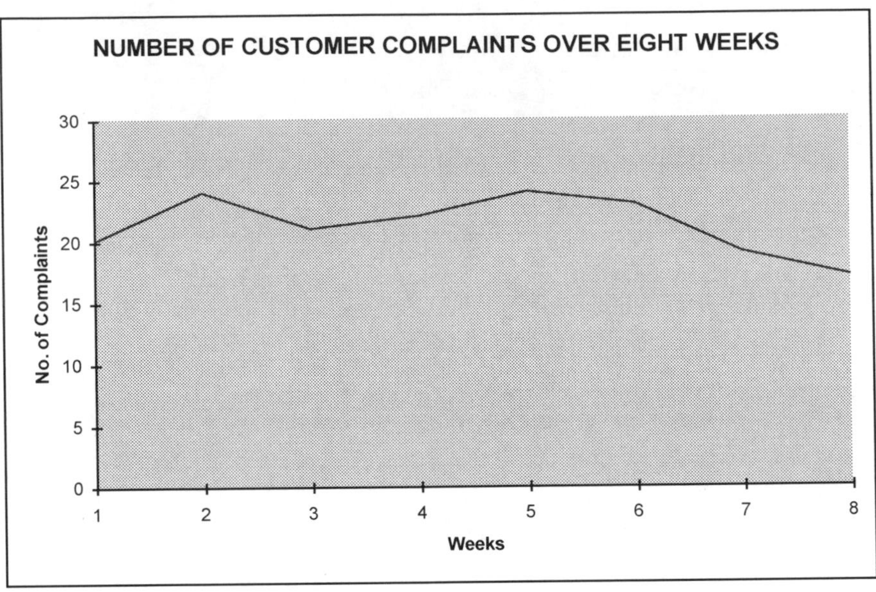

vi) Column Graph

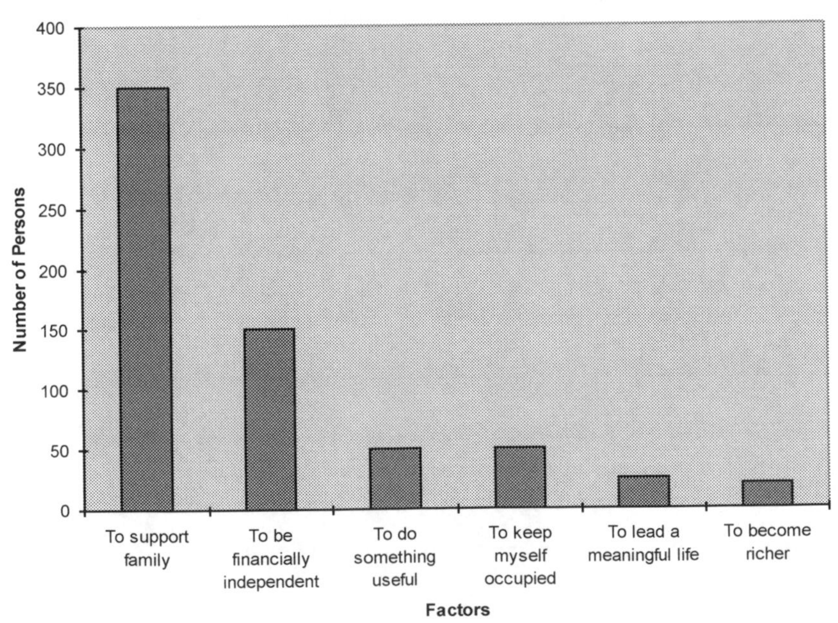

vii) Bar Graph

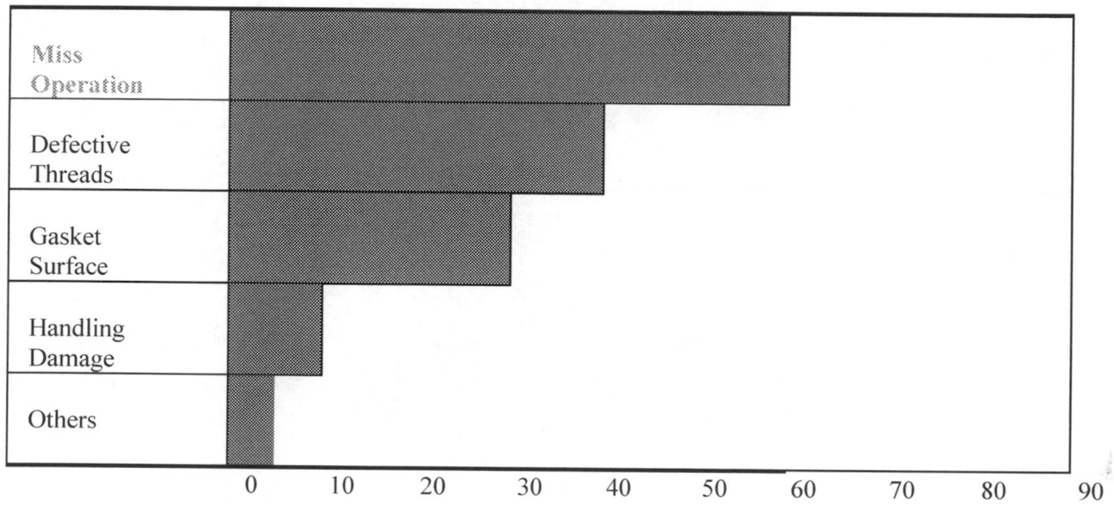

viii) Pie Graph

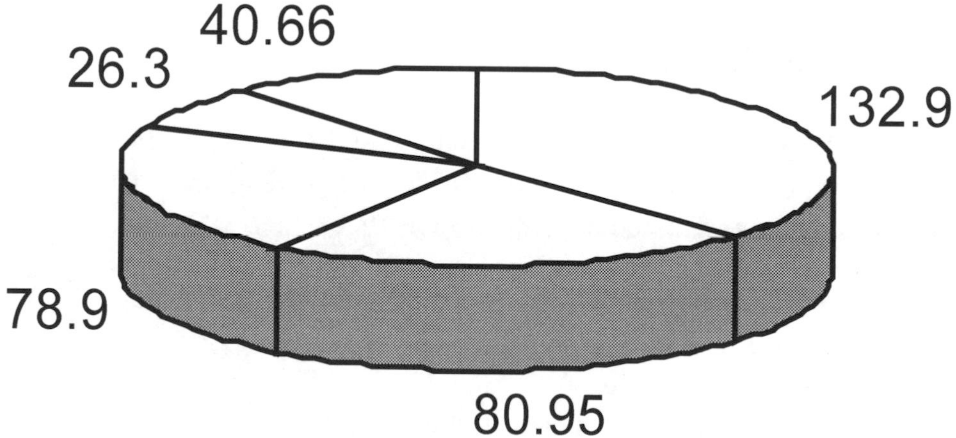

ix) Line Balancing Chart

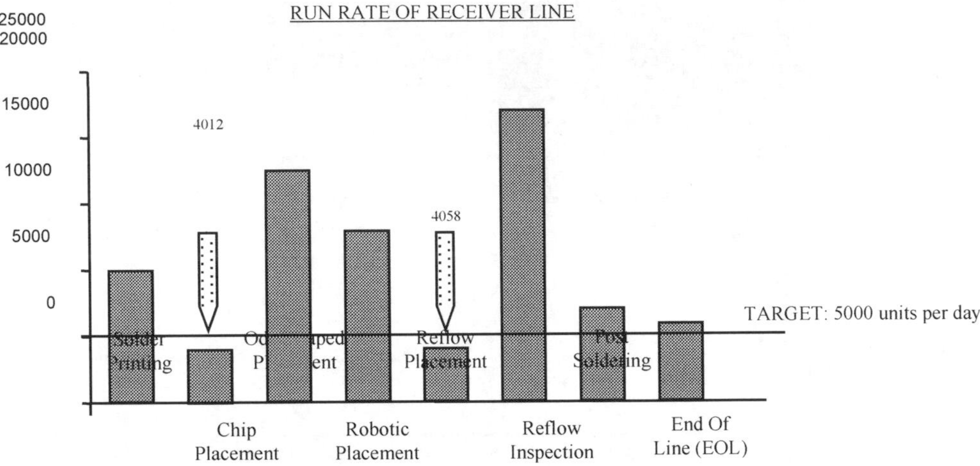

5.6 Set Target

5.6.1 Purpose of Setting Target

Once the team has established the present status and defined the problem, members must set a target for the project. The target will provide the direction the team should be heading to, and the constraints they should be working with.

The target set must be reasonable. Too high a target may discourage the team. On the other hand, members may find no challenge if the target is set too low.

Target may be expressed in percentages or units.

5.6.2 Different Approaches in Target Setting

a) Based on data collected and analyzed in the earlier stages
b) Based on benchmarking with company best
c) Based on benchmarking with industry best

d) Based on member's innovative ideas

5.6.3 Pareto Diagram

i) Introduction

In 1897, Italian economist V. Pareto presented a formula showing that the distribution of income is uneven. A similar theory was expressed diagrammatically by the U.S. economist M.C. Lorenz in 1907. Both of these scholars pointed out that by far the largest share of income or wealth is held by a very small number of people. Meanwhile, in the field of quality control, Dr J.M. Juran applied Lorenz's diagram to classify problems of quality into the vital few and trivial many, and named this method Pareto Diagram. He pointed out that in many cases, most defects and the cost of these arise from a relatively small number of causes.

Quality problem appears in the form of loss (defective items and their cost). It is extremely important to clarify the distribution pattern of the loss. Most of the loss will be due to a very few types of defects, and these defects can be attributed to a very small number of causes. Thus, if the causes of these vital few defects are identified, we can eliminate almost all the loses by concentrating on these particular causes, leaving aside the other trivial many defects for the time being. By using the Pareto Diagram, we can solve this type of problem efficiently.

In applying the Pareto Principle to QC projects, where there is a problem, there may be many causes, but the really important ones – those that greatly influence effects – are not many.

In QC projects, the Pareto Principle is mainly used to find out the 20% of the causes that have created 80% of the problem.

ii) Function of Pareto Diagram

Pareto Diagram is used to:

a) Identify critical factors of a problem out of many other possible factors
b) Confirm effectiveness of a solution by comparing the "Before" and "After" situations
c) Report findings and results of QC activities.

iii) Example of Pareto Diagram

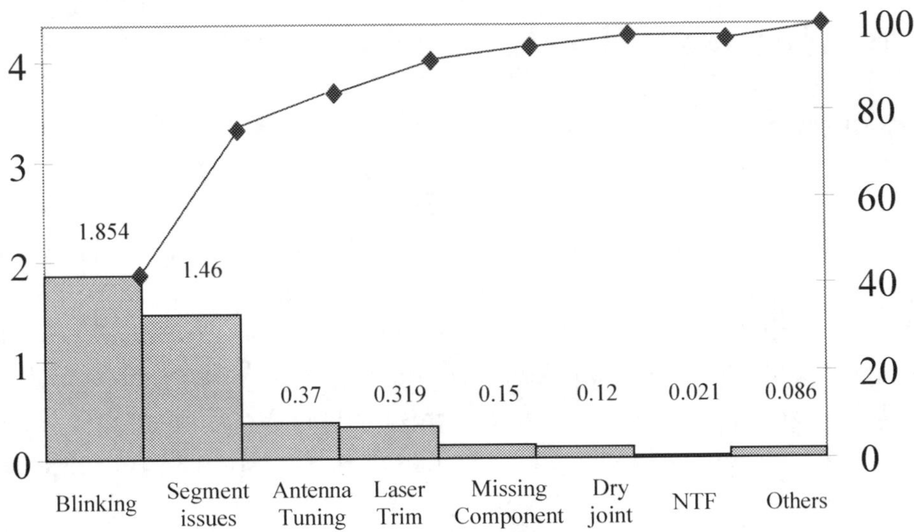

5.7 Analyze and Determine Problem

5.7.1 Different Approaches to Problem Analysis

a) Unstructured analysis of causes
b) Structured analysis of causes
c) Structured analysis of solutions

5.7.2 Cause and Effect Diagram

i) Introduction

The output or result of a process can be attributed to a multitude of factors, and a cause-and-effect relation can be found among those factors. We can determine the structure or a multiple cause-and-effect relation by observing it systematically. It is difficult to solve complicated problems without considering this structure, which consists of a chain of causes and effects and a cause-and-effect diagram is a method of expressing it simply and easily.

ii) Definition

Cause-and-effect Diagram is a diagram that shows the relation between a quality characteristic (Effect) and factors (Causes).

iii) Procedure for Making a Cause-and-Effect Diagram

a) Define problem and put on right of diagram, at the end of a horizontal line
b) Identify main causes and join to horizontal line by sloping lines
c) Brainstorm secondary causes and attach to main cause line
d) Look for root causes by identifying causes which occur more than once or which are related
e) Propose solutions to root causes

iv) Hints on Making a Cause-and-Effect Diagram

a) Identify all the relevant factors through examination and discussion by all members
a) Express the characteristic as concretely as possible
b) Make the same number of Causc-and-Effect diagrams as that of characteristics
c) Choose a measurable characteristic and factors
d) Discover factors amenable to action

v) Hints on Using a Cause-and-Effect Diagram

a) Assign an importance to each factor objectively on the basis of data

b) Try to improve the cause-and-effect diagram continually while using it

vi) Example of a Cause and Effect Diagram

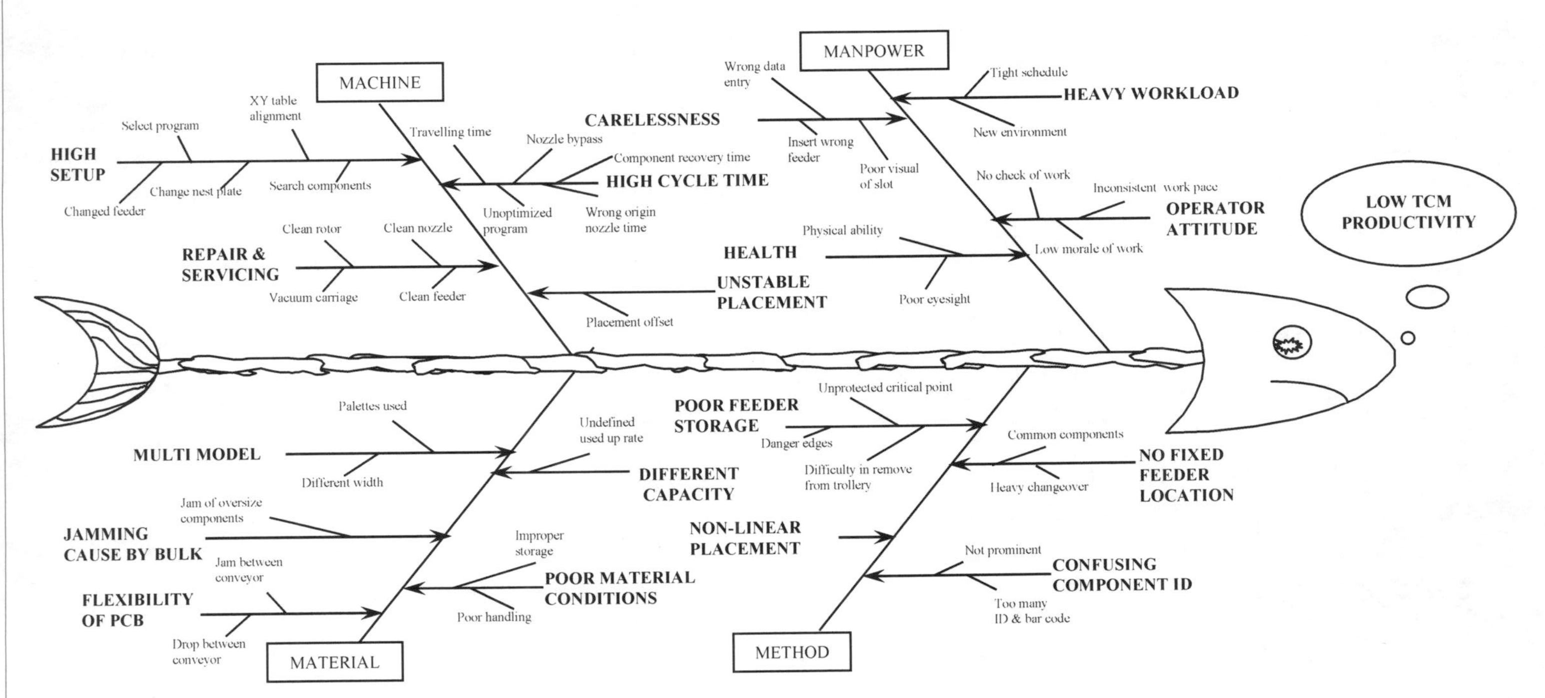

vii) Cause screening table for Low TCM productivity

Possible Cause	Main cause: Yes	Main cause: No	Remarks
MANPOWER			
1. Carelessness		3	All operators are well trained on handling and there are tracking systems to track mishandling.
2. Heavy workload		3	Our IE has studied the line balancing so as to ensure the operators are not overload by certain process.
3. Health		3	A clean working environment and a group of doctors whom they can seek help from.
4. Operator attitude		3	Operators are constantly upgraded to perform more complex work.
METHOD			
1. Poor feeder storage		3	Feeders are placed on the trolley more carefully. The trolley is pushed and kept in the room.
2. No fixed feeder location		3	Common components for different models are fixed at particular positions for convenience.
3. Confusing component ID		3	Components ID labels are placed at the obvious edge for easy checking.
4. Non-linear placement		3	Unique tube and orientation dot pictorial guide provide usual ease to prevent wrong chip placement.
MACHINE			
1. High setup time	3		Changing of feeders take up the major portion of the time.
2. Repair & service		3	Periodic preventive maintenance is performed to ensure TCM is in tip-top condition.
3. High cycle time		3	It can be reduced by optimizing the program.
4. Unstable placement		3	Offset for component is adjusted to greater accuracy.
MATERIAL			
1. Jam in bulk form		3	The bulb feeders are improved for fluent flow of components.
2. Different capacity		3	Compromise with the manufacturer for a standard amount.
3. Flexibility of PCB		3	The flexibility of PCB has nothing to do with the low productivity of TCM.
4. Poor material conditions		3	Ask the manufacturer to look into the problem.

viii) Pros and cons table for solutions of low TCM productivity

SOLUTION	PROS	CONS	SELECTED
Used fixed feeders	1. Less feeders change. 2. Less feeders are kept in the material room.	1. Pick-up time is not minimise 2. Obstructing the maintenance area in the carriage.	
Feeder loader	1. Fast in changing the feeders. 2. Can be used for storage of feeders 3. Less damage is caused when mounting of feeders.	1. Need cost to fabricate the fixture. 2. Need to occupy additional space for the storage of loader. 3. Need additional maintenance.	
Colour identification	1. Better visual of component ID 2. Ease of matching ID with feeder slot. 3. Clearer view of multi-model using the same component ID. 4. Ease for double checking 5. Ease of storage. 6. Ease of printing the tag by using a colour printer. 7. Better categorisation. 8. More systematic during changeover.	1. Fresh operator not familiarised of the colour tag. 2. Time taken to print the tags for all the feeders. 3. Tear and wear of colour-tag. 4. Match rail ID with colour tag at feeder.	√

5.7.3 Other Tools and Techniques for Cause and Effect Analysis

a) Relation Diagram
b) Solution Effect Diagram
c) Fault Tree Analysis

5.7.4 Tools and Techniques for Cause Evaluation

a) Root Cause Evaluation Matrix
b) Design of Experiment

5.7.5 Examples

i) Relations Diagram

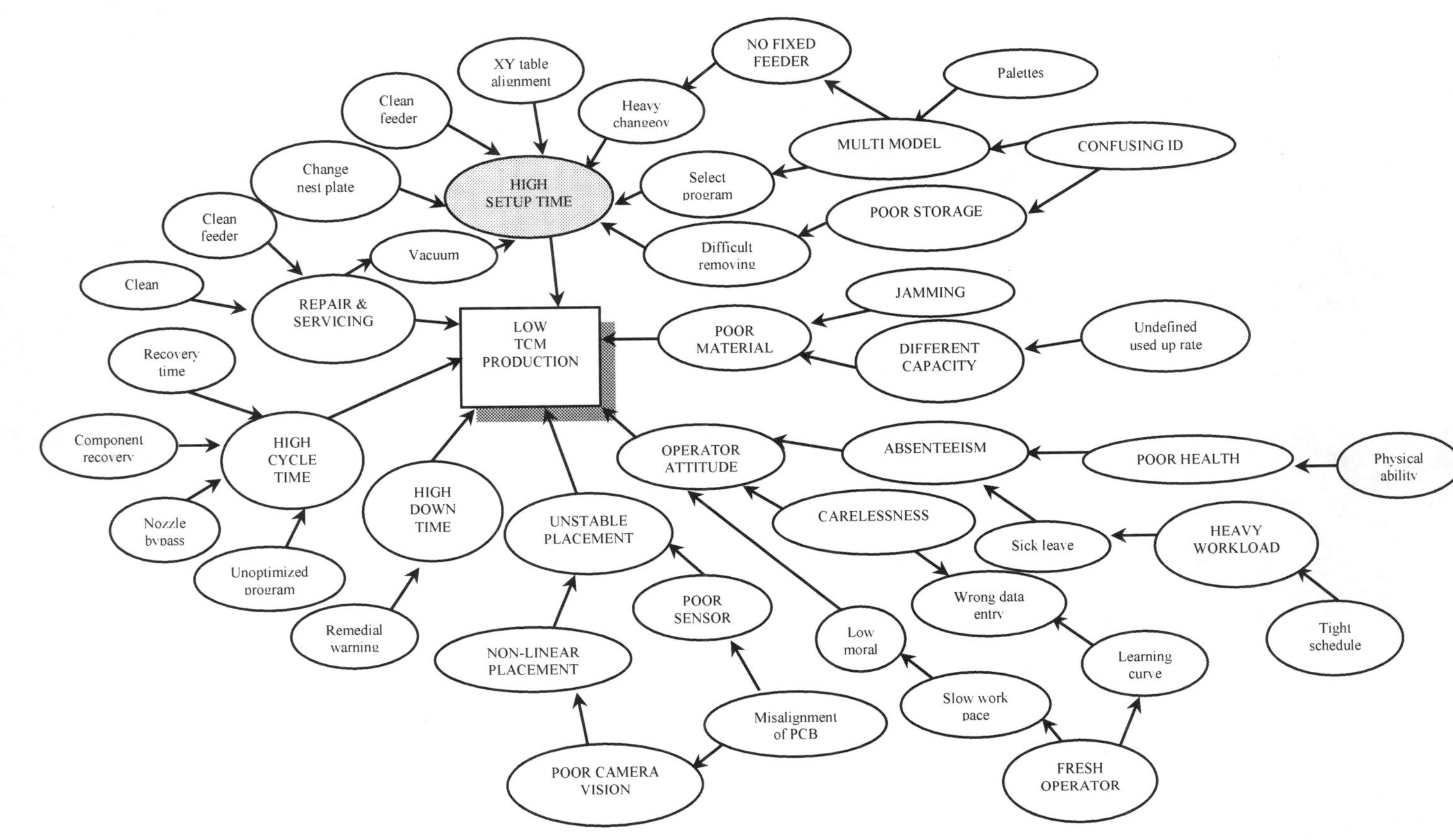

ii) Fault Tree Analysis

Graphic method of setting out causes and origins of potential problems with product or service.

Fault Tree Analysis: starting a car

symbols

- consequence of faults
- 'or' gate (this happens if one or more events take place)
- original faults
- 'and' gate (this happens if all the events below take place)

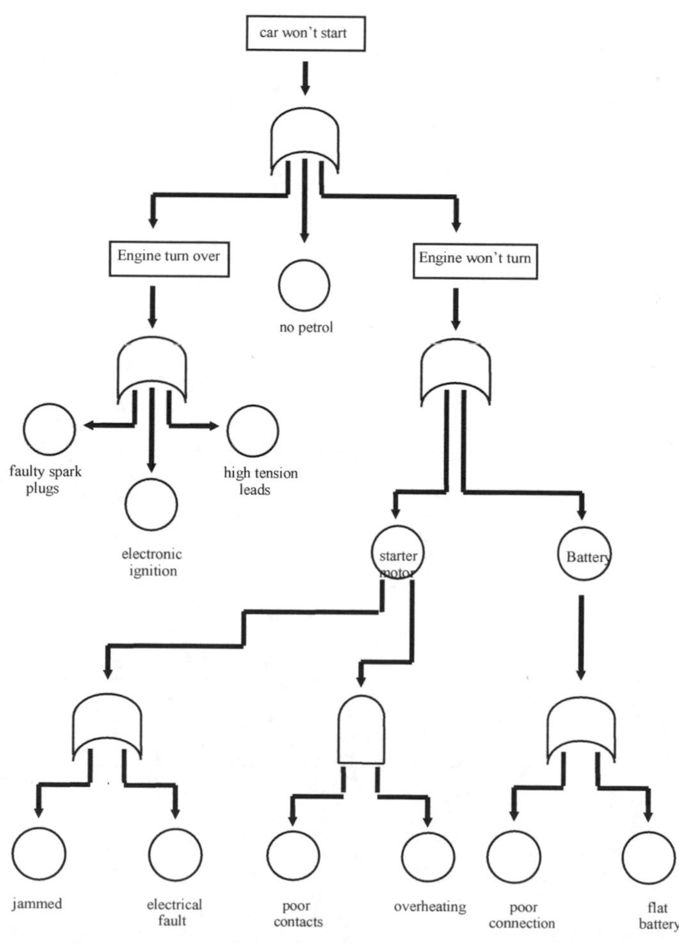

iii) Root Cause Evaluation Matrix

Root cause Evaluation Matrix for lateness in schools

● highly probable relationship = 3 points

❍ possible relationship = 2 points

▲ not a strong relationship = 1 point

	Evaluation criteria				
Causes	Certainty	Importance	Solution Known	Solution easy	Total
Poor motivation	●	❍	▲	▲	7
Poor transport	❍	▲	●	▲	7
Poor record keeping	▲	❍	●	●	9
Lack of consequences	●	●	●	●	12
Lack of awareness among staff	❍	●	●	●	11
Lack of focus on issues	❍	❍	●	●	10
Lack of system to deal with lateness	▲	●	●	●	10

iv) Design of Experiment

Title

Design of experiment (DOE) to study the correct setting for singulator to break ceramic array into single carrier.

Objectives:

To find out the most appropriate setting to achieve zero Defects Per Hundred Units (DPHU) for carrier.

Results

Variables	Level	
	-	+
A. Breaking speed (seconds)	0.8	1.8
B. Breaking angle (degree)	36	37

Run	n	Breaking speed	Breaking angle	Rejected	Accepted
1	1200	1.8	37	9	1191
2	1200	1.8	36	6	1194
3	1200	0.8	37	3	1197
4	1200	0.8	36	0	1200

	A+	A-
B+	n = 1200 Acc = 1191 Rej = 9	n = 1200 Acc = 1197 Rej = 3
B-	n =1200 Acc = 1194 Rej = 6	n = 1200 Acc = 1200 Rej = 0

Conclusion

Zero DPHU when the setting is: breaking speed is 0.8 seconds and breaking angle is 36 degrees.

5.8 Plan Solution

5.8.1 Different Approaches to Solution Planning

a) Solution for root causes
b) Solution for related causes
c) Corrective solution
d) Preventive solution

5.8.2 Decision Analysis

i) Definition

Decision Analysis is a structured approach to making decisions.

The tool provides a logical analysis of facts to support the decision. The process involves all levels of expertise in the decision in a very visible way.

ii) When to use Decision Analysis

Decision Analysis is especially useful for choosing between the attributes of things such as equipment or materials where each option is clearly defined.

iii) Steps in using Decision Analysis

a) Define decision statement
b) List criteria to consider in making the decision
c) Divide criteria into "musts" and "wants"
d) Brainstorm options to satisfy the decision statement

e) Check options against "must" criteria
f) Compare options which fulfil "must" criteria against "want" criteria, using weighted ratings
g) Present results as a table and select option with highest score

5.8.3 Other Tools and Techniques for Decision Analysis

a) Tree Diagram
b) Force Field Analysis
c) Failure Mode Effect and Criticality Analysis
d) Solution Effect Analysis

5.8.4 Technique for Preventive Solution

a) Poka Yoke

Fool-proofing devices which present problems

5.8.5 Examples

i) Decision Analysis

Choosing a computer system for Department X

Decision statement

Select a computer system which will capture all the data needed by the Management of department X

Decision criteria

Musts

- be compatible with existing hospital admissions system
- include all nursing management functions
- come with adequate training and support
- have at least one site or extensive simulation up and running

Wants

- attractive screen design
- easy to use
- good price relative to other product
- approved by RHA
- provide real time data

Selecting options

Musts	A	B	C	D	E
Compatibility	✓	✓	X	✓	✓
Functionality	✓	✓	✓	✓	✓
Training and support	✓	✓	✓	✓	✓
Track record	✓	✓	X	✓	✓

Classification of remaining options

Wants	Weight Factor	A	B	D	E	Maximum score
Attractiveness	4	32	28	24	32	40
Easy to use	6	30	30	24	42	60
Price	5	50	30	35	10	50
RHA approved	2	08	10	14	04	20
Real time	8	00	00	00	80	80
Total		120	98	111	168	250

Conclusion

The clear leader is option E, because it gives real time data. In this example, the clinicians' preference gives this a weight factor of 8, which outweighs the RHA's approval (weight factor 2).

ii) Tree Diagram

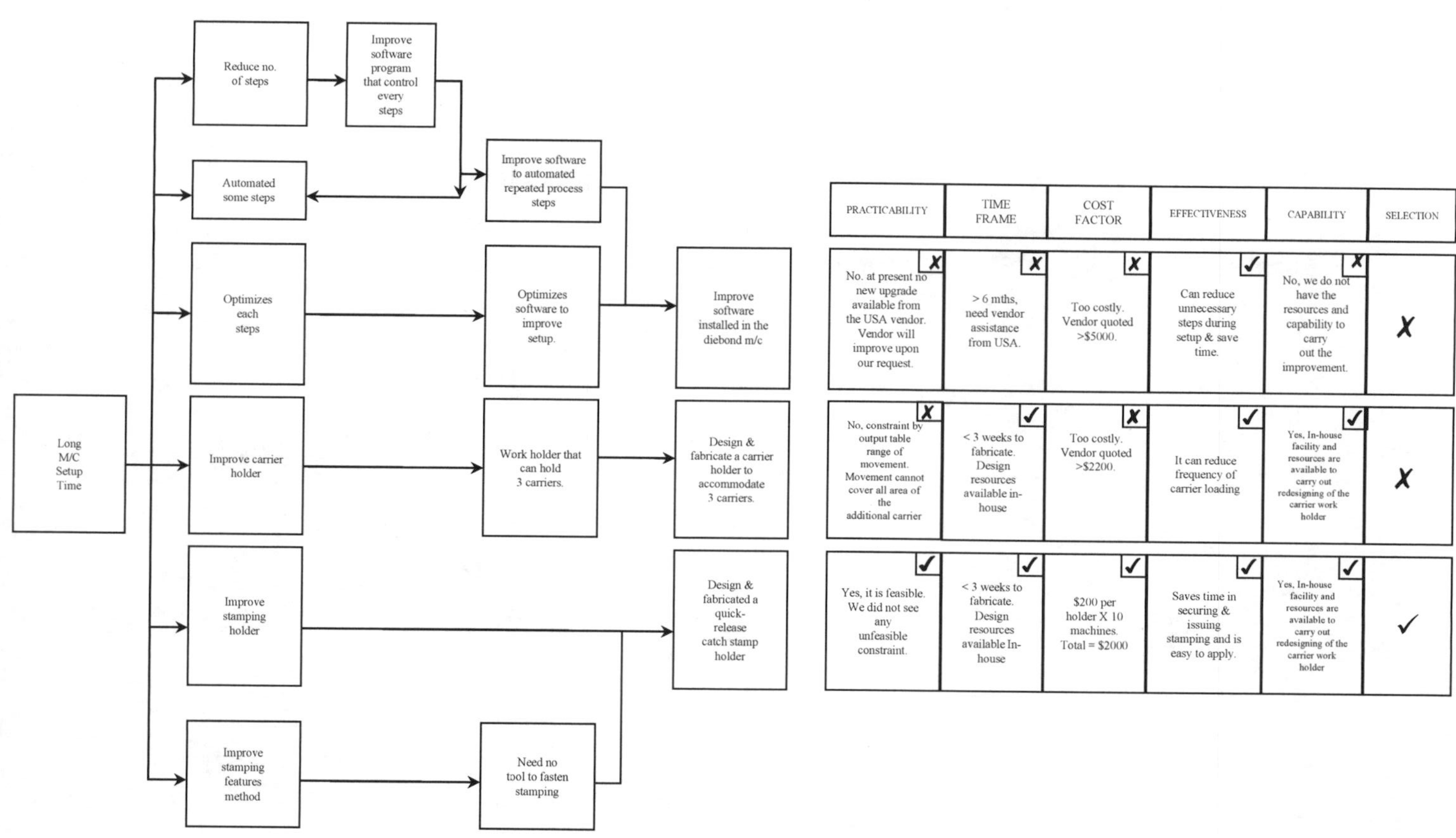

PRACTICABILITY	TIME FRAME	COST FACTOR	EFFECTIVENESS	CAPABILITY	SELECTION
✗ No. at present no new upgrade available from the USA vendor. Vendor will improve upon our request.	✗ > 6 mths, need vendor assistance from USA.	✗ Too costly. Vendor quoted >$5000.	✓ Can reduce unnecessary steps during setup & save time.	✗ No, we do not have the resources and capability to carry out the improvement.	✗
✗ No, constraint by output table range of movement. Movement cannot cover all area of the additional carrier	✓ < 3 weeks to fabricate. Design resources available in-house	✗ Too costly. Vendor quoted >$2200.	✓ It can reduce frequency of carrier loading	✓ Yes, In-house facility and resources are available to carry out redesigning of the carrier work holder	✗
✓ Yes, it is feasible. We did not see any unfeasible constraint.	✓ < 3 weeks to fabricate. Design resources available In-house	✓ $200 per holder X 10 machines. Total = $2000	✓ Saves time in securing & issuing stamping and is easy to apply.	✓ Yes, In-house facility and resources are available to carry out redesigning of the carrier work holder	✓

iii) Force Field Analysis

Method of analyzing problems in the items of the influences that affect them

Example: To introduce a quality improvement program into the organization

Total	Significance of change ✪	Possibility of Change ❁	Positive Forces	Negative forces	Possibility of Change ❁	Significance of change ✪	Total
7	3	4	People's desire to do well	Overworked	2	2	4
4	2	2	Acceptance of the inevitability of change	Fear of change	4	5	9
7	4	3	Benefits for customers	Suspicion of management's motives	3	3	6
7	4	3	Competitive pressure	Poor understanding of the need for change	4	3	7
25			Total			Total	26

✪ How significant are the consequences of change?
❁ How far is it possible to change this force?

5 very strong
4 strong
3 medium
2 low
1 weak

iv) Failure Mode Effect and Criticality Analysis

For anticipating errors in a product or process, and finding ways of preventing them.

FMECA for an advertising mailshot

Item	What could go wrong	Probability 1-10	Criticality 1-10	Effect	Prevention
Mailshot concept	Won't communicate well to the public	5	10	Reduce returns on the mailshot	Use PR company, evaluate other direct mail (benchmarking)
Mailshot design	Won't fit all constrains	7	4	Cost time to put it right	Make a physical dummy, including envelope
Database	Some names missing	10	5	Some letters will start dear ………	Put title instead of the name
Printing letters	Print quality not very good; smudges	6	3	Some letters won't look very smart	Print in batches of 50 - can catch any problems early on
Posting	post codes incomplete	10	1	Cost more to send	Add in $20 extra to the budget for the job

v) Solution Effect Diagram

Graphic tool for analyzing the likely effects of proposed solutions. Use this analysis when you are proposing changes, so that you can be clear about the consequences of solutions.

Solution Effect Analysis for Introducing Flextime

Managing Resources
HR Management
Better planning and Communication
Higher Utilization
Funding
Less Contact at work
Lonely
Self Discipline
Less Management Control
Happier
More Participation at Home
Introduce Flextime
Productivity Gains
Customer losses contact continuity
Staff need to keep temporary records
Peer Group influence reduced
Pay takes longer to calculate
Clocking In/Out System
Checking Time sheets
Quality of Work
Administration

5.9 Implement Plan and Evaluate Results

5.9.1 Roadmap to Effective Implementation of Plan and Evaluation of Results

a) Define the solution
b) Identify area for trial implementation

c) Identify implementation activities
d) Determine start and completion dates
e) Plan and allocate resources
f) Draw implementation schedule
g) Draw action plan
h) Implement trial solution
i) Evaluate results
j) Fine-tune Solution
k) Recommend solution for Standardization

5.9.2 Action Plan

i) Definition

Action Plan is a tool for breaking down objectives into tasks and deciding who will do what and when.

Action Plan is a way of planning how best to use people to achieve particular objectives. It makes sure people know exactly what their responsibilities are, and in what order.

ii) When to use Action Plan

It is particularly useful for planning initiatives where tasks fall outside the normal pattern of people's responsibilities.

iii) When not to use Action Plan

Do not use Action Plan when the project is sizable, with action points well into double figures. Use a more formalized approach such as CPA or PERT.

iv) Steps in Using Action Plan

a) Set objectives
b) Break down objectives into tasks
c) Put tasks in order, using flowchart

d) Establish due dates for each task
e) Allocate people tasks
f) Copy and distribute Action Plan to everyone involved

v) Example of Action Plan

Action Plan

Forms Management Team 1/3/2008

Action	**Start Date**	**Finish Date**	**Who**	**How**
Collect forms	8/3/08	29/3/08	All	Ask heads of Departments
List forms	29/3/08	5/4/08	JG	Database
Check duplication	29/3/08	5/4/08	TW	Manual check
Book room for next meeting	8/3/08	12/4/08	TW	
Research forms design	8/3/08	5/4/08	GA	Library
Research forms management System	8/3/08	5/4/08	BW/JG	Library, software catalogues
Circulate agenda	10/4/08	10/4/08	AB	

5.9.3 Other Tools and Techniques for Implementation of Plan

a) Gantt Chart
b) Critical Path Analysis (CPA)
c) Performance Evaluation Review Technique (PERT)

5.9.4 Tools and Techniques for Evaluation of Results

a) Run Chart
b) Control Chart
c) Process Capability Analysis

5.10 Standardization and Review

5.10.1 Roadmap to Effective Standardization and Review

a) Define the solution
b) Prepare SOP (Standard Operation Procedure)
c) Seek management approval
d) Incorporate SOP into company Quality Procedures
e) Plan standardization schedule
f) Draw action plan
g) Standardization
h) Measure results continuously
i) Identify area for continuous improvement

5.10.2 Tools and Techniques for Standardization

a) Standard Operation Procedure
b) ISO 9000 Quality Procedure
c) ISO 9000 Quality Instruction

5.10.3 Tools and Techniques for Project Review

a) Run Chart
b) Control Chart
c) Process Capability Analysis

5.10.4 Examples

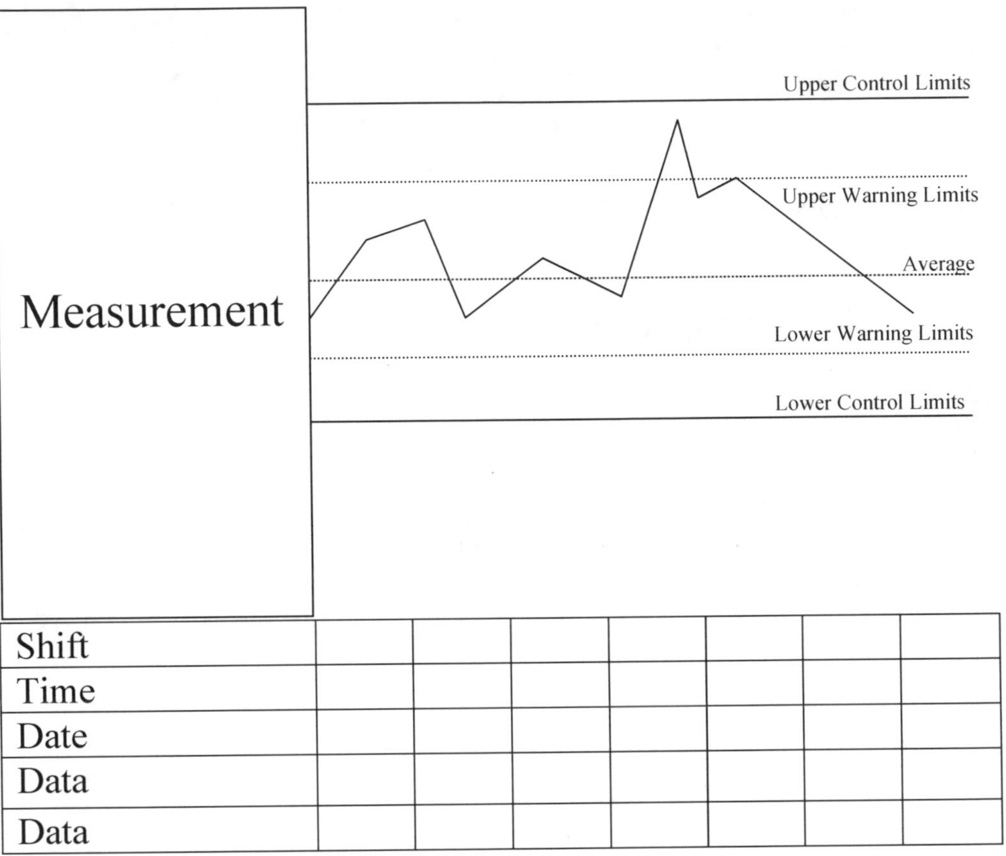

Shift							
Time							
Date							
Data							
Data							

5.11 Self-Evaluation

5.11.1 Introduction

After a project is completed, members should take some time to do a self-evaluation. They should reflect on what they have done and what they have not done, and the things they want to continue doing. Also, they should take note of what their mistakes are and avoid them when they start on their next project. By reviewing their actions, they can keep improving, both as a team as well as individually.

5.11.2 Radar Chart

Radar Chart is a graphical tool for rating performance, showing actual and ideal performance. It can be used by members to examine their improvement in knowledge and skills in QC tools. It can also be used to indicate their contribution to the team, check other performance areas and personal traits.

i) When Not to Use Radar Chart

Don't use it without agreement on how to define performance targets.

ii) Steps in Drawing Radar Chart

a) Select areas of performance
b) Define low and high performance in each area
c) Construct Radar Chart as wheel: Equal segments for each performance area; spokes as measurement scale with high performance on outside edge.
d) Rate performance in each area, individually and as a group
e) Join together rating scores and fill in performance rating
f) Select biggest gap in most critical area for improvement programme

iii) Example of a Radar Chart

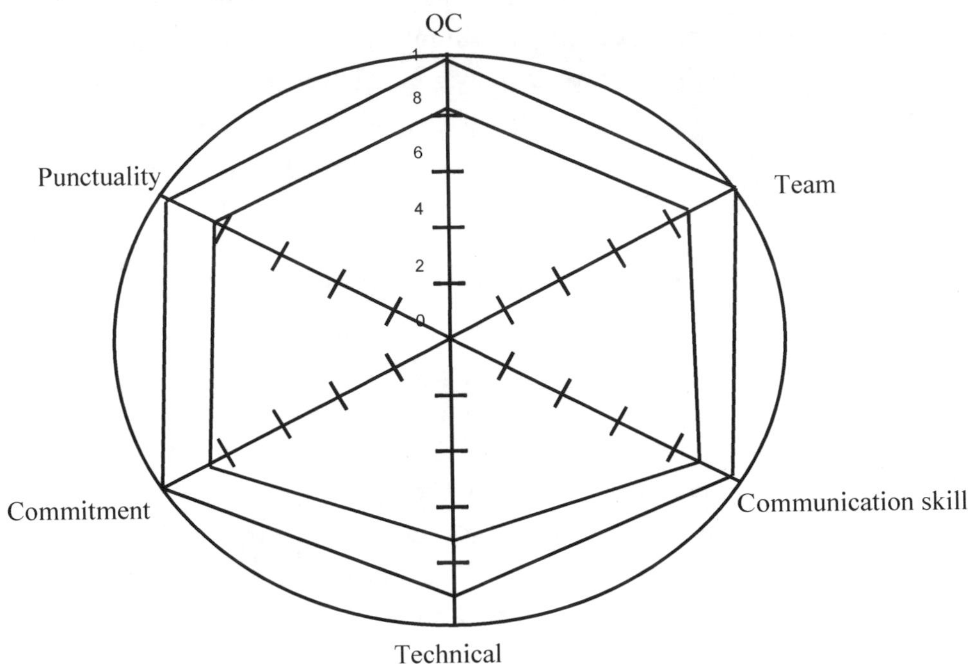

QC knowledge	8	9.8
Teamwork	8.5	10
Communicate skill	8.7	9.8
Technical skill	7	9
Commitment	8.5	10
Punctuaality	8.2	9.7

5.12 Future Project Selection

5.12.1 Proactive Action for Future Project

Members need to examine the following and take remedial actions before the start of the next project:

a) Problems encountered in working as a team
b) Difficulties encountered in completing the project
c) Critical items with significant gaps in Radar Chart

Members need to re-examine the list of projects identified at the beginning of the earlier project to confirm whether the next highest score in the project selection decision list is the most appropriate project to take on, after taking into consideration the above factors.

Some proactive actions that the team might take are:

a) Consult specialist in area of deficiency
b) Attend courses and/or take remedial actions on areas where members need improvement
c) Realign project with company objectives
d) Recruit cross functional members
e) Network critical functional areas

5.13 Conclusion

5.13.1 Two Key Elements in PDCA Cycle

a) Systematic
b) Scientific (Quantitative)

5.13.2 Five Critical Success Factors in QC Problem Solving

a) Pitch the project theme at appropriate level
b) Ensure sufficient depth and width in problem analysis
c) Generate solution with significant impact to organization
d) Disseminate solution for benchmarking
e) Take proactive action from lesson learnt

6

SIX SIGMA

6.1 Background of Six Sigma (6σ)

In 1987, Bob Galvin, CEO of Motorola, started their 6σ Quality Program, with the following goals: a) improve product and service quality 10 times by 1989, and at least 100 fold by 1991 and b) achieve 6σ capability by 1992.

The purpose is to improve customer satisfaction by reducing or eliminating defects in products, and errors and mistakes in all administrative, service and transactional processes.

In 1991, Lawrence Bossidy took over a troubled conglomerate, AlliedSignal and in 1994 used 6σ approach to radically change the way it did business, sales repeatedly rose in double digits while productivity and earnings rose dramatically

In 1995, Jack Welch, CEO of GE embarked on a 6σ program. GE achieved $2 billion in savings by end 1998, reported Wall Street Journal.

6.2 What is Six Sigma?

Sigma is a Greek letter, σ, used in mathematical statistics to represent the standard deviation of a distribution.

It is a statistic that quantifies the amount of variability or non-uniformity existing in a process, response or characteristics.

6.3 Sigma and PPM (Parts per Million)

Sigma	Parts per Million
1 σ	317,320
2 σ	45,500
3 σ	2,700
4 σ	63.5
5 σ	0.6
6 σ	0.002

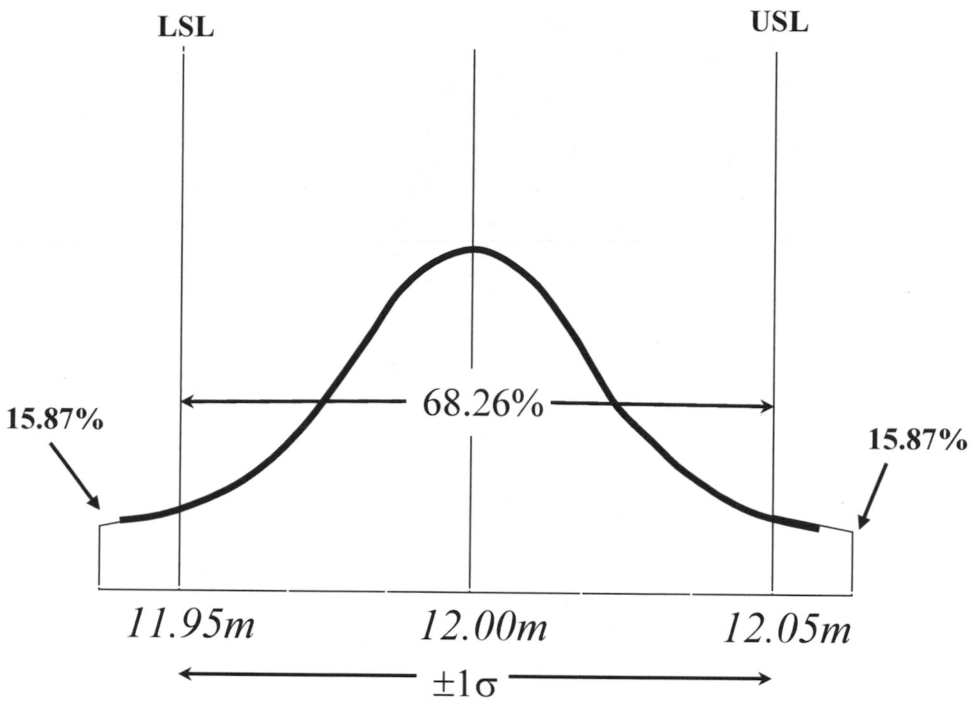
LSL
USL
68.26%
15.87%
15.87%
11.95m
12.00m
12.05m
±1σ

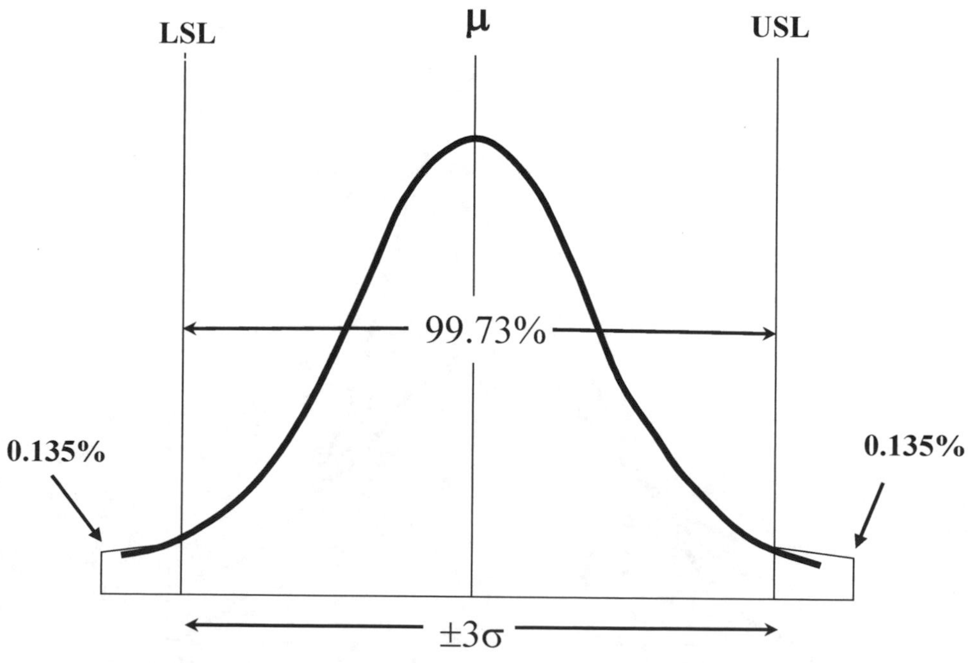
LSL
μ
USL
99.73%
0.135%
0.135%
±3σ

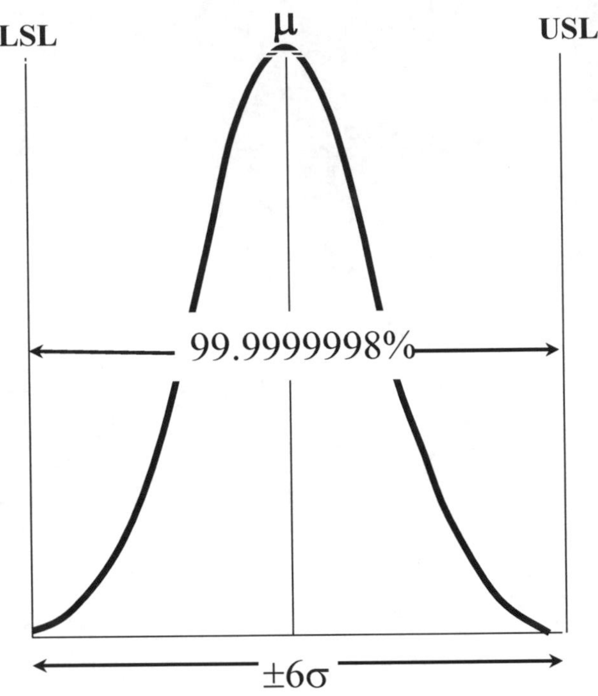
LSL
μ
USL
99.9999998%
±6σ

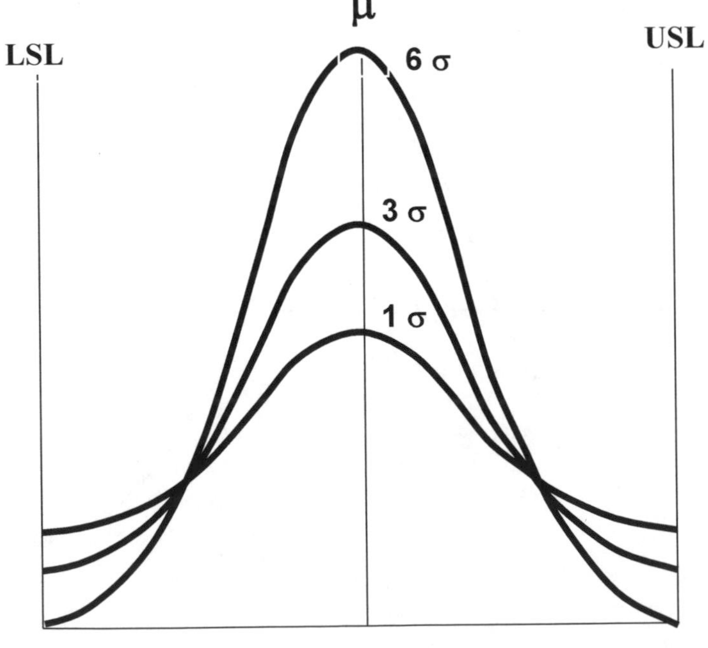
μ
LSL
USL
6 σ
3 σ
1 σ

6.4 μ with 1.5σ Shift

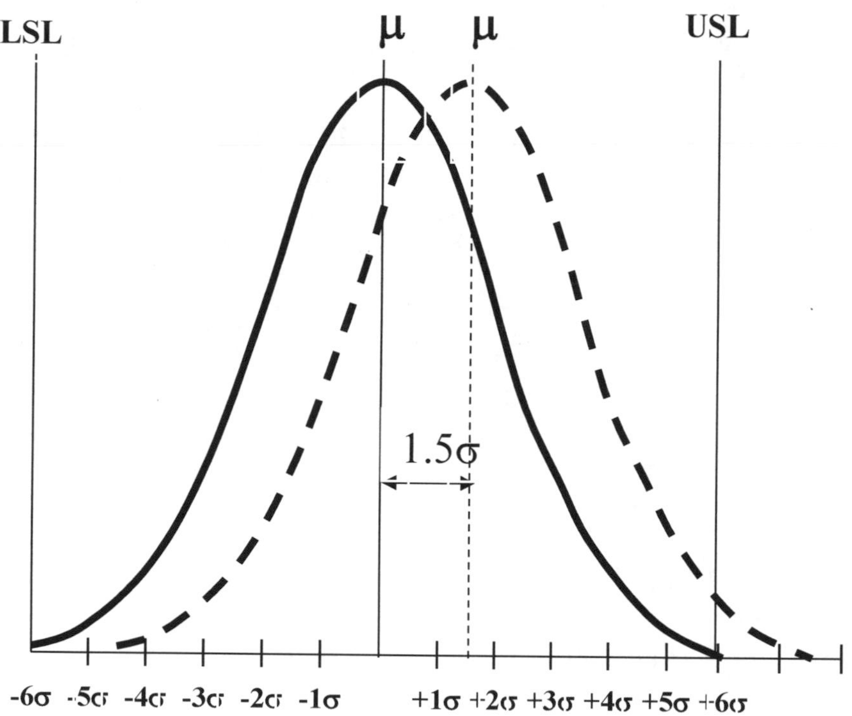

Sigma	Parts per Million	μ with 1.5σ Shift
1 σ	317,320	690,000
2 σ	45,500	308,000
3 σ	2,700	66,803
4 σ	63.5	6,210
5 σ	0.6	233
6 σ	0.002	3.4

6.5 Why Embark on Six Sigma?

6σ is a management philosophy that attempts to improve customer satisfaction to near perfection.

6σ is a measure of quality and efficiency, but furthermore, it is a measure of excellence.

For an organisation to embark on a 6σ program means delivering top quality service and product, while at the same time virtually eliminating all internal inefficiencies. It means having a common focus on excellence throughout the whole organisation

6.6 Six Sigma Strategy

a) Process Improvement
b) Process Design/Redesign
c) Process Management

a) Process Improvement: **DMAIC**

- **D**efine the problem and what the customers require
- **M**easure the defects and process operation
- **A**nalyse the data and discover causes of the problem
- **I**mprove the process to remove causes of defects
- **C**ontrol the process to make sure defects don't recur

b) Process Design/Redesign: **DMADV**

- **D**efine customer requirements and goals for the process/product/service
- **M**easure and match performance to customer requirements
- **A**nalyse and assess process/product/service design
- **D**esign and implement new processes/product/services
- **V**erify results and maintain performance

c) Process Management: **DMAC**

- **D**efine processes, key customer requirements and process "owners"
- **M**easure performance to customer requirements and key process indicators

- o **A**nalyse data to enhance measures and refine the process management mechanisms
- o **C**ontrolling performance through ongoing monitoring of inputs/operations/outputs and responding quickly to problems and process variations

6.7 Six Sigma Organisation

a) The Council
b) Project Sponsors and champions
c) The Six Sigma Coach (Master Black Belt)
d) The Project Leader (Black Belt)
e) Team Members
f) The Process Owner

a) The Council

i) Develop a strong rationale for doing Six Sigma
ii) Plan and actively participate in the implementation
iii) Create a vision
iv) Become a powerful advocate
v) Set clear objectives
vi) Hold itself and others accountable
vii) Demand solid measures of results
viii) Communicate results and setbacks

b) Project Sponsors and Champions

i) Setting a rationale and goal for improvement projects
ii) Couching on and approving changes
iii) Finding resources
iv) Advocating for the team's efforts
v) Running interference for the team
vi) Working with other managers
vii) Learning the importance of data-driven management

c) The Six Sigma Coach (Master Black Belt)

i) Communicating with Champions and Council

ii) Establish and stick to a firm schedule
iii) Dealing with resistance
iv) Estimate, measure and validate dollars and other savings
v) Help to resole team and other conflicts
vi) Gather and analyze data about team activities
vii) Help teams promote and celebrate their successes

d) The Project Leader (Black Belt)

i) Review/revise/clarify the project rationale
ii) Work with team members
iii) Select or help to select project team members
iv) Identify and find resources and data for the team
v) Support team members in implementation
vi) Making sure the team uses its time effectively
vii) Maintain the team's project schedule
viii) Support the transfer of new solutions or processes
ix) Document final project results

e) Team Members

i) Brainstorming
ii) Carry out instructions for data collection and analysis
iii) Listen actively to others
iv) Carry out assignments
v) Review the efforts of the team itself

f) The Process Owner

i) Normally the manager of a part of a particular function

People who receive the solution created by an improvement team and become the "owners" responsible for managing the improved process

6.8 The DMAIC Implementation Process

a) Define the Opportunities
b) Measuring Process Performance
c) Analyzing Data and Investigating Causes
d) Improving the Process
e) Control and Process Management

a) Define the Opportunities

i) Establish Project Charter

Guided by the Council, the Champion and the project team should select a project title that is aligned to the strategic goals and objectives of the organization established at the corporate level. The Champion can use one of the following systems to identify the project.

- o Strategic Deployment Management System (SDMS®)
- o Holistic and Integrated Management System (HIMS®)

SDMS® is a management system used to deploy strategic goals and objectives of an organisation to all functions and all levels of its employees.

HIMS® is a management system that helps organizations implement their strategic plans effectively, and achieve organizational goals, mission and vision effectively through harnessing the total factor productivity of the organizations.

<table>
<tr><td colspan="5">PROJECT CHARTER</td></tr>
<tr><td>Project Title</td><td colspan="4"></td></tr>
<tr><td>Project Facilitator</td><td colspan="4"></td></tr>
<tr><td>Project Leader</td><td colspan="4"></td></tr>
<tr><td>Team Members</td><td colspan="4"></td></tr>
<tr><td>Broad Definition of the Issue</td><td colspan="4"></td></tr>
<tr><td>Problem / Opportunity Statement</td><td colspan="4"></td></tr>
<tr><td>Project Scope, constraints, assumptions</td><td colspan="4"></td></tr>
<tr><td>Stakeholders</td><td colspan="4"></td></tr>
<tr><td>Implementation Plan</td><td colspan="2">Start Date</td><td colspan="2">End Date</td></tr>
<tr><td>Stage</td><td>Planned</td><td>Actual</td><td>Planned</td><td>Actual</td></tr>
<tr><td>DEFINE</td><td></td><td></td><td></td><td></td></tr>
<tr><td>MEASURE</td><td></td><td></td><td></td><td></td></tr>
<tr><td>ANALYZE</td><td></td><td></td><td></td><td></td></tr>
<tr><td>IMPROVE</td><td></td><td></td><td></td><td></td></tr>
<tr><td>CONTROL</td><td></td><td></td><td></td><td></td></tr>
<tr><td colspan="5">SIGNED:</td></tr>
</table>

ii) Identify customer requirements

The project team can use one of the following techniques or tools to identify the customer requirements:

- o Quality Function Deployment
- o SIPOC (Supplier-Input-Process-Output-Customer)

iii) Analyse and prioritise customer requirements

Kano Analysis can be used to classify the customer requirements into basic requirements, core competitive requirements, and breakthrough customer needs/features.

b) Measuring Process Performance

i) Select what to measure

- CTQ (Critical-To-Quality) Tree

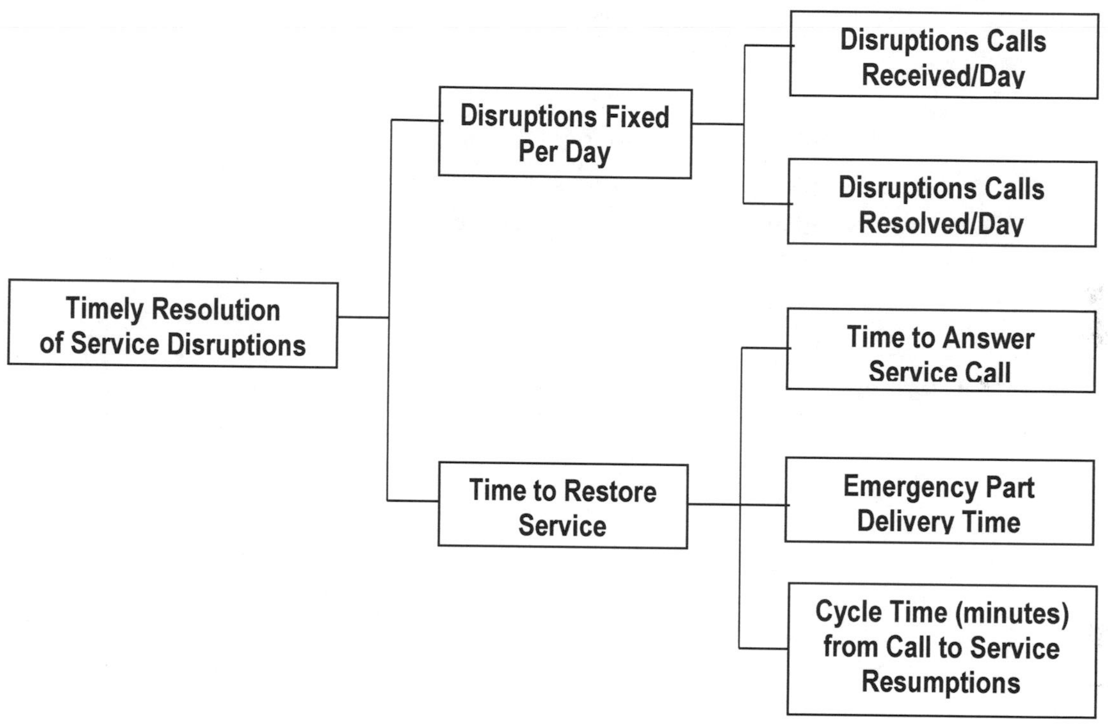

ii) Prepare data collection and sampling plan

iii) Develop baseline defect measures

- Final Yields
- First-Pass Yield
- Defects

  Defect is any failure to meet a customer requirement or performance standard. For example, poor paint job, and a lost reservation.

- Defect Opportunity

Defect Opportunity is a chance that a product or service might fail to meet a customer requirement or performance standard. For example, scratch, uneven paint, wrong colour, and stain.

- DPMO (Defects per Million Opportunities)

  The following example illustrates the DPMO of a service operation.

  - Process: Counter Services
  - Number of services observed: 668
  - Number of services with errors observed: 25
  - Number of error opportunities per serve: 5
  - DPMO = 7,485
  - Sigma = 3.94

iv) Identify improvement opportunities

Final Yield

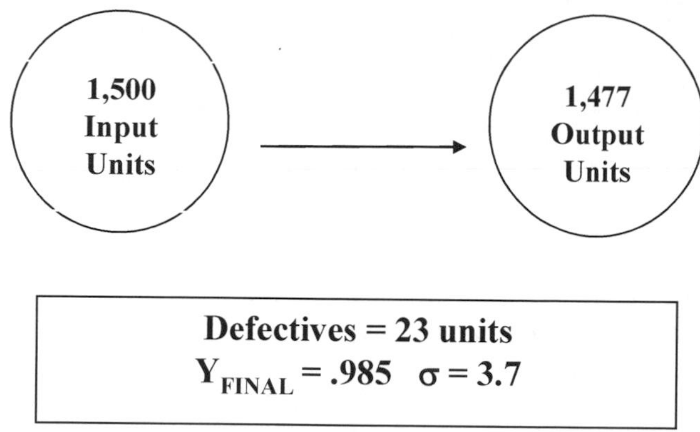

First-Pass Yield

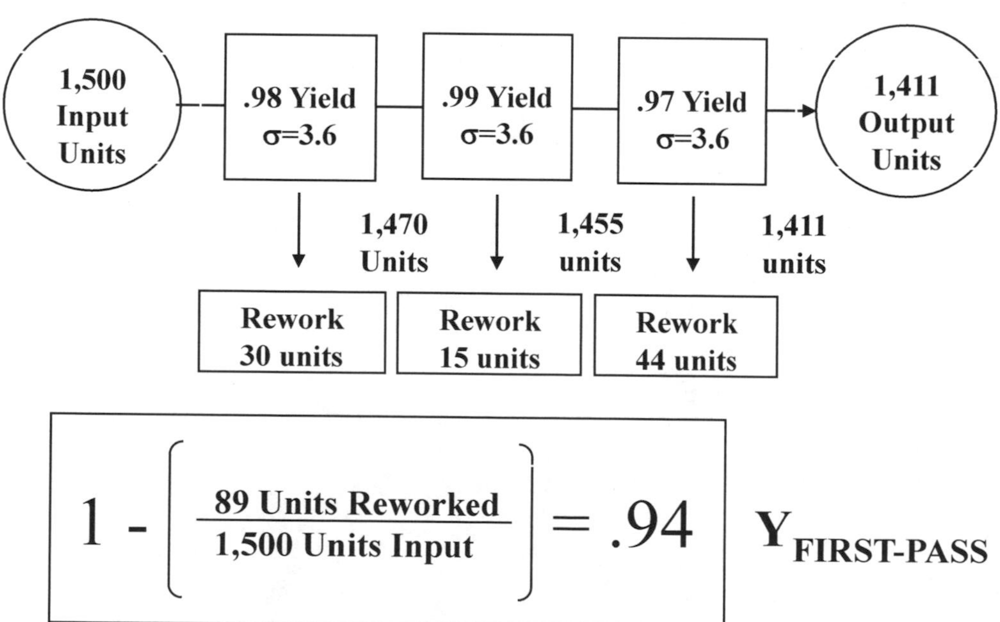

c) Analysing Data and Investigating Causes

There are two main categories of analysis:

i) Data Analysis
ii) Process Analysis

and three phases of root cause analysis:

iii) Exploring
iv) Generating hypotheses about the causes
v) Verifying or eliminating causes

Some Tools for Analysing Data and Investigating Causes

	Data Analysis	Process Analysis
Exploring	• Pareto Chart • Run Chart • Histogram	• Process Map • Deployment Map
Generating hypotheses about the causes	• Brainstorming • Cause and Effect Diagram	• Brainstorming • Value Analysis
Verifying or eliminating causes	• Scatter diagram • Stratified chart	• Data Collection Tools

d) Improving the Process

i) Generate creative solution ideas
ii) Synthesise solution ideas
iii) Analyse and select a solution
iv) Pilot test
v) Implement full scale

Some Tools and Techniques for Improving the Process

STEP	TOOLS AND TECHNIQUES
Generate creative solution ideas	Simplification, Straight-line processing, Parallel processing, alternative paths, etc
Synthesise solution ideas	Tree Diagram
Analyse and select a solution	Impact/Effort Matrix, Decision Matrix
Pilot test	Force Field Analysis, Pilot Planning Checklist, Pilot Testing Debrief
Implement full scale	Completion Checklist

e) Control and Process Management

i) Document the improvement
ii) iEstablish on-going process measure

- monitor stability, capability

Stability

Stability is a stable process that produces predictable results consistently. To ensure that the process is stable, we need to develop control charts of our indicators.

The Upper Control Limit (UCL) and Lower Control Limit (LCL) are calculated from the data. 99.7% of all expected result (common cause variation) should lie between these two limits.

Control Limits show what the process can deliver. Specification Limits are defined by the customers.

Processes that are "out of control" need to be stabilised before they can be improved.

Special causes require immediate cause-and-effect analysis to eliminate the special cause of variation.

Capability

Capability is defined as the ability of a process to produce products within specification limits.

The Upper Specification Limit (USL) and Lower Specification Limit (LSL) are determined from the customer's requirements.

The Capability of Attribute (counted) data like defects is zero defects (USL=LSL=0).

The Capability of Variable (measured) data like time, money, length, weight, is determined using customer's specifications

Cp, the process capability index, is the 6σ range of the variation within the process. Cp = (USL-LSL)/6σ

Cpk, accounts for process centering. Cpk = min of (USL-X)/3σ or (X-LSL)/3σ

Typically, when Cp and Cpk are over 1.0, the process is capable.

± 6σ implies Cp = 2, Cpk = 2, ppm = 0.002

iii) Improve and sustain the process

- adopt or adapt best practices – benchmarking
- process re-engineering
- design for six sigma

Average Control Chart

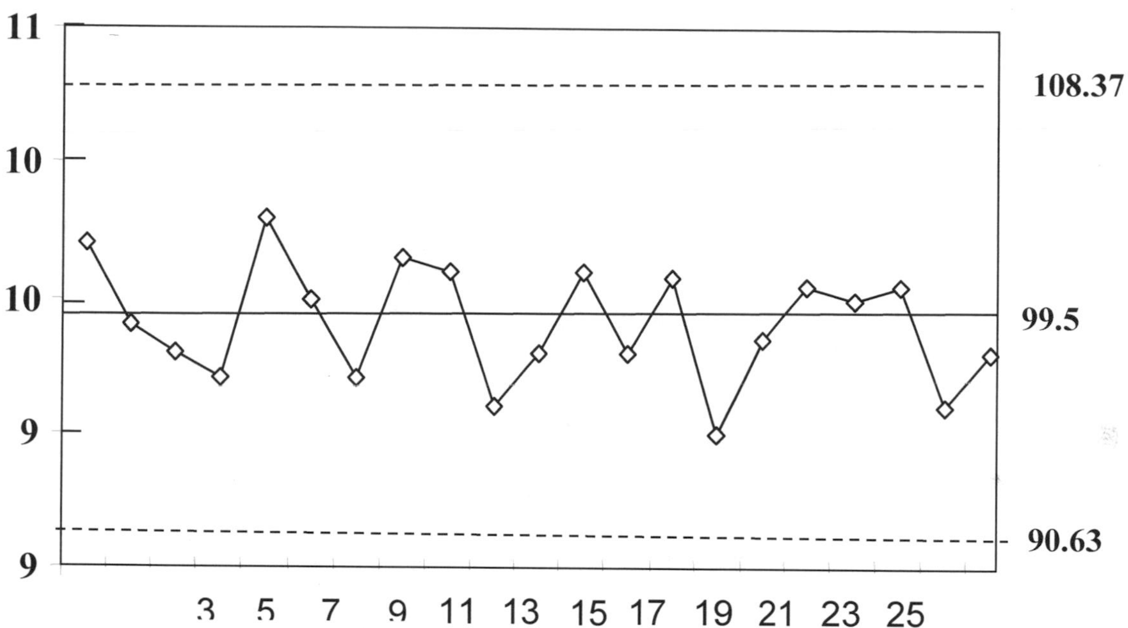

Sigma Control Chart

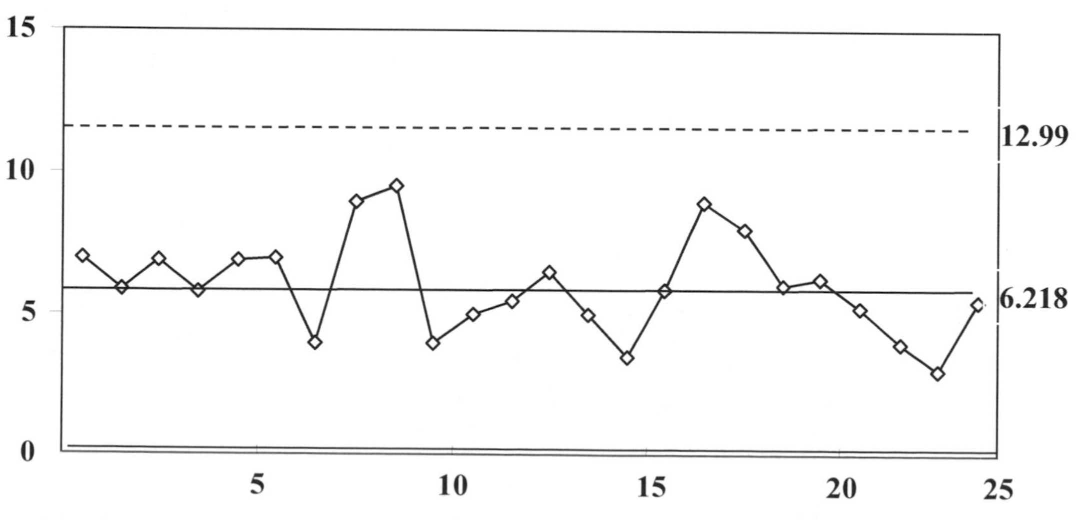

6.9 Process Design / Redesign

a) **D**efine customer requirements and goals for the process/product/service

b) **M**easure and match performance to customer requirements

c) **A**nalyse and assess process/product/service design

d) **D**esign and implement new process/product/service

e) **V**erify results and maintain performance

Some Tools for Process Design / Resign

- Quality function Deployment (QFD) - House of Quality
- Design of Experiments (DOE) - used to find optimal operating conditions to achieve a desired output
- Failure Modes and Effects Analysis (FEMA) - anticipate problems so you can take steps to counteract them, and reduce or eliminate the risks
- Benchmarking

House of Quality

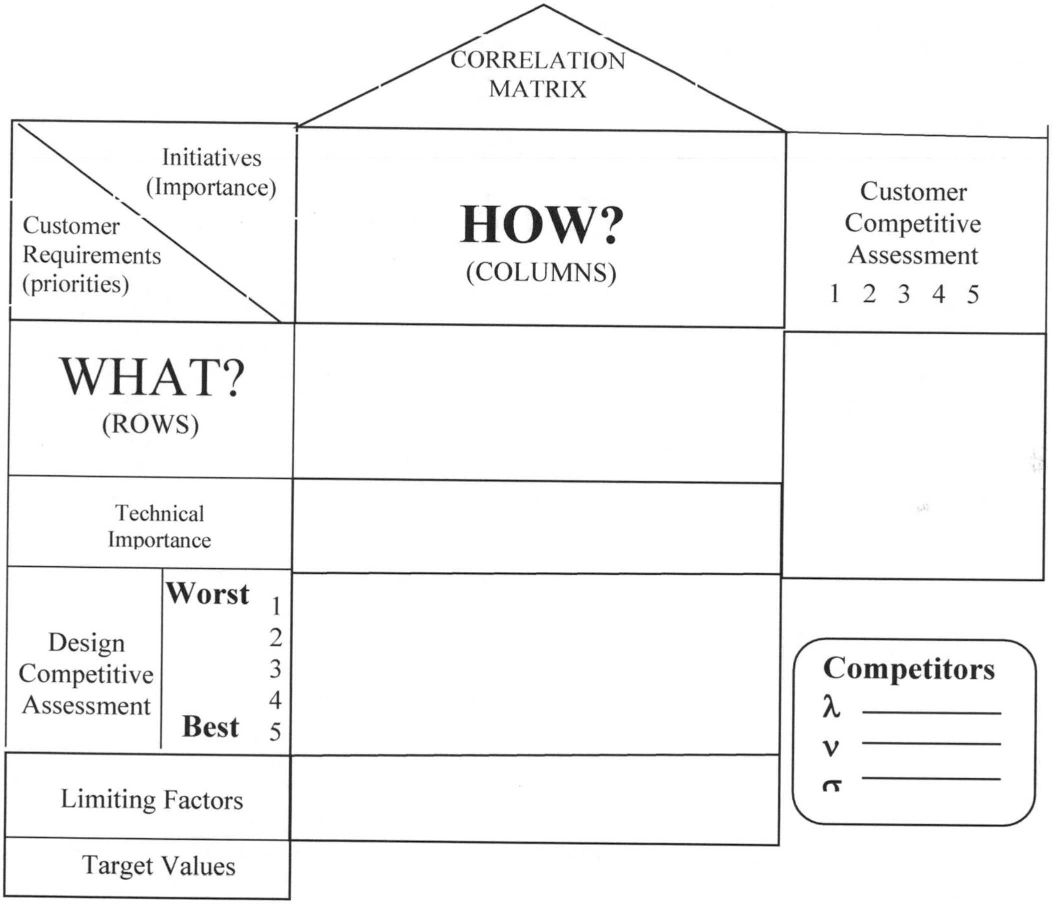

CORRELATION MATRIX

Initiatives (Importance)

Customer Requirements (priorities)

HOW?

(COLUMNS)

Customer Competitive Assessment

1 2 3 4 5

WHAT?

(ROWS)

Technical Importance

Design Competitive Assessment

Worst 1

2

3

4

Best 5

Competitors

λ ______

ν ______

σ ______

Limiting Factors

Target Values

7

BENCHMARKING

7.1 Introduction

Benchmarking has been around for a long time.

In 1907, BHP is believed to have compared its steel-making processes with those of steel-makers in Europe.

In the 1930s, before Toyota made its first motor vehicles, its executives visited American Ford plants to learn about mass production.

In the 1950s, Toyota executives returned and studied the inventory management system of some American supermarkets. This evolved into the Kanban system of production.

In the late 1970s, Xerox was shocked to discover that Fuji-Xerox was selling copiers at a price equivalent to what it cost US Xerox simply to manufacture the copiers. This discovery spearheaded a successful program to reduce costs in the US manufacturing process. Xerox later incorporated benchmarking as a key element in their corporate-wide improvement movements.

The successes of some of the pioneering organizations that have made breakthrough gains have focused attention on benchmarking. Today, many organizations use benchmarking to help drive continuous improvement movements. In the USA this has been heavily promoted through the American Quality Award and in Singapore by the Singapore Quality Award.

7.2 Definition

a) The search for industry best practices that lead to superior performance (Robert C. Camp, Xerox)

b) An ongoing process for emulating best-in-class practices, products, and services to help achieve superior performance and competitive advantage (Florida Power & Light Co.)

c) The continuous process of analyzing the best practices in the world for the purpose of establishing and validating process goals and objectives leading to world-class levels of achievement through process improvement (IBM Corp.)

d) An improvement process in which a company measures its performance against that of best-in-class companies, determines how those companies achieved their performance levels, and uses the information to improve its own performance. The subjects that can be benchmarked include strategies, operations, processes, and procedures. ("The Quality Glossary," Quality Progress, February 1992, page 20.)

7.3 Types of Benchmarking

a) Internal Benchmarking

You can benchmark internally by comparing your area with other departments, business units, or locations within your own organization.

Example:	Finance Office against Human Resources Office on service quality
Advantage:	Easy to find partners
Disadvantages:	Narrow focus generally means opportunities for break-through improvements are missed
	Internal politics may cause reluctance for genuine information sharing

e) External Benchmarking

i) Competitive Benchmarking

You benchmark externally against Competitors.

Example:	ABC bank against XYZ bank on service quality
Advantage:	Clear focus on performance measured
Disadvantages:	Difficult to gain agreement to share information
	Information tends to show "where" rather than "how" to improve business performance
	Comparing with others that are all in the same industry may limit creative solution

ii) Industry Benchmarking

You benchmark against other organizations in the same industry that may not be competitors, because of differences in product mix, etc.

Example:	ABC airline against XYZ port on handling of customer complaints
Advantages:	Easier to identify willing partners
	Better chance of open sharing of information
Disadvantage:	Limit to chances of break-through gains

iii) Generic Benchmarking

You benchmark against organizations that are not in the same industry which employ similar processes with a particular performance emphasis, such as the cycle time in developing new products/services, cost-effectiveness in filling customer orders.

Example:	ABC supermarket against XYZ manufacturing co. on logistic management
Advantages:	Greatest opportunity for break-through improvement ideas that will give competitive advantage
	Few concerns about giving away competitive information
Disadvantages:	Hardest to locate partners who have something of use to you
	Hardest to incorporate into your own business processes in a practical way

iv) Process Benchmarking

Process Benchmarking refers to business processes and is indistinguishable, for practical purposes, from Generic Benchmarking

v) Functional Benchmarking

Functional Benchmarking generally refers to a function in the organization, such as Logistic Management (a function is a collection of processes). To do Functional Benchmarking, one needs to disintegrate the function into business processes. Hence, it too ends up being similar to Generic Benchmarking.

7.4 Benchmarking Process

a) AT&T 9-Step Benchmarking Process

i) Project conception
ii) Planning

- o Determine what to benchmark
- o Develop project plan

i) Preliminary data collection

- o Identify performance variables and collect secondary data
- o Measure own process

iii) Best-in-class Selection
iv) Best-in-class Data Collection
v) Assessment
vi) Implementation Planning
vii) Implementation
viii) Re-calibration

ix)

b) Eastman Kodak Company's Benchmarking

i) iLeadership

- o Build leadership team commitment
- o Commission the benchmarking team

ii) Plan

- o Identify critical performance measures
- o Identify comparative operations

iii) Analyze

- o Measure your own performance
- o Determine data collection method and collect data
- o Analyze and compare data to determine gaps

iv) Implement

- o Communicate findings and recommendations
- o Develop plans to meet and surpass superior operations
- o Implement plans and monitor progress

v) Nurture

- o Review competitive position

c) IBM's Benchmarking Process

i) Self-Introspect (Process Management)

- o Clarify your customers and output
- o Define appropriate benchmarking measurements
- o Review (and refine) your processes or product definitions

ii) Pre-Benchmarking (Preparation)

- o Prioritize and select what is to be benchmarked
- o Choose your benchmarking "partners"
- o Set the level of data collection

iii) Benchmarking (Execution)

- o Collect data and organize them
- o Calculate gaps from baseline
- o Estimate future attainable level of achievement

iv) Post-Benchmarking (Project Management)

- o Present benchmarking results
- o Set goals and action plan
- o Implement actions and assure success

v) Review/Reset (Progress Assessment)

- o Review ongoing benchmarking integration
- o Assess progress toward goals
- o Reset goals and return to step 1.

d) Xerox's Benchmarking Process

Phase I Planning

i) Identify benchmarking subject
ii) Identify benchmarking partners
iii) Data collection
  a) Determine data collection method
  b) Collect data

Phase II Analysis

iv) Determine current competitive gap
v) Project future performance
vi) Communicate findings and gain acceptance

Phase III Integration

vii) Establish functional goals
viii) Develop action plans

Phase IV Action

ix) Implement plans and monitor progress
x) Recalibrate benchmark

e) Generic Benchmarking Process

i) Recognize Need for Change

a) Gain management commitment
b) Select lead team and train

ii) Identify Processes to Benchmark

a) Review business priorities
b) Decide broadly which areas to benchmark
c) Gain approval of the decision

iii) Select Teams and Train

a) Train preparation teams

iv) Analyze Your Own Processes within the Defined Broad Area

a) Conduct analysis
b) Decide what issues are most important
c) Prepare information gathering tools for visit, including questionnaire

v) Partner Selection Process

a) Search for partners
b) Contact potential partners

vi) Build Relationship and Conduct the Visit

a) Exchange preliminary information with partner
b) Organize visit
c) Conduct visit
d) Debrief

vii) Analyze Gaps and Develop Implementation Strategy

a) Communicate preliminary findings
b) Analyze implications
c) Design improvement strategy
d) Design improvement projects
e) Communicate
f) Gain agreement
g) Execution

7.5 The Benchmarking Code of Conduct

The International Benchmarking Clearinghouse, the Strategic Planning Institute Council on Benchmarking, and The Benchmarking Centre has adopted a common code of conduct recommended for all companies engaged in benchmarking.

a) Principle of Legality

- If there is any potential question on the legality of an activity, don't do it.
- Avoid discussions or actions that could lead to or imply an interest in restraint of trade, market and/or customer allocation schemes, price fixing, dealing arrangements, bid rigging, or bribery. Don't discuss costs with competitors if costs are an element of pricing.

- o Refrain from the acquisition of trade secrets by any means that could be interpreted as improper, including the breach or inducement of a breach of any duty to maintain secrecy. Do not disclose or use any trade secret that may have been obtained through improper means or that was disclosed by another in violation of a duty to maintain its secrecy or limit its use.
- o Do not, as a consultant or client, extend one benchmarking study's findings to another company without first obtaining permission of the parties to the first study.

b) Principle of Exchange

- o Be willing to provide the same type and level of information that you request from your benchmarking partner to that partner
- o Communicate fully and early in the relationship to clarify expectations, avoid misunderstandings, and establish mutual interest in the benchmarking exchange.
- o Be honest and complete

c) Principle of Confidentiality

- o Treat benchmarking interchange as confidential to the individuals and companies involved. Information must not be communicated outside the partnering organizations without the prior consent of the benchmarking partner who shared the information.
- o A Company's participation in the study is confidential and should not be communicated externally without their prior permission.

d) Principle of Use

- o Use information obtained through benchmarking only for purposes of formulating improvement of operations or processes within the companies participating in the benchmarking study.

e) Principle of First-Party Contact

- o Initiate benchmarking contacts, whenever possible, through a benchmarking contact designated by the partner company.
- o Respect the corporate culture of partner companies and work within mutually agreed procedures.

f) Principle of Third-Party Contact

- o Obtain an individual's permission before providing his or her name in response to a contact request.

g) Principle of Preparation

- o Make the most of your benchmarking partner's time by being fully prepared for each exchange.
- o Help your benchmarking partners prepare by providing them with a questionnaire and agenda prior to benchmarking visits.

h) Principle of Completion

- o Follow through with each commitment made to your benchmarking partner in a timely manner.
- o Complete each benchmarking study to the satisfaction of all benchmarking partners as mutually agreed.

i) Principle of Understanding and Action

- o Understand how your benchmarking partner would like to be treated, and treat them accordingly.

8

TOTAL QUALITY MANAGEMENT (TQM)

8.1 Evolution of Quality System

Tremendous development in the field of quality has spanned the entire 20th century. The first signs of a quality consciousness date back to the 17th century when the guild act was passed in England requiring craftsmen to have their products tested and appropriately marked depending on their quality. Since then quality remained restricted to inspection first by the operators (operator quality control) in the manufacturing industry till the end of the 19th century, and later by the foremen (foremen quality control) till the early decades of the 20th century.

With the development of Control Charts by Dr. Walter A. Shewhart of Bell Laboratories in 1920 the first major change was seen as the focus shifted from inspection to process control. Statistical Quality Control (SQC), the fourth stage was thus developed. This was during World War II when there were tremendous mass production requirements. SQC still remains a very powerful Quality Control tool.

The next phase of development up to the early 80s is total quality control when firms develop a specific decision-making and operating framework for product quality, which was effective enough to take suitable action on the quality control findings.

Today, Total Quality Management (TQM) is widely adopted by most American and Japanese organizations. TQM is a management approach to long-term success through customer satisfaction. It is based on the participation of all members of an organization to excel in all dimensions of products and services that are important to the customer. Thus we find that with evolution of quality, responsibility for quality has passed from solely the quality department to everybody in the organization including the management whose commitment should be apparent.

In summary, the three phases of Quality Management development over the years are:

- Phase I – Inspection orientated quality control
- Phase II – Process orientated quality control
- Phase III – Total Quality Management

8.2 Background Knowledge

i) Definition of Quality

ISO 9000:2000 defines quality as the "degree to which a set of inherent characteristics fulfils requirements". Quality is a composite of specified and expected characteristics of a product and/or service.

"Quality" is also defined in various ways and in various time periods as shown in Chapter 3.

ii) Quality Assurance and Quality Control

Quality assurance is a total company-wide philosophy. It means working to a planned and regularly monitored system of actions and controls and is applied to all those activities, which significantly affect or impact the quality of a product, service or activity and the efficiency of achievement of this quality.

Ultimately, all these planned and systematic activities and controls are aimed at providing: what is wanted, when it is wanted and what is wanted at an acceptable price.

It is a management tool within the organization and a means to providing confidence to the customer.

Quality Control, however, are operational techniques and activities aimed both at monitoring a process and at eliminating causes of unsatisfactory performance in various stages.

iii) Inspection Orientated Quality Control

The rationales of this approach are: to prevent shipment of non-conforming products, to involve only one department (quality assurance), and to minimize / eliminate incoming inspection by introducing Supplier Certification programs.

This is typically the product control and essentially leads to segregation of the good and the bad parts. For the company it is a means to ensure that only products conforming to requirements are placed on the market.

The following are its deficiencies: inspection was necessary; impossible to be 100% effective; delay or lack of feedback to operators on quality problems; and QA as police department not helpers.

iv) Process Orientated Quality Control

Further refinement to the inspection or product quality control is the process oriented quality control. The common beliefs are: we can prevent problems by controlling the processes; that quality was the responsibility of the manufacturing department; and the role of QA should be to act on behalf of management and also the end user of the product to assure product quality.

The underlying principle of this approach is that control must start with the investigations and tests to determine the possibility of improving quality characteristics during manufacturing cycle.

The goal is to control the manufacturing process. It involves all the departments that affect the manufacturing process: purchasing, engineering, manufacturing, marketing and subcontractors.

The deficiencies of the process-orientated quality control are that they: did not address the product design; did not focus on the customer; and did not address the other non-manufacturing areas.

8.3 Introduction to Total Quality Management

i) What is Total Quality Management (TQM)?

In Total Quality Management, all functions and staff focus on continuous process improvement, resulting in increased customer satisfaction. Quality Assurance and Quality Improvement are thus important elements of TQM.

Generally, TQM is:

- o A management philosophy supported with an operating methodology
- o Concerned with involving and supporting all staff
- o Based on initiatives and actions by management (top-down approach)
- o A strategy directed to customer satisfaction and to create staff participation
- o To facilitate "doing the right things the first time"
- o An effective problem identification and corrective action approach, leading to continuous quality improvements in supply, administration, operations and customer service.
- o A new long-term organizational way of life (culture) with greater staff satisfaction, competence and commitment.
- o Evolving from traditional quality control and quality assurance.

ii) TQM and ISO 9000 Quality Management System

The certification to ISO 9000 should be viewed as the beginning rather than the end of the quality development process. Research shows that during the 1980s most companies in the United Kingdom developed towards TQM through a program of accreditation of ISO 9000. Accreditation to ISO 9000 leads to the establishment of a Quality Management System that does not address all the key elements of TQM

Hence, implementing a quality system such as ISO 9000 is not the same as achieving TQM. However, it is a good foundation for a TQM program.

The criteria of the quality awards (world class standards, such as the USA National Quality Award as described in Chapter 1) are often regarded as the closest definition for a TQM system.

8.4 Four Key Elements of Total Quality Management

i) Total Quality is Customer Driven

- o Find out customers' needs and expectations
    - Ask questions
    - Listen to feedback
    - Be open (feedback isn't always positive)
- o Establish formal and informal communication systems
- o Set standards based on feedback

ii) Total Quality is Continuous Improvement

- o Improve every aspect of the organization continuously
    - Meet changing needs and expectations of customers
    - Ensure efficient and effective customer-supplier relationship (both internal and external)
    - Improve processes continuously through Quality Circles (QC), Quality Improvement Teams (QIT), Cross Functional Teams (CFT), Staff Suggestion Schemes (SSS), Six Sigma (6σ), Benchmarking, and innovation, etc.
- o Move continuous improvement from reactive to proactive
- o Continuous improvement depends on training

iii) Total Quality is Total Involvement

- o Total commitment from everyone in the organization – from the highest to the lowest levels
- o Participative management – teamwork (QC, QIT, CFT, committees, etc)
- o Strategic Deployment Management System (SMDS®) – knowing the big picture and understanding the value of your own contribution
- o Ownership – managing your own work and taking pride and ownership in what you do
- o Recognizing the accomplishments of others

iv) Total Quality is Societal Networking

- o Network learning
  - From within company, customers, suppliers
  - From national, regional and international infrastructure
- o Benchmarking
- o Do not reinvent the wheel

8.5 TQM Implementation

i) Total Management Commitment

- o Leadership by example
- o Followership by observation
- o Resources, time, and be seen
- o World Class Standard (WCS): Leadership

ii) Total Quality Steering Committee

- o Teamwork vs Hierarchical
- o Trained in Total Quality
- o Need for Continued Learning
- o WCS: Leadership

iii) Develop Vision Statement and Guiding Values

- o Vision : Ideal, Generic
- o Values : Policy to achieve vision
- o WCS: Leadership

iv) Set Broad Objectives and Deploy to whole Organization

- o Flow from mission and vision

- o Describe organization's strategy
- o Cascade down to entire organization through Strategic Deployment Management System
- o Measure both outcomes and performance drivers
- o Form a bridge between the vision/mission and the specific tactics
- o Quality objectives vs Financial objectives
- o WCS: Planning

v) Publicize and Communicate

- o Maximize effort, eliminate rumours
- o Demonstrate by action that management is serious about its implementation
- o Paradigm shift program
- o Moving Towards Productivity and Quality Excellence program
- o WCS: Leadership

vi) Identify Strength and Areas for Improvement (AFI)

- o Assessment using WCS criteria
- o Clarify and verify issues
- o Capitalize on strength identified
- o Identify AFI in system/process approach - integration, prevention, improvement/ evaluation cycle
- o Identify AFI in system/process deployment - all functions, levels, consistency
- o Identify AFI in result/trend - positive, sustained, benchmarked
- o Prioritization of improvement effort
- o All WCS categories, including Information and Processes

vii) Identify Advocates and Resistors

- o Critical to ensure success at first try
- o Make use of Advocates while working around Resistors
- o Advocator/Resistor issue is temporary

viii) Establish Baseline for Employee Attitudes and Satisfaction

- o Employees are internal customers
- o WCS: People

ix) Establish Baseline for Customer Satisfaction

- o For survival
- o At the heart of Total Quality
- o WCS: Customers

x) Identify Projects

- o Strategic Deployment Management System (SDMS®) - organization's objectives and departmental goals)
- o Organization's strengths and weaknesses
- o Personalities of those involved
- o Project's probability of success
- o WCS: Planning

xi) Train the Teams

- o House of Continuous Improvement (HOCI®)
- o Productivity, Quality, 5S Housekeeping, 8 Wastes, QC, 6s, Benchmarking
- o Road Map to Effective Implementation of QC Project
- o WCS: People

xii) Tailor Implementation

- o Approach taken must fit the organization's needs, culture, strength and weakness
- o Incorporate PDCA cycle

xiii) Provide Team Feedback to Steering Committee

- o Ensure instructions aren't misunderstood
- o New teams are unknown entities

xiv) Collect and Act on Customer Feedback

- o Sources: Warranty Data, Sales Results, Customer Service Department, Distributors, Unsolicited Customer Feedback, Customer Visits, Customer Satisfaction Surveys, User Groups, etc
- o Feedback for continuous improvement
- o WCS: Customers

xv) Collect and Act on Employee Feedback

- o Sources: Formal Survey, Management Sensing and Listening, Internal Customer Input, Human Resources Records, etc
- o Feedback for continuous improvement
- o WCS: People

xvi) Change the Infrastructure

- o Change in organization structure: Business systems, processes and procedures; Union rules; Awards and recognition programs; etc
- o Standardize optimized systems, processes and procedures

xvii) Reassess Organization with WCS Criteria

- o Identify gaps for continuous and breakthrough improvements
- o Plan gap closure starting from step (i)

xviii) Implement Continuous and Breakthrough Improvement Programs

- o Don't reinvent the wheel
- o Benchmarking
- o Knowledge sharing
- o Breakthrough initiatives

8.6 TQM Implementation Model

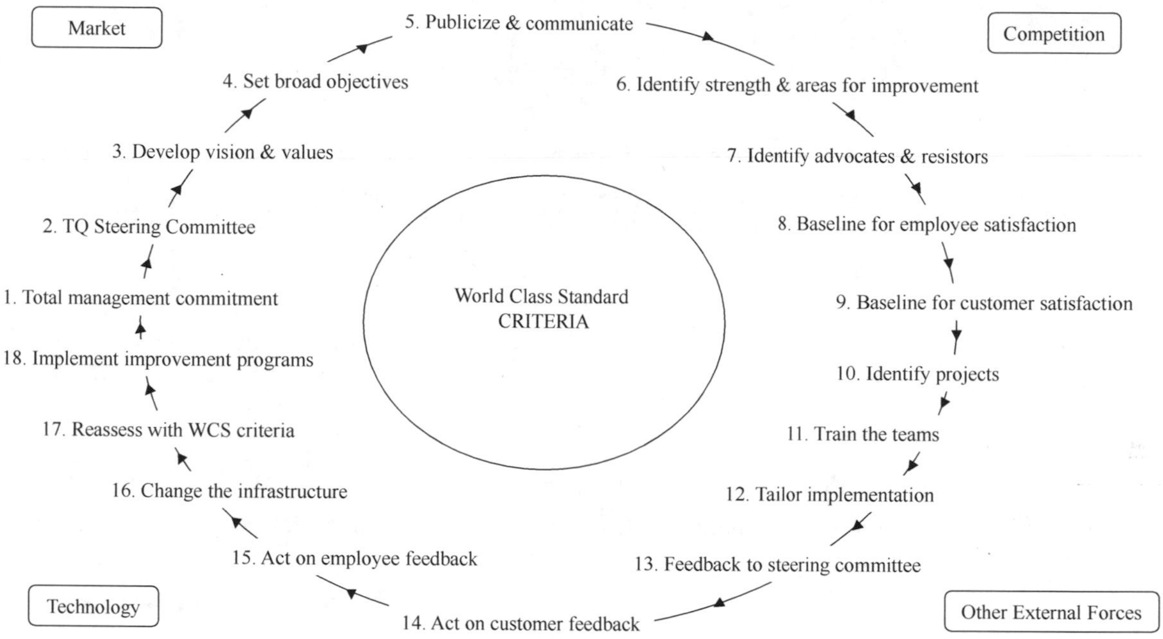

9

TOTAL PRODUCTIVE MAINTENANCE

9.1 Introduction

The concept of PM (Preventive Maintenance) was introduced in 1951. PM is a program of planned inspections, replacements and repairs designed to prevent expensive catastrophic failures and control deterioration. Before PM, companies generally practiced BM (Breakdown Maintenance), which means fixing equipment only after it has broken down.

Over the years the PM approach gradually changed to meet the new demands of the industry. The concept of MI (Maintainability and Methods Improvement) was introduced to promote modifications or procedures that make the same breakdown less likely to happen again. The concept of MP (Maintenance Prevention) was aimed at involving the equipment designers in building better equipment that is easier to maintain.

Finally, the PM, MI, and MP approaches were consolidated under the new definition of PM, which in this case stands for Productive Maintenance.

9.2 Definition

Total Productive Maintenance (TPM) was defined in 1971 by the Japan Institute of Plant Engineers (JIPE) as follows:

"TPM is designed to

- o maximize equipment effectiveness (improving overall efficiency) by establishing a comprehensive productive maintenance system covering the entire life of the equipment, spanning all equipment-related fields (planning, use, maintenance, etc) and,

- o with the participation of all employees from top management down to shop-floor workers, to promote productive maintenance through voluntary small-group activities."

By definition it includes the following five (5) points:

1. Maximizes the effectiveness of each piece of equipment
2. Builds a comprehensive Productive Maintenance (PM) system
3. Brings together people from all departments concerned with equipment
4. Involves everyone from top executives to frontline workers
5. Carries out PM through autonomous small group activities

9.3 Six Aims of TPM

- o Build a disciplined workplace free of minor flaws
- o Create efficient production line
- o Build reliable production line
- o Create production lines with individuality (lines that please workers)
- o Train workers to know their equipment thoroughly
- o Create workplaces that aim for their targets

9.4 Scope of TPM Activities

i) Installing Equipment

Planning, costing, selection, installation, start-up

ii) Equipment Operation

Correct operation, work-flow adjustment, preventing recurrent shut-downs, 5Ss

iii) Equipment Maintenance

- o Daily Maintenance: Cleaning, oiling, tightening, proper operating procedures, daily inspection
- o Regular Maintenance: Regular inspections and regular maintenance
- o Predictive Maintenance: Propensity studies, nonconformance detection, equipment diagnosis
- o Breakdown Maintenance: Early detection and correction, and crisis management
- o Corrective maintenance: Improving equipment, lightening loads, enhancing precision, speeding up operation, simplifying procedures, monitoring conditions, improving maintenance procedures

iv) Equipment improvements made based on feedback from maintenance repairs and modifications

v) Maintenance training and skill enhancement

vi) Enhanced safety and sanitation and better working conditions through equipment maintenance

9.5 Eliminating Equipment Losses

The Six Big Losses

- o Breakdown losses
- o Setup and adjustment Losses
- o Idling and minor stoppage losses
- o Speed loss
- o Quality defects and rework
- o Start-up/yield losses

i) Breakdown Losses

Breakdowns are caused by all sorts of factors, but usually we notice only the big problems and overlook the many slight defects that also contribute to them; such as loose screws, abrasion, debris, and contaminants.

ii) Setup and Adjustment Losses

Setup and adjustment losses are stoppage losses occurring during setup procedures such as retooling, etc.

iii) Idling and Minor Stoppage Losses

Idling and minor stoppages are caused by temporary problems in the equipment

iv) Speed Loss

Speed loss occurs when there is a difference between the speed at which a machine is designed to operate and its actual operating speed.

v) Quality Defects and Rework

Quality defects and rework are losses in quality caused by malfunctioning production equipment.

vi) Start-up/Yield Losses

Start-up/yield losses are those incurred because of the reduced yield between the time the machine is started up and when stable production is finally achieved. Their extent depends on the stability of processing conditions, worker training, loss incurred by test operations and other factors.

9.6 Measurement of Equipment Effectiveness

TPM uses an Output Operating Rate (OPR) to measure Equipment effectiveness as shown below:

$$\text{OPR} = \frac{(\text{Planned Cycle Time} \times \text{Number of Defect-Free Products})}{\text{Planned Operating Time}}$$

Overall Equipment Effectiveness (OEE) can also be measured using the following formula:

OEE = Availability x Performance Rate x Quality Rate

i) Availability (Operating Rate)

The operating rate tells us what percentage of time equipment is actually running when we need it. This is expressed in the following formula:

$$\text{Availability} = \frac{\text{Loading Time - Downtime}}{\text{Loading Time}} \times 100\%$$

For example, the loading time for a given day is 480 minutes and downtime totals 100 minutes (60 minutes due to breakdowns, 30 minutes for retooling, and 10 minutes due to adjustments).

$$\text{Availability} = \frac{480 - 100}{480} \times 100\% = 79\%$$

ii) Performance Rate

The performance rate is based on the operating speed rate and the net operating time. The operating speed rate tells us how fast a machine is running (in terms of cycle time) compared to its ideal or designed speed. When the performance rate shows a speed reduction, it reflects a hidden loss.

Performance Rate = (Operating Speed Rate) x (Net Operating Rate)

$$\text{Operating Speed Rate} = \frac{\text{Ideal Cycle Time}}{\text{Actual Cycle Time}} \times 100\%$$

$$\text{Net Operating Rate} = \frac{\text{Output x Actual Cycle Time}}{\text{Loading Time - Downtime}} \times 100\%$$

For example, if the standard cycle time per item is 0.5 minutes and the actual cycle time per item is 0.8 minutes.

$$\text{Operating Speed Rate} = \frac{0.5 \text{ minutes}}{0.8 \text{ minutes}} \times 100\%$$

$$= 62.5\%$$

If the number of processed items per day is 400, the actual cycle time per item is 0.8 minutes, and the operating time is 400 minutes, then

$$\text{Net Operating Rate} = \frac{400 \text{ items} \times 0.8 \text{ minutes}}{400 \text{ minutes}} \times 100\%$$

$$= 80\%$$

Performance Rate = 62.5% x 80% = 50%

If the rate of quality products is 98%, then the overall equipment effectiveness is:

OEE = Availability x Performance Rate x Quality Rate

= 79% x 50% x 98%

= 38.7%

9.7 Case Study for Discussion

Who is responsible for the Metro train maintenance?

It has been a practice for the Metro Corporation to maintain and operate the Metro train business. However, lately, while the operational profitability of the company is on the rise, the breakdown rate of the train has been increasing and showing signs of more problems to come.

The board of directors are concerned if the operational profitability will continue along the present trend while the train maintenance cost is expected to go up tremendously. In fact, the board is more concerned about the negative feedback on the train disruption from the travelers. They have become more vocal recently in the social media.

The board has asked the management of the company to put up a proposal to address these problems. Can you help the management with your proposal?

10

ISO 9000 QUALITY MANAGEMENT SYSTEM

10.1 Introduction

The International Organization for Standardization (ISO) is a specialized international agency for standardization. ISO is made up of the national standard bodies of 91 countries and has its headquarters in Geneva, Switzerland. The ISO 9000 Series was first published in 1987.

The intent of the ISO series is to establish a worldwide acceptable Quality System. The focus is on generic Quality Management, including Quality Systems, Quality Assurance and supporting technologies. This allows for world trade to have the same Quality System and encourages fewer trade barriers.

There is nothing within the ISO 9000 Series that mandates the implementation of the standard. At this time the ISO 9000 Series Quality Systems is strictly voluntarily. However, some governments and companies within the European Community have indicated that they require or give preference to companies that are registered to ISO 9000 Series Quality System. In essence, if your competitor is registered and you are not, then you are out of the competition.

History of ISO 9000	
Year	Event
1959	MIL-Q-9858 Quality Program Requirements
1962	NASA NPC 200-2 Quality Program Provisions for Space System Contractors
1950's & 1960's	Ministry of Defense and Central Electricity Board (UK) introduces BS 5179 and BS 5750
1960's	Department of Defense (US) imposed quality systems requirements on suppliers
1970's	The Food & Drug Administration (US) imposed quality systems requirements on suppliers
1980's	ISO 9000 series was introduced (TC 176) in 1987.
1990's	ISO 9000 series was accepted by many countries as their National Standards because it was adopted as the European Standards and Europe without frontier by end 1992. The first revision was issued in 1994
2000's	The family of standards was re-organized into 4 main standards and issued in December 2000.

10.2 ISO 9000:1994 Quality Management System

The ISO 9000 standards set the basic rules for a quality management system, from conception to implementation. They provide guidelines and spell out the requirements of a quality management system and determine the key elements of such a system.

ISO 9000 standards are not product standards but quality management system standards. They are generic in applications. Besides manufacturing, they have been applied to service industries such as banks, transport, construction information technology companies and educational institutions.

ISO 9000 is a generic term that represents the five standards, i.e., ISO 9000, 9001, 9002, 9003 and 9004, which establish the requirements for a company's Quality Management System.

The ISO protocols require that all standards be reviewed at least every five years to determine whether they should be confirmed, revised or withdrawn. The 1994 versions of the ISO 9000 family are revised by ISO's Technical Committee TC176 and the new version was published in December 2000.

10.3 ISO 9000:2000 Quality Management System

i) Background to the Changes

Extensive surveys have been carried out on a worldwide basis in order to understand better the needs of all user groups. The revised standards will take into account all previous experience with quality management systems. They will result in closer alignment of the quality management system with the needs of the day to day running of the organization.

It has long been recognized that investment in quality management systems, in addition to responding to customer expectations, has resulted in benefits to the efficiency of the organization, its operations and economic performance, as well as to the quality of the products and services. Specifically, the revised standards will be of great help for organizations wishing to go beyond simple compliance with Quality Management System requirements for certification purposes. They can be readily applied to small, medium and large organizations in the public and private sectors and will be equally applicable to users in industrial, service, software and other areas.

ii) Essential Changes to the ISO 9000 Series

The key points in the 27 standards and documents are integrated into four primary standards. Sector needs are addressed while maintaining the generic nature of the standards.

The four primary standards are:

- ISO 9000: Quality management systems – Fundamentals and vocabulary
- ISO 9001: Quality management systems – Requirements
- ISO 9004: Quality management systems – Guidance for Performance Improvement
- ISO 19011: Guidelines on Quality and Environmental Auditing

The revised ISO 9001 and ISO 9004 standards are developed as a "consistent pair" of standards. Whereas the revised ISO 9001 will more clearly address the QMS requirements for an organization to demonstrate its capability to meet customer needs, the revised ISO 9004 is intended to lead beyond ISO 9000 towards the development of a comprehensive QMS, designed to address the needs of all interested parties.

Both standards will use a common vocabulary as defined in ISO 9000:2000, which describes the underlying fundamentals. A logical, systematic approach has been adopted in formulating the definitions used in ISO 9000:2000, with the intention of generating a more consistent terminology that is "user friendly".

The 1994 version of the ISO 9001, ISO 9002, and ISO 9003 standards were consolidated into a single revised ISO 9001:2000 standard.

Clause 1.2 "Application" will permit the exclusion of some clauses of ISO 90001:2000 where the related processes are not performed by the organization, and these requirements do not affect the organization's ability to provide products that meet customer and applicable statutory or regulatory requirements.

ISO 19011 parts 1, 2 and 3 were revised jointly with ISO 14010, 14011 and 14012. The combined ISO 19011: Guidelines on Quality and Environmental Auditing was published in 2002.

iii) The "Consistent Pair" of Quality Management Standards

The revised ISO 9001 and 9004 are being designed to constitute a "consistent pair" of standards. Their structure and sequence will be identical in order to facilitate an easy and useful transition between them.

The primary aim of the "consistent pair" is to relate modern quality management to the processes and activities of an organization, including the promotion of continual improvement and achievement of customer satisfaction. Furthermore, it is intended that the ISO 9000 standards have global applicability.

Therefore, the factors that are driving the revision process, among others, are:

- o Applicability to all product categories and to all sizes of organizations. (Note that the ISO 9000:2000 definition of "product" also includes "services")
- o Simple to use, clear in language, readily translatable and easily understandable.
- o Ability to connect QMS to organizational processes.
- o Provision of a natural stepping stone towards TQM.
- o Greater orientation toward continual improvement and customer satisfaction.
- o Compatibility with other management systems, such as ISO 14000 for environmental management.
- o Need to provide a consistent basis and address the primary needs and interests of organizations in specific sectors such as aerospace, automotive, medical devices, telecommunications and others.

In this way, all organizations, whether private or public, large or small, producing manufactured goods, services, or software, are being offered tools with which to achieve internal and external benefits.

iv) Permissible Exclusion (Clause 1.2 Application)

All requirements of the Standard are generic and are intended to be applicable to all organizations, regardless of type, size and product provided.

When any requirement(s) of the Standard cannot be applied due to the nature of an organization and its product, this can be considered for exclusion.

Where exclusions are made, claims of conformity to the Standard are not acceptable unless these exclusions are limited to requirements within clause 7, and such exclusions do not affect the organization's ability or responsibility, to provide products that meet customer and applicable regulatory requirements.

The Most likely clauses to be considered for permissible exclusions are: 7.3 Design and development; 7.5.2 Identification and traceability; 7.5.3 Customer property; and 7.6 Control of measuring and monitoring devices.

v) Documented Procedures

"Documented procedures" mean that the procedures have to be established, documented, implemented and maintained. Documented procedures required in this International Standard are:

- 4.2.3 Control of documents
- 4.2.4 Control of quality records
- 8.2.2 Internal audit
- 8.3 Control of nonconformity
- 8.5.2 Corrective action
- 8.5.3 Preventive action

The extent of the quality management system documentation can differ from one organization to another due to

a) the size of organization and type of activities,
b) the complexity of processes and their interactions, and
c) the competence of personnel

vi) Quality Management Principles

Major changes in the revised ISO 9000 standards are in the increased focus on top management commitment and customer satisfaction, the emphasis on processes within the organization, and the introduction of continual improvement concepts.

The revisions of ISO 9001 and 9004 are based on eight quality management principles that reflect best management practices. These eight principles are:

- Customer focused organization

Organizations depend on their customers and therefore should understand current and future customer needs, should meet customer requirements and strive to exceed customer expectations.

- Leadership

Leaders establish unity of purpose and direction of the organization. They should create and maintain the internal environment in which people can become fully involved in achieving the organization's objectives.

- Involvement of people

People at all levels are the essence of an organization and their full involvement enables their abilities to be used for the organization's benefit.

- Process approach

A desired result is achieved more efficiently when activities and related resources are managed as a process.

- System approach to management

Identifying, understanding and managing interrelated processes as a system contributes to the organization's effectiveness and efficiency in achieving its objectives.

- Continual improvement

Continual improvement of the organization's overall performance should be a permanent objective of the organization.

- Factual approach to decision making

Effective decisions are based on the analysis of data and information.

- Mutually beneficial supplier relationship

An organization and its suppliers are interdependent and a mutually beneficial relationship enhances the ability of both to create value.

10.4 ISO 9001:2000/08 Quality Management System Model

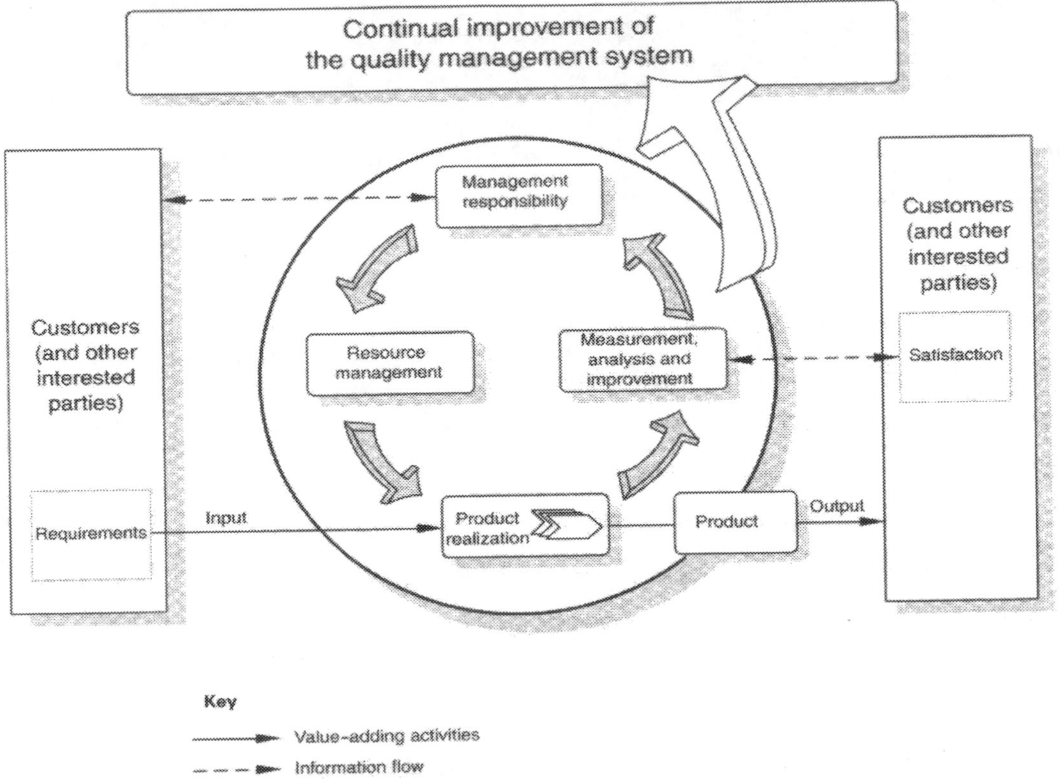

10.5 ISO 9001:2000/08 Quality Management System Structure

The ISO 9000:2000 QMS structure is organized into the following five key sections:

a) 4. Quality Management System
b) 5. Management responsibility
c) 6. Resource management
d) 7. Product realization
e) 8. Measurement, analysis and improvement

10.6 Changes in ISO 9001:2008 Quality Management System

ISO 9001 was last revised in 2001. Apparently the standard was so near perfection that few changes were proposed in the latest revision. The following is the summary of the proposed changes since the last revision in 2001.

Clause No	Clause Title	Proposed Changes in ISO 9001:2008
0.2	Process approach	Wording change to emphasize that processes must be capable of achieving desired outputs
1.1	Scope	Wording change to clarify that "product" can also mean "intermediate product" and a note to explain that statutory and regulatory requirements may be expressed as legal requirements
4.1	General requirements	Notes will be included to clarify the requirements regarding "outsourcing" and its relationship with "purchasing"
4.2.1	General documentation requirements	Notes will be included to emphasize that "documentation" can also include "records" and that mandatory procedures may be in the form of combined documents, or that requirements may be covered by more than one document
4.2.3	Document control	Note to clarify that only external documents affecting the QMS need to be controlled
5.5.2	Management representative	Clarification that the MR must be a member of the organization's own management
6.2.1	Human resources	Clarification that competence requirements apply to any personnel whose work affects the QMS
6.3	Infrastructure	Clarifies that this includes information system
6.4	Environment	Clarification of circumstances that are covered by this clause
7.2.1	Customer related processes	Clarification of what may be covered by "post delivery activities"

7.3.1	Design and development planning	Clarification that review, validation and verification all have distinct purposes but may be conducted and recorded either separately or in a combined way if appropriate
7.3.3	Design and development outputs	Clarification that product preservation requirements must be considered
7.5.4	Customer property	Clarification that intellectual property and personal data are covered by the clause
7.6	Control of monitoring and measuring devices	Re-titled. Replace "devices" with "equipment". Explanation of its applicability to software.
8.2.1	Customer satisfaction	Note offers examples of how perception data may be captured
8.2.3	Monitoring and measurement of processes	Clarification that identifies that consideration be given to product conformity and QMS effectiveness

10.7 ISO9001:2008 Quality Management System

i) Contents

Section	Title
1	**Scope**
1.1	General
1.2	Application
2	**Normative Reference**
3	**Terms and Definitions**
4	**Quality Management System**
4.1	General Requirements
4.2	Documentation requirements
4.2.1	General
4.2.2	Quality Manual
4.2.3	Control of documents

4.2.4	Control of records
5	**Management Responsibility**
5.1	Management commitment
5.2	Customer focus
5.3	Quality policy
5.4	Planning
5.4.1	Quality objectives
5.4.2	Quality management system planning
5.5	Responsibility, authority and communication
5.5.1	Responsibility and authority
5.5.2	Management representative
5.5.3	Internal communication
5.6	Management review
5.6.1	General
5.6.2	Review input
5.6.3	Review output
6	**Resource Management**
6.1	Provision of resources
6.2	Human resources
6.2.1	General
6.2.2	Competence, awareness and training
6.3	Infrastructure
6.4	Work environment
7	**Product Realization**
7.1	Planning of product realization
7.2	Customer-related processes
7.2.1	Determination of requirements related to the product
7.2.2	Review of requirements related to the product
7.2.3	Customer communication
7.3	Design and development

7.3.1	Design planning
7.3.2	Design inputs
7.3.3	Design outputs
7.3.4	Design review
7.3.5	Design verification
7.3.6	Design validation
7.3.7	Design changes
7.4	Purchasing
7.4.1	Purchasing control
7.4.2	Purchasing information
7.4.3	Verification of purchased product
7.5	Production and service provision
7.5.1	Control of production and service provision
7.5.2	Validation of processes for production and service provision
7.5.3	Identification and traceability
7.5.4	Customer property
7.5.5	Preservation of product
7.6	Control of measuring and monitoring devices
8	**Measurement, Analysis and Improvement**
8.1	General
8.2	Monitoring and measurement
8.2.1	Customer satisfaction
8.2.2	Internal audit
8.2.3	Measuring and monitoring of processes
8.2.4	Measuring and monitoring of product
8.3	Control of non-conformity
8.4	Analysis of data
8.5	Improvement
8.5.1	Continual improvement
8.5.2	Corrective action
8.5.3	Preventive action

ii) ISO9001:2008 QMS Clause 1: Scope

1.1 General

ISO9001 specifies requirements for a QMS where an organization:

a) needs to demonstrate the ability to consistently supply products and services which meet requirements, and
b) aims to enhance customer satisfaction.

1.2 Application

This clause allows organizations to claim that relevant sub-clauses do not apply. However, these exclusions can only be claimed against clause 7.

iii) ISO9001:2008 QMS Clause 2: Normative Reference

This clause is for information and states that the prime reference document for explanation of terms used is "ISO 9000:2005, Quality management systems – Fundamentals and vocabulary".

It also states that where references are made to undated standards, the latest version applies.

iv) ISO9001:2008 QMS Clause 3: Terms and Conditions

This is for information purposes, and states the terms given in ISO9000 apply and that the term "product" can also mean "service".

v) ISO9001:2008 QMS Clause 4: Quality Management System

4.1 General Requirements

You must establish a QMS which is kept up to date and continually improved.

This clause requires that you must:

a) Determine the processes involved,
b) Determine the sequence of operations,
c) Determine ways by which you can be sure that the processes are working correctly,
d) Ensure that you have sufficient resources for the processes and their monitoring, and
e) Can show that you monitor and improve your system.

This clause clarifies the requirements for controls of outsourced products.

4.2 Documentation Requirements

4.2.1 General

The clause defines that the types of documentation that you must include in your system:

a) Statements of a quality policy and quality objectives,
b) A quality manual
c) Documented procedures required by the Standard, and
d) Records required by the Standard to prove that you meet its requirements plus any others that you decide you need, in order to operate your business properly.

4.2.2 Quality Manual

You must have an up to date quality manual that includes:

a) The scope of the QMS, including details of and justification for any exclusion,
b) The documental procedures established for the QMS or reference to them, and
c) A description of the interaction between the processes.

4.2.3 Control of Documents

a) You must ensure that only the correct version of the documents is available for use. They must be reviewed and approved prior to use.
b) You must periodically review them for ongoing suitability (are they still legible, relevant, etc)
c) For external documents, only those that are required for the planning and operation of the system are meant to be included.

4.2.4 Control of Records

a) You must make sure that you keep sufficient records to prove that you are operating your QMS correctly.
b) You must have a procedure which ensures that the records are suitably controlled with regards to:

- defining what records are required,
- how and where they are stored,
- ensuring that they can be retrieved, and
- describing their retention time and subsequent disposal.

vi) ISO9001:2008 QMS Clause 5: Management Responsibility

5.1 Management Commitment

a) You must define the commitment of your top management to the development and implementation of the system,
b) You must have a quality policy,
c) You must have quality objectives,

d) You must conduct management review, and
e) You must ensure that you make sufficient resources available.

5.2 Customer Focus

a) You must define the commitment of your top management to determining, meeting, and enhancing customer satisfaction.
b) You must describe how you ensure "customer focus".

5.3 Quality Policy

You must have a relevant policy for quality of your products/services:

a) It is one of the most important facets of your quality system. It is the top level document of the system.
b) It should define your approach to quality in an achievable and demonstrable way.
c) Your policy must ensure that you have a system for establishing and reviewing quality objectives.
d) You must review your quality policy.

5.4 Planning

5.4.1 Quality Objectives

Top management must ensure that:

a) You have adequate resources to achieve the required level of quality.
b) You define your objectives for quality using measurable terms.

5.4.2 Quality Management System Planning

Top management must ensure that:

a) You have provided the resources needed in order to ensure that your objectives for quality are planned and identified.
b) When changes are made to your system, the changes must be made in a controlled way so that your system continue to meet the requirements of ISO 9001 standard

5.5 Responsibility, Authority and Communication

5.5.1 Responsibility and Authority

a) You must identify the responsibilities of the key functions within your organization.
b) You should describe the key duties of the top management.
c) Employees should be aware of who they report to and who reports to them (if relevant). They should be aware of the general structure of the organization.

5.5.2 Management Representatives

Top management must appoint a "quality champion" who must be a member of the management team, and whose responsibilities include:

a) ensuring the QMS processes are operating correctly,
b) reporting the performance of QMS to the top management, and
c) promoting awareness of customer requirements.

5.5.3 Internal Communication

Top management must ensure that there is adequate communication between the various levels of staff and between different departments.

5.6 Management Review

5.6.1 General

Top management must review the QMS, at planned intervals, to ensure its continuing suitability, adequacy and effectiveness. The review shall include assessing opportunities for improvement and the need for changes to the system.

5.6.2 Review Input

You must define what the inputs are for your review process. The standard lists some areas which you need to address:

a) results of audits,
b) customer feedback,
c) process performance and product conformity,
d) status of preventive and corrective actions,
e) follow-up actions from previous management reviews,
f) changes that could affect the quality management system, and
g) recommendation for improvement.

5.6.3 Review Output

You must define what the outputs are. The standard lists some areas that you must address:

a) improvement of the effectiveness of the management system,
b) improvement of product/services that you supply, and
c) resources needed.

vii) ISO9001:2008 QMS Clause 6: Resource Management

6.1 Provision of Resources

You must ensure that you provide adequate resources:

a) to implement the required processes and to improve them, and
b) to enhance customer satisfaction.

6.2 Human Resources

6.2.1 General

You must ensure that you have adequately trained and experienced staff to conduct the required work.

6.2.2 Competence, Awareness and Training

You must:

a) Identify what skills are required for the tasks which affect product quality,
b) provide training or take other actions to satisfy these needs,
c) evaluate the effectiveness of the action taken,
d) ensure employees are aware of the relevance and importance of their activities, and
e) maintain appropriate records of education, training, skills and experience.

6.3 Infrastructure

You must determine, provide and maintain the infrastructure needed to achieve conformity to product requirements. Infrastructure includes, as applicable,

a) building, workplace and associated utilities,
b) process equipment (both hardware and software), and
c) supporting services (such as transport or communication).

6.4 Work Environment

You must determine and manage the work environment needed to achieve conformity to product requirements.

viii) ISO9001:2008 QMS Clause 7: Product Realization

7.1 Planning of Product Realization

You must:

a) determine the quality objectives and requirements for the product,
b) plan all processes needed to provide your products/services,
c) plan the required inspection and testing activities,
d) identify what records needed to provide evidence that the product has been properly produced.

7.2 Customer-related Processes

7.2.1 Determination of Requirements related to the Product

You must determine:

a) requirements specified by the customer,
b) requirements not stated by the customer but necessary for specified or intended use,
c) statutory and regulatory requirements related to the product, and
d) any additional requirements determined by the organization.

7.2.2 Review of Requirements related to the Product

You must ensure that:

a) product requirements are defined,
b) contract or order requirements differing from those previously expressed are resolved,
c) you have the ability to meet the defined requirements, and
d) maintain records of the results of the review and actions arising from the review.

7.2.3 Customer Communication

You must ensure effective communication with customers in relation to:

a) product information,
b) enquiries, contracts or order handling, including amendments, and
c) customer feedback, including customer complaints.

7.3 Design and Development

7.3.1 Design and Development Planning

You must ensure that you identify:

a) the design and development stages,
b) the review for each design and development stage, and
c) the responsibilities and authorities for design and development.

7.3.2 Design Inputs

You must identify the design inputs which include:

a) functional and performance requirements,
b) applicable statutory and regulatory requirements,
c) where applicable, information derived from previous similar designs, and
d) other requirements essential for the design.

7.3.3 Design Outputs

You must specify the design outputs which must:

a) meet the input requirements,
b) provide appropriate information for purchasing, production and for service provision,
c) contain or reference product acceptance criteria, and
d) specify the characteristics of the product that are essential for its safe and proper use.

7.3.4 Design Review

You must review the progress the design activities at suitable stages so as:

a) to evaluate the ability of the results of design to meet requirements, and
b) to identify any problems and propose necessary actions.

7.3.5 Design Verification

a) You must verify your designs to ensure that the design meets the design input requirements.
b) Your plan should state how and when you plan to do this.

7.3.6 Design Validation

a) You must ensure that the product or service works correctly in practice.
b) Your plan should state how and when you plan to do this.

7.3.7 Control of Design Changes

a) You must ensure that any changes are reviewed and recorded.
b) You must consider the effect that the changes may have on any sections of the design work already completed or under way.

7.4 Purchasing

7.4.1 Purchasing Control

a) You must evaluate and select suppliers based on their ability to supply product in accordance with your requirements.

b) You must establish criteria for selection, evaluation and re-evaluation.
c) You must keep records of the results of evaluations and any necessary actions arising from the evaluation.

7.4.2 Purchasing Information

You must ensure that your purchase order clearly describes the product to be purchased, which can include

a) requirements for approval,
b) requirements for qualification of personnel, and
c) quality management system requirements.

7.4.3 Verification of Purchased Product

a) You must ensure that the purchased product supplied to you meets specified purchase requirements through receiving or in-process inspection or testing.
b) For inspection or testing to be conducted at vendor's premise, you must specify when and how this to be done in the purchase order.

7.5 Production and Service Provision

7.5.1 Control of Product and Service Provision

You must plan and control the processes of producing your products or services, which include:

a) information that describes the characteristics of the product,
b) work instructions,
c) the use of suitable equipment,
d) the use of monitoring and measuring devices,
e) the implementation of monitoring and measurement, and
f) the implementation of release, delivery and post-delivery activities

7.5.2 Validation of Processes for Production and Service Provision

This section is concerned with processes which produce items that can not be tested directly. In this case, you must:

a) define criteria for review and approval of the processes,
b) ensure approval of equipment and qualification of personnel,
c) ensure use of specific methods and procedures,
d) establish requirements for records, and
e) revalidation

7.5.3 Identification and Traceability

a) You must identify the product by suitable means throughout product realization to ensure accidental mix-ups.
b) Where traceability is a requirement, you must be able to trace exactly which materials from which supplier were used in which goods. This may also extend to knowing which operators were involved.

7.5.4 Customer Property

a) You must exercise care with customer property while it is under your control or being used by you.
b) You must identify, verify, protect and safeguard customer property provided for use or incorporation into the product.
c) If any customer property is lost, damaged or otherwise found to be unsuitable for use, you must report to the customer and keep the records.
d) Customer property can include intellectual property.

7.5.5 Preservation of Product

a) You must preserve the conformity of product during internal processing and delivery to the intended destination. This preservation shall include identification, handling, packaging, storage and protection.
b) Preservation shall also apply to the constituent parts of a product.

7.6 Control of Monitoring and Measurement Devices

a) You must identify what measurements need to be made, and what equipment must be used.
b) When measuring equipment is used to inspect or set up the product that you manufacture, you must ensure that they are accurate for the purpose.
c) Measuring equipment must be calibrated at specific intervals, or prior to use.
d) Calibration results must be recorded.

ix) ISO9001:2008 QMS Clause 8: Measurement, Analysis and Improvement

8.1 General

You must plan and implement the monitoring, measurement, analysis and improvement processes needed

a) to demonstrate conformity of the product,
b) to ensure conformity of the quality management system, and
c) to continually improve the effectiveness of the quality management system

This shall include determination of applicable methods, including statistical techniques, and the extent of their use.

8.2 Monitoring and Measurement

8.2.1 Customer Satisfaction

a) Customer satisfaction is one of the measurements of the performance of the quality management system.
b) You must monitor information relating to customer perception as to whether you have met customer requirements.
c) You must identify the methods for obtaining and using this information.

8.2.2 Internal Audit

a) You must conduct internal audits at planned intervals to determine whether your quality management system conforms to the requirements of this Standard.
b) You must plan the audit program.
c) You must define the audit criteria, scope, frequency and methods.
d) You must ensure objectivity and impartiality of the audit process.
e) Auditors shall not audit their own work.
f) You must have a procedure to control these activities.

8.2.3 Monitoring and Measurement of Processes

a) You must apply suitable methods for monitoring and measurement of the quality management system processes.
b) These methods must demonstrate if the ability of the processes achieves the planned results. When planned results are not achieved, corrective action must be taken to ensure conformity of the product.

8.2.4 Monitoring and Measurement of Product

a) You must monitor and measure the characteristics of the product at appropriate stages to verify that product requirements have been met.
b) You must keep records of the measurement to provide evidence of conformity and indication of the person authorizing release of the product.
c) You must ensure that you do not release product until all of the required activities have been conducted.

8.3 Control of Nonconforming Product

a) You must ensure that product which does not conform to product requirements is identified and controlled to prevent its unintended use or delivery.
b) You must deal with nonconforming product by one or more of the following ways:

- o by taking action to eliminate the detected nonconformity,
- o by authorizing its use, release or acceptance under concession by a relevant authority and, where applicable, by the customer,
- o by taking action to preclude its original intended use or application.

c) You must keep records of the nature of nonconformities and any subsequent actions taken.
d) When nonconforming product is detected after delivery or use has started, you must take action appropriate to the effects of the nonconformity.
e) You must have a procedure to control these activities.

8.4 Analysis of Data

You must collect and analyze appropriate data to demonstrate the suitability and effectiveness of the quality management system. These data include:

a) customer satisfaction
b) conformity to product requirements
c) characteristics and trends of processes and products, and
d) suppliers

8.5 Improvement

8.5.1 Continual Improvement

You must continually improve the effectiveness of the quality management system through the use of the quality policy, quality objectives, audit results, analysis of data, corrective and preventive actions and management review.

8.5.2 Corrective Action

You take corrective actions to eliminate the causes of nonconformities encountered and to prevent their recurrence. A documented procedure must be established to define the requirements for:

a) reviewing nonconformities (including customer complaints),
b) determining the causes of nonconformities,
c) evaluating the need for action to ensure that nonconformities do not recur,
d) determining and implementing action needed,
e) records of the results of action taken and
f) reviewing corrective action taken.

8.5.3 Preventive Action

You take preventive action to eliminate the causes of potential nonconformities in order to prevent their occurrence. A documented procedure must be established to define requirements for:

a) determining potential nonconformities and their causes,
b) evaluating the need for action to prevent occurrence of nonconformities,
c) determining and implementing action needed
d) records of results of action taken, and
e) reviewing preventive action taken.

10.8 From ISO9001:2008 to ISO9001:2015

i) Introduction

In 2012, ISO TC 176 - responsible for ISO 9001 development - celebrated 25 years of implementing ISO 9001, and concluded that it is necessary to create a new QMS model for the next 25 years. The revised standard ISO 9001:2015 was published by ISO on 23 September 2015.

The scope of the standard has not changed, however, the structure and core terms were modified to allow the standard to integrate more easily with other international management systems standards.

The 2015 version is also less prescriptive than its predecessors and focuses on performance. This was achieved by combining the process approach with risk-based thinking, and employing the Plan-Do-Check-Act cycle at all levels in the organization.

ii) Reasons for Change

- Adapt to a changing world
- Reflect the increasingly complex environments in which organizations operate
- Provide a consistent foundation for the future
- Ensure the new standard reflects the needs of all relevant interested parties
- Ensure alignment with other management system standards

iii) Key Changes

Some of the key changes include:

- Greater emphasis on building a management system suited to each organization's particular needs
- A requirement that those at the top of an organization be involved and accountable, aligning quality with wider business strategy
- Risk-based thinking throughout the standard makes the whole management system a preventive tool and encourages continuous improvement
- Less prescriptive requirements for documentation: the organization can now decide what documented information it needs and what format it should be in
- Alignment with other key management system standards through the use of a common structure and core text

iv) Key Feature Changes

- 10-clause structure and core text for all Management System Standards (MSS)
- More compatible with services and non-manufacturing users

- Clearer understanding of the organization's context is required - "one size doesn't fit all"
- Process approach strengthened/more explicit
- Concept of preventive action now addressed throughout the standard by risk identification and mitigation

- The term documented information replaces the terms document and record
- Control of externally provided products and services replaces purchasing / outsourcing
- Increased emphasis on seeking opportunities for improvement

v) Key Benefits of Common Clause Structure

- All ISO management systems standards will look the same with the same structure (some deviations)
- Provides the option of integrating management systems
- Standardized core definitions

10.9 ISO9001:2015 Quality Management System

i) Contents

Section	Title	PDCA
1	**Scope**	
2	**Normative references**	
3	**Terms and definitions**	
4	**Context of the organization**	**PLAN**
4.1	Understanding the organization and its context	
4.2	Understanding the needs and expectations of interested parties	
4.3	Determining the scope of the quality management system	
4.4	Quality management system and its processes	
5	**Leadership**	
5.1	Leadership and commitment	
5.2	Policy	
5.3	Organizational roles, responsibilities and authorities	
6	**Planning**	
6.1	Actions to address risks and opportunities	
6.2	Quality objectives and planning to achieve them	
6.3	Planning of changes	
7	**Support**	
7.1	Resources	
7.2	Competence	
7.3	Awareness	
7.4	Communication	
7.5	Documented information	

8	**Operation**	**DO**
8.1	Operational planning and control	
8.2	Requirements for products and services	
8.3	Design and development of products and services	
8.4	Control of externally provided processes, products and services	
8.5	Production and service provision	
8.6	Release of products and services	
8.7	Control of nonconforming outputs	
9	**Performance evaluation**	**CHECK**
9.1	Monitoring, measurement, analysis and evaluation	
9.2	Internal audit	
9.3	Management review	
10	**Improvement**	**ACTION**
10.1	General	
10.2	Nonconformity and corrective action	
10.3	Continual improvement	

ii) Clause 4: Context of the organization

a) Clause 4.1

Determine what the relevant external and internal issues are for your organization, and that are relevant to its strategic direction

b) Clause 4.2

Identify the relevant interested parties and their relevant requirements

c) Clause 4.3 and 4.4

The requirement for the scope is now better defined, must be documented and consider:

- external and internal issues
- requirements of relevant interested parties
- the products and services covered (must also be stated in scope)

- allowing applicability of specific requirements
- justification for any case where a requirement cannot be applied (exclusion)

iii) Clause 5: Leadership

a) Clause 5.1.1

Leadership is required to ensure:

- take accountability for the effectiveness of the quality management system
- ensure the quality policy and quality objectives are compatible with the context and strategic direction of the organization
- ensure the integration of the QMS requirements into the organization's business processes
- promote the use of the process approach and risk-based thinking
- ensure that the QMS achieves its intended results
- engage, direct and support persons to contribute to the effectiveness of the QMS
- supporting relevant management roles
- promotion of improvement

b) Clause 5.1.2

Top management needs to ensure customer satisfaction through:

- customer and applicable statutory and regulatory requirements being determined and met
- risk and opportunities are being addressed
- the focus on products and services meeting customers and other requirements

c) Clause 5.2

- Explicit requirement to apply the policy

d) Clause 5.3

- Explicit requirement for relevant roles to be assigned, communicated and understood

- No requirement for a specific management representative and the responsibility now resides with top management to assign and manage
- Requirement for defining responsibility and authority for ensuring processes are delivering their intended outputs

iv) Clause 6: Planning

a) Clause 6.1

- Considering the issues raised and relevant interested parties' requirements identified (4.1 and 4.2), this clause requires the determination of risks and opportunities which need to be addressed, actions to be taken and evaluation of the effectiveness of these actions

b) Clause 6.2

Objectives should be:

- established for processes relevant to the QMS
- in line with customer requirements
- in line with products and services conformity
- monitored, communicated & updated

c) Clause 6.3

- Changes to the QMS should be carried out in a planned manner
- The standard has evolved to enable organizations to adapt to changing environments or circumstances

Note: It is important to know that change is addressed in the following clauses:

- Clause 6.3 - Planning/implementing changes to the QMS
- Clause 7.1.6 - Organizational knowledge - for addressing changing needs and trends, with respect to knowledge
- Clause 8.1 - Controlling operational changes, planned and unintentional
- Clause 8.5.6 - Addressing changes affecting products & services

v) Clause 7: Support

a) Clause 7.1

There should be adequate resources to ensure effectiveness of the QMS. Resource considerations now include:

- o internal resources
- o external providers
- o people
- o monitoring and measuring resources
- o organizational knowledge required to ensure the processes provide conforming products and services
- o external communication

b) Clause 7.3 and 7.4

Relevant persons doing work under the organization's control need to have awareness and communication (internal and external) of the QMS and benefits of improving performance

c) Clause 7.5.1

Requirements that used to be required for a quality manual have been enhanced and made more flexible to allow for the use of documented information needed for the quality management system

d) Clause 7.5.2

Enhanced requirement for the creation and updating of documented information, e.g. description, format & suitability

e) Clause 7.5.3

Control of documented information – now explicitly includes confidentiality, integrity and access

vi) Clause 8: Operation

a) Clause 8.1.b

- o Explicit requirement for establishing criteria for processes

b) Clause 8.2.1

- o Explicit considerations are now linked to: customer communications; customer property, and contingency actions

c) Clause 8.2.2

- o Determination of requirements; this requires a process and is explicit with regard to substantiating claims for products and services being offered

d) Clause 8.3

- o This section on design and development of products and services has substantively changed and simplified

e) Clause 8.3.2

- o Design and development has been restructured to allow for a more process orientated approach
- o Involvement of customers and users as part of design planning to be considered

f) Clause 8.3.3

- o Design and development inputs – explicit requirements for internal and external resource needs, potential consequences of failure, level of control expected by customers

g) Clause 8.3.4

- o Design and development controls – new clause combining Reviews, Verification & Validation

h) Clause 8.5.5

- o Post-delivery activities is a new clause

i) Clause 8.5.6

- o A new requirement for the control of changes is addressed in the slide introducing the concept of change

j) Clause 8.6

- o The release of products and services is now part of the operational requirements

k) Clause 8.7

- o The control of nonconforming output is more explicit; it now considers the options to apply correction and corrective action
- o Nonconforming product changed to nonconforming output

vii) Clause 9: Performance evaluation

a) Clause 9.1.1

- o In 8.1 ISO 9001:2008 (clause 8.1) there was a requirement for planning. This is replaced with identifying what needs monitoring and measuring, and the methods to be used

b) Clause 9.1.3

- o There are specific requirements for analysis and evaluation when using results as inputs to management review
- o Effective implementation of planning and actions to address risks and opportunities are new requirements in this clause

c) Clause 9.2

- o Internal audit program now has explicit considerations for: quality objectives, customer feedback and changes impacting the organization; management responsibility for action is now implicit whereas previously this was explicit
- o An auditor is now required to be impartial versus in the previous version they could not audit their own work

d) Clause 9.3

- o There are now additional requirements for management review. These include:
- o changes in external and internal issues (such as strategic direction)
- o performance concerning external providers
- o adequacy of resources for effective QMS and effectiveness of actions taken addressing risks & opportunities

e) Clause 9.3.1

- o Management reviews should be aligned to the strategic direction of the organization

f) Clause 9.3.3

- o Management review outputs have been enhanced to include many of the new areas of focus

viii) Clause10: Improvement

a) Clause 10.1

- o This clause is new. It addresses more comprehensive opportunities for improvement; not only continual improvement
- o Addresses improvement of products and services and future needs and expectations
- o Emphasis is now on improving processes to prevent nonconformities and improving products and services

b) Clause 10.2

- o The nonconformity referred to in this clause concerns the entire QMS and not specifically the products or services which are addressed under clause 8.7

c) Clause 10.2.1

- o New emphasis is placed on nonconformity and corrective action
- o Consequences are now included thus actions taken now recognize the potential occurrence of a similar nonconformity elsewhere
- o Risks and opportunities now need to be updated when required following a nonconformity

d) Clause 10.2.2

- o Documented information is now required on the nature of the nonconformity and subsequent actions taken

e) Clause 10.3

- o Opportunities shall be addressed as part of continual improvement

11

ISO 14000 ENVIRONMENTAL MANAGEMENT SYSTEM

11.1 Introduction

Organizations are becoming increasingly concerned with the potential impact of their activities, processes, products, and services on the environment. They face increasing pressure, both internal and external, to alter their business management plans to give environmental protection greater priority. Organizations' efforts to address environmental concerns can be given more order and consistency through the implementation of an Environmental Management System (EMS).

The ISO 14000 is perhaps the most comprehensive EMS initiative ever taken. This standard is expected to be in the international environmental quality benchmark for conducting business in the global marketplace of the 21st century.

11.2 Overview of ISO 14000 Standards

The overall aim of the ISO 14000 Standard is to support environmental protection and prevention of pollution in balance with socio-economic needs.

An EMS provides the framework for the organization to examine issues such as the allocation of resources, assignment of responsibilities and on-going evaluation of practices, procedures and processes systematically, and to achieve continuous improvement in environmental performance through effective management of their environmental impacts.

While Quality Management System (QMS) deals with customers' needs, EMS addresses the needs of a broad range of interested parties and the evolving needs of society for environmental protection. This standard, however, shares common management system principles with the ISO 9000 series of QMS.

The organization may elect to use an existing management system consistent with the ISO 9000 series as a basis for its environmental management system. The application of various management systems, however, may differ due to different purposes and different interested parties.

11.3 Environmental Risk and Sustainable Development

Environmental Risk

The management of risk is a vital function of modern business. Effective risk management of business processes is fundamental to a successful business.

Environmental risk is associated with each interaction of an organization with the environment. The impacts are either direct or indirect.

Direct impacts are normally associated with the activities of a specific site, for example:

- Production of wastes
- Air emissions and effluent discharges
- Use of energy and water

Indirect impacts are either upstream or downstream of the organization and often exceed the direct impacts. For example:

- Pollution associated with electricity generation resulting from energy use
- Pollution associated with the production of goods and services utilized by the organization
- Polluting effects of products when used
- Wastes produced by the organization (landfill or incineration issues)

Sustainable Development

Environmental issues are often managed purely on an operational and reactive basis, yet the environment is clearly a strategic issue. There is an international consensus that all countries of the world must reduce their impact on the environment; they only disagree on how the reduction should be achieved. However, they are all broadly in agreement on the principle of "sustainable development".

Sustainable development can be defined as the development that meets the needs of the present without compromising the ability of future generations to meet their needs. There are five basic principles of sustainable development:

- The precautionary approach (development consistent with scientific and technical understanding of environmental issues),
- Prevention of pollution,
- Conservation of natural resources
- Equivalence of standards of environmental management across the world
- The polluter pays

11.4 Development of ISO 14000 Standards

- Developments in the area of EMS started in the early 1990s
- In 1992, the British Standard BS 7750 was introduced
- European Commission launched the Eco-Management and Audit Scheme (EMAS) in 1993
- Countries around the world, following the lead set by BSI, started developing EMS standards
- In 1993, the International Organization for standardization (ISO) established a Technical Committee (TC207) to develop and produce a set of unified, voluntary standards for environmental management
- The two EMS Standards, ISO 14001 and ISO 14004 were published as international standards on 1st September 1996
- The three Environmental Auditing Standards were also published as international standards on 1st October 1996

11.5 ISO 14000 Series

The initial set of standards developed is as follow:

ISO 14001	Environmental Management Systems – specifications with guideline for use
ISO 14004	Environmental Management Systems – general guidelines on principles, systems and supporting techniques
ISO 14010	General Principles of Environmental Auditing
ISO 14011	Audit Procedures
ISO 14012	Qualification Criteria for Environmental Auditors
ISO 14024	Environmental Labeling
ISO 14031	Environmental Performance Evaluation
ISO 14040	Life-Cycle Assessment – Principles and Guidelines
ISO 14050	Terms and Definitions

The most important set of standards are ISO 14001 and ISO 14004.

ISO 14001 is the standard that specifies the core requirements for environmental management systems and is intended to be used as a conformance standard for EMS certification. ISO 14001 shares common system requirement principles with ISO 9001.

ISO 14004 is a guideline standard addressing a broad range of environmental management issues. It provides simple guidelines for establishing and implementing EMS.

Another useful standard in the series is ISO 14011, which provides guidelines on environmental auditing procedures. This standard bears a common linkage to the quality system auditing procedures outlined in the standard ISO 19011.

11.6 ISO 14000 EMS Principles

Principle 1: Commitment and Policy

An organization should define its environmental policy and ensure commitment to its Environmental Management System

Principle 2: Planning

An organization should formulate a plan to fulfill its environmental policy.

Principle 3: Implementation

For effective implementation an organization should develop the capabilities and support mechanisms necessary to achieve its environmental policy, objectives, and targets.

Principle 4: Measurement and Evaluation

An organization should measure, monitor and evaluate its environmental performance.

Principle 5: Review and Improvement

An organization should review and continually improve its EMS, with the objective of improving its overall environmental performance.

11.7 ISO 14001 Environmental Management System (EMS)

ISO 14001 requires organizations to identify the environmental aspects of their activities, products or services and to evaluate the resulting impacts on the environment so that objectives and targets can be set for controlling significant impacts and for improving environmental performance.

ISO 14001 specifies the EMS requirements that on organization must meet in order to achieve certification by a third party – the certification body.

The requirements contained within Section 4 of ISO 14001 and the elements are:

4.1 General
4.2 Environmental Policy
4.3 Planning
4.3.1 Environmental Aspects
4.3.2 Legal and Other Requirements
4.3.3 Objectives and Targets

4.3.4	Environmental Management Program
4.4	Implementation and Operation
4.4.1	Structure and Responsibility
4.4.2	Training, Awareness, and Competence
4.4.3	Communications
4.4.4	Environmental Management System Documentation
4.4.5	Document Control
4.4.6	Operational Control
4.4.7	Emergency Preparedness and Response
4.5	Checking and Corrective Action
4.5.1	Monitoring and Measurement
4.5.2	Nonconformance and Corrective and Preventive Action
4.5.3	Records
4.5.4	Environmental Management System Audit
4.6	Management Review

a) Clause 4.1: General

This clause describes the intended purposes of the EMS, that is, to improve in environmental performance. By the continuous process of reviewing and evaluating, an EMS will be improved with the intended result of improving its environmental performance.

b) Clause 4.2 Policy

The intention of this clause is that by making the organization's environmental policy available to the public, the organization is very clearly setting highly visible environmental objectives. By this, the organization demonstrates commitment and accountability which could be verified, examined and even criticized if it fails to deliver the promises made.

Thus, the policy is intended to be the main "driver" of the EMS and all other elements of the system will follow on naturally from it.

The environmental policy must be reviewed by the top management. This is to ensure that the ultimate responsibility for, and commitment to, an EMS belongs to the highest level of management within the organization.

c) Clause 4.3: Planning

i) Clause 4.3.1: Environmental Aspects

The intent behind this sub-clause is to ensure that an organization has the capability and mechanisms to identify continually any environmental aspects it has and then to attach a level of significance to those aspects in a structured and logical way.

Because the environmental behavior of a supplier, or indeed a customer, could well turn out to be not of the same level of responsibility exercised by the implementing organization, such "indirect" or remote activities may well be of far more significance than that of the "direct" impacts of the organization itself. It therefore makes sense for an organization to include such "indirect" environmental aspects within its system and, using the same methodology, attach a level of significance.

ii) Clause 4.3.2: Legal and Other Requirements

These sub-clause requirements are included in the standards because it is recognized that an organization could well fall down on its environmental performance if it did not possess sufficient knowledge of applicable environmental laws, or codes of practice, within its industry sector. These codes of practice are the "other requirements".

An organization must comply with local and national legislation. By definition, legislation exists to control significant environmental impacts; otherwise the legislation would not come into being. Thus, because of this implied significance, compliance with legislative requirements is the baseline for certification to ISO 14001.

iii) Clause 4.3.3: Objectives and Targets

Although the organization may have an environmental policy and may have identified those aspects of its business which have a significant environmental impact, it needs to translate such findings into clear achievable objectives, measured by specific targets. In practical terms, each significant environmental impact should have an associated objective and target set against it for the control of, and minimization of, that impact. This then is the intention and purpose of this sub-clause.

iv) Clause 4.3.4: Environmental Management Programs

The purpose of this sub-clause is to ensure that the organization has allocated responsibilities and resources and set time-scales for ensuring that the activities described in the preceding sub-clauses will happen as planned and also that new activities will be subjected to such environmental management controls. This ensures that the environmental consequences of any new developments are considered at the earliest possible stage. To allow such a program to be monitored, it therefore makes sense for the organization to document and make visible and available, such a plan or program to all involved employees,

d) Clause 4.4: Implementation and Operation

i) Clause 4.4.1: Structure and Responsibility

This sub-clause is included to ensure that personnel are assigned specific responsibilities for a part, or parts, of the EMS and has a very clear-cut reporting structure (with no ambiguities). For example, when monitoring emissions to atmosphere, it should be clear who actually performs the task, with contingency plans for responsibility if the named person is away ill or on vacation.

The sub-clause also requires that top management appoints an individual to be the "management representative", with specific ownership for the well-being of the EMS and co-ordination of all environmental activities.

ii) Clause 4.4.2: Training, Awareness and Competence

This sub-clause is designed to enable an organization not only to identify training needs, as appropriate, but also to measure the success of that training. All individuals need some form of training to enable them to perform a new task.

Awareness is the product (or end result) of any training given – if personnel are more aware of the consequences of their action they are far more likely to follow procedures.

Competence is usually a term describing an individual's capability to absorb training and to apply the resultant awareness to the tasks that they perform. So, although several individuals may appear to be equally receptive during a training session, there may well be big differences in performance when the knowledge from the training is put into practice. Some will do better than others – that is they will be more competent – and this is an area on which this sub-clause requires the implementing organization to focus.

iii) Clause 4.4.3: Communication

Communication, both internal and external, is extremely important and if it is not formally addressed, may have negative effects on the success of the EMS.

Internal communication is necessary for information flow, particularly to departments that may not be at the forefront of the EMS. External messages are just as important. Such communication needs to be coordinated to get across a consistent message to the media, suppliers and customers, as well as the other stakeholders.

iv) Clause 4.4.4: EMS Documentation

For a system to be audited, there must be a minimum level of documentation available to demonstrate that the system exists and can be followed through by anyone who wishes to do so. However, this sub-clause uses phases such as "describing the core elements" and "provides direction" to ensure that a top-heavy documented system is not the aim of this sub-clause. There is encouragement from the accreditation bodies and certification bodies alike to ensure that an EMS is not too focused on documentation alone. A balance must be struck between failure to document essentials and a bureaucratic system that does not add any value or meaning to the system.

v) Clause 4.4.5: Document Control

The purpose of document control in any management system is to ensure that when, for example, an operator follows a procedure, that procedure is the most up-to-date available, and that an out-of-date procedure cannot be followed accidentally. In an EMS, following an outdated procedure could lead to adverse environmental consequences, so some method must be in place to control documentation.

vi) Clause 4.4.6: Operational Control

The purpose of operational control is to ensure that those environmental aspects that are deemed to be significant (as identified earlier in clause 4.3 Planning) are controlled in such a way that the objectives and targets have a fair chance of being achieved.

Such control will invariably be described and documented in procedures but need only be appropriate to the nature, complexity and degree of significance of the function, activity or process that they address. Such control should include direct and indirect environmental impacts.

vii) Clause 4.4.7: Emergency Preparedness and Response

The intent behind this sub-clause is that an organization must have in place plans of how to react in an emergency situation. Waiting until an emergency occurs and then formulating a plan is plainly not a good idea. The emergency plans or procedures may not work in practice and this failure may lead to an environmental incident.

e) Clause 4.5: Checking and Corrective Action

i) Clause 4.5.1: Monitoring and Measurement

A program or activity for environmental improvement cannot said to be achieving anything unless the starting point is known, the objective and target are defined and progress in between start and finish is somehow measured. This sub-clause requires an organization to monitor and measure its environmental targets at regular intervals. Unless there is such regular monitoring, an environmental objective may not be achieved. Furthermore, the organization may not recognize this as a problem nor take the necessary corrective actions.

ii) Clause 4.5.2: Nonconformance and Corrective and Preventive Action

Nonconformance in the system must be recognized and acted upon. The root cause should be investigated and controls put in place to make sure the nonconformance do not happen again. Although this is the overriding purpose of this sub-clause, care must be taken to ensure that the corrective actions that are taken by the organization are commensurate with the environmental impact encountered and that committing excess time and resources to problems of a low magnitude is avoided.

iii) Clause 4.5.3: Records

The purpose of this sub-clause is to ensure that the organization keeps records of its activities. For example, in the event of a dispute with a regulatory body, not having records to demonstrate compliance with discharge consents could spell trouble for the organization. A potentially heavy fine may be reduced if objective evidence in the form of records is produced which demonstrates – if not absolute control – then due diligence. It therefore makes sense for the organization to decide which records it needs to keep, and for how long, commensurate with the risks involved if they did not keep such records. In any event, legislative requirements will dictate that some records are kept for minimum specified time periods.

iv) Clause 4.5.4: Environmental Management System Audits

Internal audits are now an established management tool in many businesses. The concept of self-policing is recognized as an important mechanism by the organization with any form of management system, including EMS.

Accreditation bodies insist that third-party certification bodies must determine the amount of reliance that can be placed upon the organization's internal audit. Such audits should be carried out in much greater depth than the external assessment body could hope to achieve and, indeed, this is an area upon which the certification body places much emphasis. The completeness and effectiveness of internal audits are major factors in demonstrating to the certification body that the EMS is being well managed.

f) Clause 4.6: Management Review

The purpose of this sub-clause is to consider, in a structured and measured way, all of the preceding steps that have been taken by the organization and to ask fundamental questions such as:

- Is the organization doing and achieving what has been stated in the environmental policy?
- Are objectives and targets that are set for environmental performance being achieved?
- If objectives and targets are not achieved, why not?
- Are appropriate corrective actions taking place?

These questions, and more, should be asked by top management. The ideal vehicle for such an inward-looking review is a formalized management review with an itemized agenda, minutes being taken and a report being issued to all interested parties.

A guideline for the time interval between reviews is 3 to 6 months in the early stages of implementation followed by annual reviews once the system becomes more mature. In reality, the time intervals should be determined by events.

11.8 Benefits of an Effective ISO 14001 EMS

- Improved compliance with legislative and regulatory requirements
- Reduction in liability/risk
- Pollution prevention and waste reduction
- A framework for continuous environmental performance improvement
- Community goodwill
- Attract high-quality work force

11.9 Relationship between ISO 14000 and ISO 9000

The common belief among professionals in the international standards arena is that the ISO 14000 EMS and its auditing standards, and the ISO 9000 QMS and its auditing standards, ultimately should be harmonized in some manner. A drive towards more efficient auditing will spur efforts to eliminate multiple audits, since there is a strong desire among industry members that there should only be one audit for management systems.

Integrating implementation of the standards at the operational level could help cut costs by making certification efforts more economical and audits less disruptive for auditees.

However, there are several key differences, making ISO 14001 more demanding. ISO 14001 sections missing from ISO 9001 include: specific policy requirements, environmental aspect identification, setting objectives and targets at all relevant levels, and the requirements that a company commit to complying with appropriate legislation and to prevention of pollution. As a result, ISO 14001 has legal implications missing from ISO 9000 and must take into account a broader array of stakeholders.

11.10 ISO 14001:2015 Environmental Management System

i) Why was ISO 14001 revised?

All ISO standards are reviewed every five years to establish if a revision is required in order to keep it current and relevant for the marketplace. ISO 14001:2015 is designed to respond to latest trends and ensure it is compatible with other management system standards.

The main changes in ISO 14001:2015 are:

- Increased prominence of environmental management within the organization's strategic planning processes
- Greater focus on leadership
- Addition of proactive initiatives to protect the environment from harm and degradation
- Improving environmental performance added
- Lifecycle thinking when considering environmental aspects
- Organizations need to control or influence outsourced processes.
- Addition of a communications strategy
- ISO common framework for management systems

ii) Benefits to Business or Organization

There are many reasons why an organization should take a strategic approach to improving its environmental performance. Users of the standard have reported that ISO 14001 helps:

- Demonstrate compliance with current and future statutory and regulatory requirements
- Increase leadership involvement and engagement of employees
- Improve company reputation and the confidence of stakeholders through strategic communication
- Achieve strategic business aims by incorporating environmental issues into business management
- Provide a competitive and financial advantage through improved efficiencies and reduced costs

- o Encourage better environmental performance of suppliers by integrating them into the organization's business systems

iii) PDCA Model

The PDCA Model provides an iterative process used by organizations to continual improvement. It can be briefly described as follows:

Plan – establish environmental objectives and processes necessary to deliver results in accordance with the organization's environmental policy

Do – implement the processes as planned

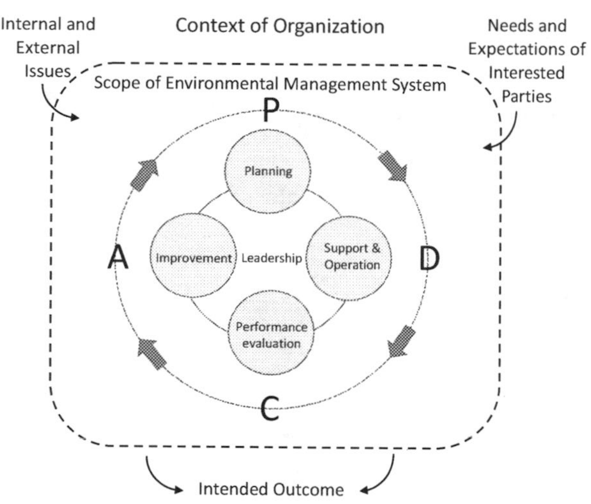

Check – monitor and measure processes against the environmental policy, including its commitment, environmental objectives, and operating criteria and report the results

Act – take actions to continually improve relationship between PDCA and the framework in this International Standard

iv) ISO 14001:2015 Contents

ISO 14001 specifies the Environmental Management System requirements that an organization must meet in order to achieve certification by a third party – the certification body.

The clauses and titles of ISO 14001 Environmental Management System are:

1.	Scope
2.	Normative reference
3.	Terms and conditions
4.	Context of the organization
4.1	Understanding the organization and its context
4.2	Understanding the needs and expectations of interested parties
4.3	Determining the scope of the XXX management system
4.4	Environmental management system
5	Leadership
5.1	Leadership and commitment
5.2	Policy
5.3	Organizational roles, responsibilities and authorities
6	Planning
6.1	Actions to address risks and opportunities
6.1.1	General
6.1.2	Environmental aspects
6.1.3	Compliance obligation
6.1.4	Planning action
6.2	Environmental objectives and planning to achieve them
6.2.1	Environmental objectives
6.2.2	Planning action to achieve environmental objectives
7	Support
7.1	Resources
7.2	Competence
7.3	Awareness
7.4	Communication
7.4.1	General
7.4.2	Internal communication

7.4.3	External communication
7.5	Documented information
7.5.1	General
7.5.2	Creating and upgrading
7.5.3	Control of documented information
8	Operation
8.1	Operational planning and control
8.2	Emergency preparedness and response
9	Performance evaluation
9.1	Monitoring, measurement, analysis and evaluation
9.1.1	General
9.1.2	Evaluation of compliance
9.2	Internal audit
9.2.1	General
9.2.2	Internal audit program
9.3	Management review
10	Improvement
10.1	General
10.2	Nonconformity and corrective action
10.3	Continual improvement

v) Clause 4: Context of the organization

a) Clause 4.1: Understanding the organization and its context

The organization shall determine external and internal issues that are relevant to its purpose and that affect its ability to achieve the intended outcome(s) of its environmental management system.

b) Clause 4.2: Understanding the needs and expectations of interested parties

The organization shall determine:

- the interested parties that are relevant to the environmental management system;
- the relevant requirements of these interested parties.

c) Clause 4.3: Determining the scope of the environmental management system

The organization shall determine the boundaries and applicability of the environmental management system to establish its scope. When determining this scope, the organization shall consider:

- o the external and internal issues referred to in 4.1;
- o the requirements referred to in 4.2

The scope shall be available as documented information.

d) Clause 4.4: Environmental management system

The organization shall establish, implement, maintain and continually improve an environmental management system, including the processes needed and their interactions, in accordance with the requirements of this International Standard.

vi) Clause 5: Leadership

a) Clause 5.1 Leadership and commitment

Top management shall demonstrate leadership and commitment with respect to the environmental management system by:

- o ensuring that the environmental policy and environmental objectives are established and are compatible with the strategic direction of the organization;
- o ensuring the integration of the environmental management system requirements into the organization's business processes;
- o ensuring that the resources needed for the environmental management system are available;
- o communicating the importance of effective environmental management and of conforming to the environmental management system requirements;
- o ensuring that the environmental management system achieves its intended outcome(s);
- o directing and supporting persons to contribute to the effectiveness of the environmental management system;
- o promoting continual improvement;

- o supporting other relevant management roles to demonstrate their leadership as it applies to their areas of responsibility.

b) Clause 5.2: Policy

Top management shall establish an environmental policy that:

- o is appropriate to the purpose of the organization;
- o provides a framework for setting environmental objectives;
- o includes a commitment to satisfy applicable requirements;
- o includes a commitment to continual improvement of the environmental management system.

The environmental policy shall:

- o be available as documented information;
- o be communicated within the organization;
- o be available to interested parties, as appropriate.

c) Clause 5.3: Organizational roles, responsibilities and authorities

Top management shall ensure that the responsibilities and authorities for relevant roles are assigned and communicated within the organization.

Top management shall assign the responsibility and authority for:

- o ensuring that the environmental management system conforms to the requirements of this International Standard;
- o reporting on the performance of the environmental management system to top management.

vii) Clause 6: Planning

a) Clause 6.1: Actions to address risks and opportunities

When planning for the environmental management system, the organization shall consider the issues referred to in 4.1 and the requirements referred to in 4.2 and determine the risks and opportunities that need to be addressed to:

- o give assurance that the environmental management system can achieve its intended outcome(s);
- o prevent, or reduce, undesired effects;
- o achieve continual improvement.

The organization shall plan:

a) actions to address these risks and opportunities;

b) how to

  - o integrate and implement the actions into its environmental management system processes;
  - o evaluate the effectiveness of these actions.

b) Clause 6.1.1: General

The organization shall establish, implement and maintain the processes needed to meet the requirements in 6.1.1 and 6.1.4.

When planning for the environmental management system, the organization shall consider:

a) the issues referred to in 4.1

b) the requirements referred to in 4.2

and determine the risks and opportunities related to its environmental aspects (see 6.1.2), compliance obligations (see 6.1.3) and other issues and requirements, identified in 4.1 and 4.2, that need to be addressed to:

- o give assurance that the environmental management system can achieve its intended outcomes;

- o prevent or reduce undesired effects, including the potential for external environmental conditions to affect the organization;
- o achieve continual improvement.

c) Clause 6.1.2: Environmental aspects

Within the defined scope of the environmental management system, the organization shall determine the environmental aspect of its activities, products and services that it can control and those that can influence, and their associated environmental impacts, considering a life cycle perspective.

When determining environmental aspects, the organization shall take into account:

- o change, including planned or new developments, and new or modified activities, products and services
- o abnormal conditions and reasonable foreseeable emergency situations.

d) Clause 6.1.3: Compliance obligations

The organization shall

- o determine and have access to the compliance obligations related to its environmental aspects,
- o determine how these compliance obligations apply to the organization
- o take these compliance obligations into account when establishing, implementing, maintaining and continually improving its environmental management system

e) Clause 6.1.4: Planning action

The organization shall plan:

a) to take actions to address its:

- o significant environmental aspects,
- o compliance obligations,
- o risks and opportunities identified in 6.1.1

b) how to:

- o integrate and implement the activities into its environmental management system processes (see 6.2, clause 7, clause 8, and 9.1) or other business processes.
- o evaluate the effectiveness of these actions (see 9.1)

When planning these activities, the organization shall consider its technological options and its financial, operational and business requirements.

f) Clause 6.2: Environmental objectives and planning to achieve them

g) Clause 6.2.1: Environmental objectives

The organization shall establish environmental objectives at relevant functions and levels.

The environmental objectives shall:

- o be consistent with the environmental policy;
- o be measurable (if practicable);
- o take into account applicable requirements;
- o be monitored;
- o be communicated;
- o be updated as appropriate.

The organization shall retain documented information on the environmental objectives.

h) Clause 6.2.2: Planning action to achieve environmental objectives

When planning how to achieve its environmental objectives, the organization shall determine:

- o what will be done
- o what resources will be required
- o who will be responsible
- o when it will be completed
- o how the result will be evaluated

The organization shall consider how actions to achieve its environmental objectives be integrated into the organization's business processes.

viii) Clause 7: Support

a) Clause 7.1: Resources

- o The organization shall determine and provide the resources needed for the establishment,
- o implementation, maintenance and continual improvement of the environmental management system.

b) Clause 7.2: Competence

The organization shall:

- o determine the necessary competence of person(s) doing work under its control that affects its environmental performance;
- o ensure that these persons are competent on the basis of appropriate education, training, or experience;
- o where applicable, take actions to acquire the necessary competence, and evaluate the effectiveness of the actions taken;
- o retain appropriate documented information as evidence of competence.

c) Clause 7.3: Awareness

Persons doing work under the organization's control shall be aware of:

- o the environmental policy;
- o their contribution to the effectiveness of the environmental management system, including the benefits of improved environmental performance;
- o the implications of not conforming with the environmental management system requirements.

d) Clause 7.4: Communication

e) Clause 7.4.1: General

The organization shall establish, implement, and maintain the processes needed for internal and external communication relevant to environmental management system, including:

- o on what it will communicate
- o when to communicate
- o with whom to communicate
- o how to communicate

f) Clause 7.4.2: Internal Communication

The organization shall:

- o internally communicate information relevant to the environmental management system among the various levels and functions of the organization, including changing to the environmental management system, as appropriate
- o ensure its communication processes enable persons doing work under the organization's control to contribute to continual improvement

g) Clause 7.4.3: External Communication

The organization shall externally communicate information relevant to environmental management system, as established by the organization's communication processes and as required by its compliance obligations.

h) Clause 7.5: Documented information

i) Clause 7.5.1: General

The organization's environmental management system shall include:

- o documented information required by this International Standard;
- o documented information determined by the organization as being necessary for the effectiveness of the environmental management system.

NOTE The extent of documented information for an environmental management system can differ from one organization to another due to:

- o the size of organization and its type of activities, processes, products and services;
- o the complexity of processes and their interactions;
- o the competence of persons.

j) Clause 7.5.2: Creating and updating

When creating and updating documented information the organization shall ensure appropriate:

- o identification and description (e.g. a title, date, author, or reference number);
- o format (e.g. language, software version, graphics) and media (e.g. paper, electronic);
- o review and approval for suitability and adequacy.

k) Clause 7.5.3: Control of documented information

Documented information required by the environmental management system and by this International Standard shall be controlled to ensure:

- o it is available and suitable for use, where and when it is needed;
- o it is adequately protected (e.g. from loss of confidentiality, improper use, or loss of integrity).

For the control of documented information, the organization shall address the following activities, as applicable:

- o distribution, access, retrieval and use;
- o storage and preservation, including preservation of legibility;
- o control of changes (e.g. version control);
- o retention and disposition.

Documented information of external origin determined by the organization to be necessary for the planning and operation of the environmental management system shall be identified, as appropriate, and controlled.

NOTE Access can imply a decision regarding the permission to view the documented information only, or the permission and authority to view and change the documented information.

ix) Clause 8: Operation

a) Clause 8.1: Operational planning and control

The organization shall plan, implement and control the processes needed to meet requirements, and to implement the actions determined in 6.1 and 6.2, by:

- establishing operating criteria for the processes;
- implementing control of the processes in accordance with the operating criteria;

The organization shall control planned changes and review the consequences of unintended changes, taking action to mitigate any adverse effects, as necessary.

The organization shall ensure that outsourced processes are controlled.

The organization shall ensure environmental requirements are consistent with a life cycle perspective.

b) Clause 8.2: Emergency preparedness and response

The organization shall establish, implement and maintain the processes needed to prepare for or response to potential emergency situation identified in 6.1.1.

The organization shall:

- prepare to respond by planning actions to prevent or mitigate adverse environmental impacts from emergency situations
- respond to actual emergency situations
- take actions to prevent or mitigate the consequences of emergency situations, appropriate to the magnitude of the emergency situations and the potential environmental impacts
- periodically test the planned response actions, where practicable
- periodically review and revise the processes and planned response actions, in particular after the occurrence of emergency situations or test
- provide relevant information and training related to emergency preparedness and response, as appropriate, to relevant interested parties, including persons working under its control

The organization shall maintain documented information to the extent necessary to have confidence that the processes are carried out as planned.

x) Clause 9: Performance evaluation

a) Clause 9.1: Monitoring, measurement, analysis and evaluation

b) Clause 9.1.1: General

The organization shall monitor, measure, analyse and evaluate its environmental performance.

The organization shall determine:

o what needs to be monitored and measured
o the methods for monitoring, measurement, analysis and evaluation, as applicable to ensure valid results
o the criteria against which the organization will evaluate its environmental performance and appropriate indicators
o when the monitoring and measuring shall be performed
o when the results for monitoring and measuring shall be analysed and evaluated

The organization shall ensure that calibrated or verified monitoring and measuring equipment is used and maintained, as appropriate.

The organization shall evaluate its environmental performance and the effectiveness of the environmental management system.

The organization shall communicate relevant environmental performance information both internally and externally as identified in it communication programmes and as required by its compliance obligations.

The organization shall retain appropriate documented information as evidence of the monitoring, measurement, analysis and evaluation results.

c) Clause 9.1.2: Evaluation of compliance

The organization shall establish, implement, and maintain the processes needed to evaluate fulfilment of its compliance obligations.

The organization shall:

- o determine the frequency that compliance will be evaluated
- o evaluate compliance and take action if needed
- o maintain knowledge and understanding of its compliance status

The organization shall retain documented information as evidence of the compliance evaluation results.

d) Clause 9.2: Internal audit

e) Clause 9.2.1: General

The organization shall conduct internal audits at planned intervals to provide information on whether the environmental management system:

a) conforms to:

- o the organization's own requirements for its environmental management system;
- o the requirements of this International Standard/this Technical Specification;

b) is effectively implemented and maintained.

f) Clause 9.2.2: Internal Audit Program

The organization shall:

- o plan, establish, implement and maintain an audit programme(s) including the frequency, methods, responsibilities, planning requirements and reporting, which shall take into consideration the importance of the processes concerned and the results of previous audits;
- o define the audit criteria and scope for each audit;
- o select auditors and conduct audits to ensure objectivity and the impartiality of the audit process;

- o ensure that the results of the audits are reported to relevant management;
- o retain documented information as evidence of the implementation of the audit programme and the audit results.

g) Clause 9.3: Management review

- o Top management shall review the organization's environmental management system, at planned intervals, to ensure its continuing suitability, adequacy and effectiveness.
- o The management review shall include consideration of:

a) the status of actions from previous management reviews;

b) changes in external and internal issues that are relevant to the environmental management system;

c) information on the environmental performance, including trends in:

- o nonconformities and corrective actions;
- o monitoring and measurement results;
  - o audit results;

d) opportunities for continual improvement.

The outputs of the management review shall include decisions related to continual improvement opportunities and any need for changes to the environmental management system.

The organization shall retain documented information as evidence of the results of management reviews.

xi) Clause 10: Improvement

a) Clause 10.1 General

The organization shall determine opportunities for improvement (see 9.1, 9.2 and 9.3) and implement necessary actions to achieve the intended outcome of its environmental management system.

b) Clause 10.2: Nonconformity and corrective action

When a nonconformity occurs, the organization shall:

a) react to the nonconformity and, as applicable:

- take action to control and correct it;
- deal with the consequences;

b) evaluate the need for action to eliminate the causes of the nonconformity, in order that it does not recur or occur elsewhere, by:

- reviewing the nonconformity;
- determining the causes of the nonconformity;
- determining if similar nonconformities exist, or could potentially occur;

c) implement any action needed;

d) review the effectiveness of any corrective action taken;

e) make changes to the environmental management system, if necessary.

Corrective actions shall be appropriate to the effects of the nonconformities encountered.

The organization shall retain documented information as evidence of:

- the nature of the nonconformities and any subsequent actions taken;
- the results of any corrective action.

c) Clause 10.3: Continual improvement

The organization shall continually improve the suitability, adequacy and effectiveness of the environmental management system.

12

WORLD-CLASS ORGANIZATION STANDARDS

12.1 USA National Quality Award Model

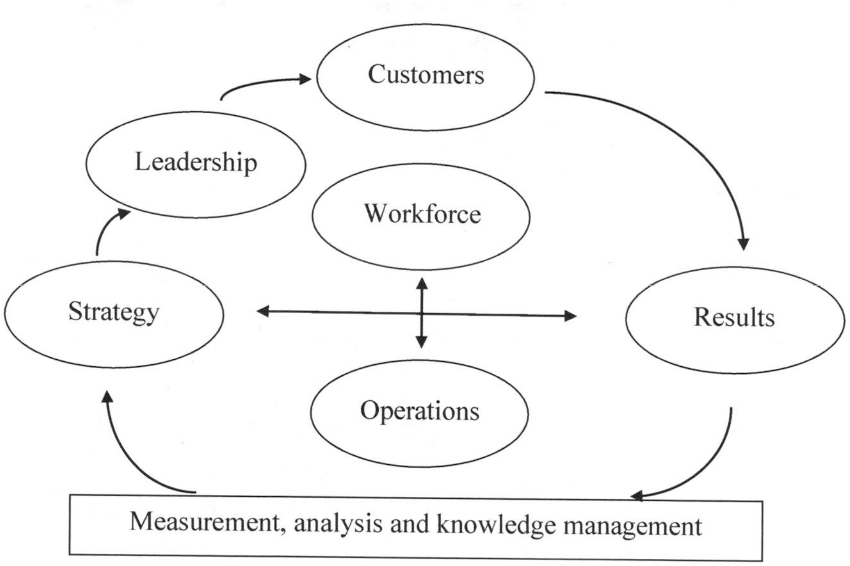

12.2 European EFQM Excellence Model

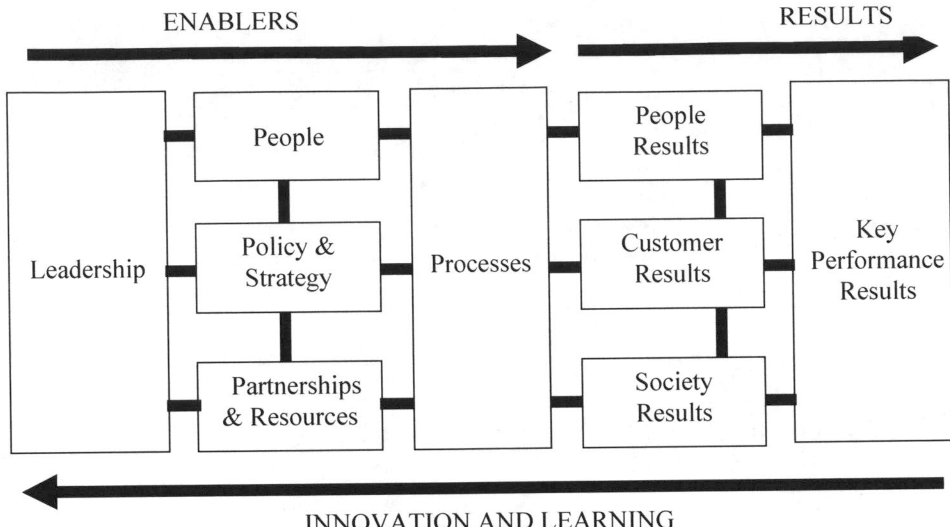

12.3 Japanese Deming Prize Model

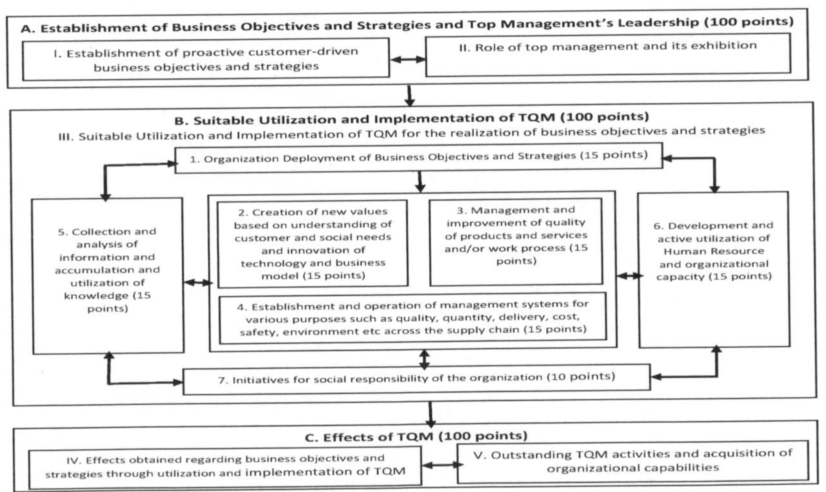

12.4 Singapore Quality Award Model

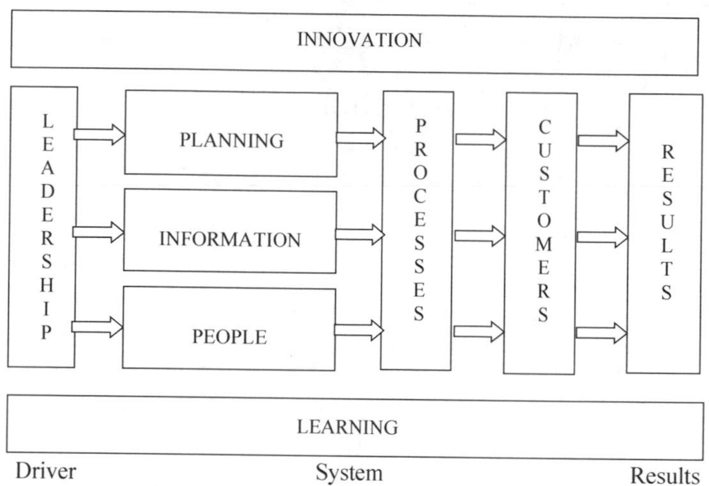

The Singapore 2017 Business Excellence Framework (BEF)

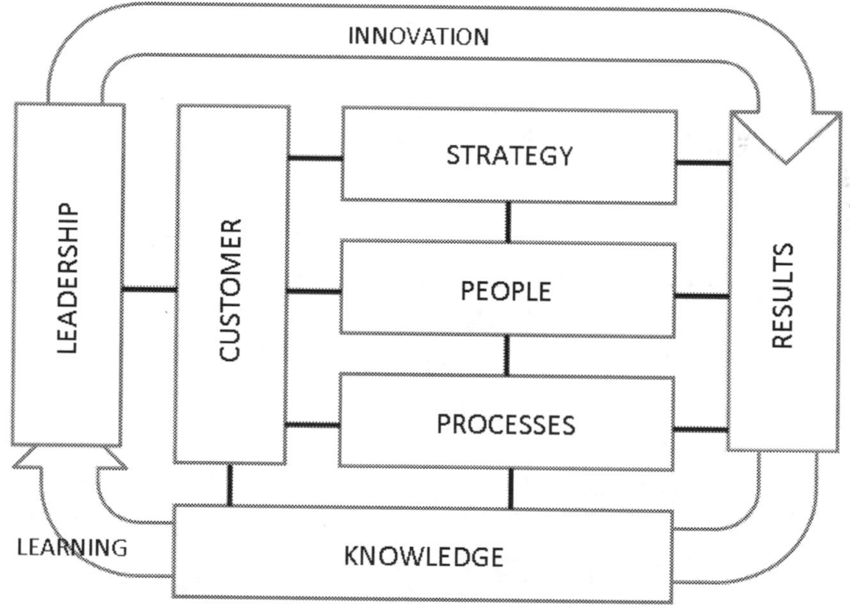

12.5 Comparison of World-Class Organization Standards

<table>
<tr><th>US NQA</th><th>EFQM</th><th>DEMING</th><th>SQA</th><th>2017 BEF</th></tr>
<tr><td>Leadership</td><td>Leadership</td><td>Top Management Leadership</td><td>Leadership</td><td>Leadership</td></tr>
<tr><td>Measurement, analysis and knowledge management</td><td>Resources</td><td>Information, analysis and utilization of IT</td><td>Information</td><td>Knowledge</td></tr>
<tr><td>Strategy</td><td>Policy and strategy</td><td>Business objectives and strategies</td><td>Planning</td><td>Strategy</td></tr>
<tr><td>Workforce</td><td>People</td><td>Human resources utilization</td><td>People</td><td>People</td></tr>
<tr><td rowspan="2">Operations</td><td>Process</td><td rowspan="2">TQM utilization and implementation</td><td rowspan="2">Processes</td><td rowspan="2">Processes</td></tr>
<tr><td>Partnership</td></tr>
<tr><td>Customers</td><td>Partnership</td><td>Customer-driven objectives and strategies</td><td>Customers</td><td>Customers</td></tr>
<tr><td>Results</td><td>Key performance results,
People results,
Customer results,
Society results</td><td>Effects of TQM</td><td>Results</td><td>Results</td></tr>
</table>

12.6 Singapore Quality Award

a) Introduction

The Singapore Quality Award (SQA) is the highest accolade given to organizations for business excellence. The Award is conferred upon the "best of the best" in recognition of their attainment of world-class standard of performance excellence.

The SQA is administered by the Singapore Productivity and Standards Board (PSB) with active sponsorship, support and participation from the private sector in terms of finance and expertise. The Prime Minister is the Patron of the Award.

The SQA is managed by the Governing Council, which draws up policies and guidelines for the award program and approves the Award recipients. Members of the council are drawn from the Award Member organizations.

The Governing Council is supported by a Management Committee, which comprises experienced assessors and business practitioners from the Award Members and Award recipients. The Committee reviews the Award criteria, develops the system for training and certifying the assessors and shortlists Award applicants.

b) The Award Criteria Purposes

The SQA criteria form the basis for the evaluation and feedback to applicants on their performance. The criteria promotes:

- Understanding of the requirements for business and organizational excellence
- Enhancement of organizational performance practices and capabilities
- Sharing of best practice information among organization

c) Core Values

i) Visionary Leadership

An organization's senior leaders need to set directions and create a customer focus, clear and visible values and high expectations. They need to develop strategies, systems, and methods for achieving excellence, stimulating innovation and building knowledge and capabilities. The values and strategies should guide all activities and decisions of the organization. The leaders should inspire and motivate the entire workforce and should encourage involvement, development and learning, innovation and creativity of all employees. By being personally involved in activities such as planning, communications, coaching, performance reviews and employee recognition, the senior leaders should serve as role models in the organizations.

ii) Customer-Driven Quality

Quality is judged by the customers. An organization should therefore take into account all product and service features and attributes that contribute value to its customers and lead to customer satisfaction, referral and loyalty. It should pay attention to current as well as future customer and market requirements, and respond to them efficiently and effectively. Care should be taken to manage customer relationship and measure customer satisfaction. Being customer-driven is thus a strategic concept that is directed towards expanding market base and retaining customer.

iii) Innovation Focus

Innovation is about making changes to the organization's products, services, processes, technologies and management practices so as to create new, significant values for the organization's stakeholders. Innovation should focus on leading the organization to new dimensions of performance. Innovation is not only the purview of research and development departments but also important for key product and service processes including the support processes. Organizations need to be structured in such a way that innovation becomes part of the culture and daily work.

iv) Organizational and Personal Learning

To achieve the highest level of performance, the approach to organizational and personal learning must be executed well. The term organizational learning refers to continuous improvement of existing approaches and processes as well as adaptation to change, leading to new goals and approaches. Learning needs to be embedded in the way the organization operates. An organization should also invest in employee personal learning through education, training and opportunities for sustained and continuous growth.

v) Valuing People and Partners

An organization should seek creative ways to involve employees in enhancing performance and customer satisfaction. Meeting the organization's performance goals requires a fully committed and skilled workforce. Reward and recognition systems need to reinforce employee participation in achieving the organization's performance objectives. The health, well-being and motivation of employees should also form part of the organization's continuous improvement objectives and activities.

Organizations need to build internal and external partnerships for mutual benefit. Strong partnerships internally (e.g. cross-functional teaming and collaborating with unions) and externally (e.g. with customers and suppliers) can help the organizations to achieve their performance goals, boost their operational effectiveness and establish new market opportunities.

vi) Agility

Today's competitive markets demand a capacity for rapid change and flexibility. Organizations face ever-shorter cycles for introduction of new or improved products and services. Increasingly, speed and flexibility in responding to customers are critical requirements. Major improvements in response time often require simplification of work units and processes and the ability to change rapidly from one process to another. A major success factor in meeting competitive challenge is the design-to-introduction cycle time. Organizations also need to carry out stage-to-stage integration of activities from research to commercialization.

vii) Knowledge-Driven System

The achievement of superior performance requires the use of data, information and increasingly, knowledge to enhance judgement and enable better decision-making. The data, information and knowledge needed for performance management can be obtained from many sources including customers, product and service performance, operations, markets, comparisons and benchmarking, suppliers, employees and financial records.

A major consideration in performance management involves the selection and use of performance measures and indicators that lead to improved performance. A comprehensive set of indicators linked to performance requirements provides a clear basis for aligning all activities to its organizational goals and business objectives.

viii) Societal Responsibility

An organization should be responsible to the society, community and the environment and practice good corporate citizenship. These cover business ethics, the protection of public health, safety and the environment, community services and the sharing of best practices with the business community. These include consideration of the potential adverse impact on public health, safety and the environment as a result of the organization's operations as well as the life cycle of its products and services. In addition, organizations need to emphasize resources and waste reduction at the sources.

ix) Results Orientation

An organization's performance system needs to focus on results that are guided and balanced by the interests of all stakeholders – customers, employees, shareholders, suppliers and partners and the community. This will help to ensure that actions and plans meet stakeholders' needs without adverse impact on any stakeholder. Using a balanced composite of performance indicators, organizations can effectively communicate requirements, monitor actual performance and marshal support for improving results.

x) Systems Perspective

All activities and functions of an organization are linked to a larger system, and the outputs depend on how the organization manages the system and develops the relationship within and around it. An organization therefore needs to manage its whole enterprise as well as its related components, to achieve performance improvement. This systems approach will enable the organization to optimize the interrelationships of its functions and to focus on the value-added factors of all processes within a larger context. It also promotes the development of a preventive culture by emphasizing continuous improvement and corrective action at early stages of all activities. The SQA criteria provide organizations with a system perspective of managing and improving performance. The core values and the seven Award categories form the building blocks of the system that allow for synthesis and alignment of all requirements to the organization's overall objectives and goals.

d) Award Framework

The core values are integrated into a comprehensive framework comprising seven categories which make up the SQA model. The seven categories are:

1. Leadership
2. Planning
3. Information
4. People
5. Processes
6. Customers
7. Results

The model has the following basic elements:

i) Driver

Senior executives set the organizational directions and seek future opportunities for the organization.

ii) System

The system comprises a set of well-defined processes for meeting the organization's performance requirements.

iii) Results

The results deliver an ever-improving customer value and organizational performance.

e) Key Characteristics of Award Criteria

i) The Criteria are Non-prescriptive

They do not describe how an organization is to be managed or organized and are non-prescriptive. This is because:

- The focus is on outcomes derived by adopting appropriate methods, tools, or techniques. Organizations are encouraged to develop and demonstrate creative, adaptive and flexible approaches for meeting basic requirements.
- The selection of tool, techniques and systems, usually depend upon many factors such as business size, business type, the organization's stage of development and employee capabilities.

ii) The Criteria are Comprehensive

The criteria address all internal and external requirements of an organization. Accordingly, the processes of all work units are tied to these requirements. New or changing strategies may be readily adapted within the same set of criteria requirements

iii) The Criteria Emphasize Learning Cycles

The criteria call for learning (improvement) cycles in all parts of the organization. The cycles have four stages: planning, execution of plans, assessment of progress and improvement based on the assessment findings.

iv) The Criteria Emphasize Alignment

The criteria support a systems perspective to maintain organizational-wide goal alignment. This is achieved through the integrated structure of the core values, the criteria, and the results-oriented cause-and-effect linkage among the criteria. Alignment in the criteria is built around connecting and reinforcing measures derived from the organization's strategy. These measures are linked to customer value and overall performance.

v) The Criteria Support Goal-Based Diagnostic

The criteria and the scoring guidelines form a two-part diagnostic (assessment) system. The criteria are a set of 21 performance-oriented requirements. The guidelines spell out the assessment dimensions – Approach, Deployment and Results – and the key factors used in the assessment relative to each dimension. An assessment thus provides a profile of the strengths and areas for improvement for an organization relative to the requirements. This diagnostic assessment is a useful management tool that goes beyond most performance reviews and is applicable to a wide range of strategies and management systems.

12.7 The SQA Criteria: Excellence Indicators

1. Leadership

1.1 Senior Managers have developed a clear vision and mission which are easily understood and which drive the organization towards excellence.

1.2 Senior Managers are personally involved in communicating the organization goals and quality corporate values to all levels of employees.

1.3 The vision, mission and goals of the organization are regularly reinforced to all levels of employees through a variety of programmes as well as in day-to-day activities.

1.4 Senior Managers are personally and visibly involved in performance improvement activities.

1.5 Senior Management cascades organization goals systematically to all levels of the organization.

1.6 Senior Managers are personally involved in recognition of teams and individuals for their contributions to quality and performance improvement.

1.7 Senior Managers encourage staff and provide opportunities for them to try new ideas, experiment, innovate and take responsible risks.

1.8 Employees at all levels confirm that Senior Management strongly supports and drives corporate culture.

1.9 Employees show a strong sense of identity and commitment towards the organization's vision, and practise the corporate values in their day-to-day work.

1.10 Senior Managers evaluate their own leadership through various sources of feedback (e.g. 360^0 appraisal) and take actions to improve their leadership.

1.11 The organization has a well-defined policy and goals in relation to its contribution to the community and the environment in which it operates. It has programmes (e.g. community service, donations to charity, environmental conservation activities, hosting educational visits, etc.) to involve employees in achieving its public responsibility objectives.

2. Planning

2.1 Planning is a systematic and closed-loop process, involving regular review and modifications when necessary.

2.2 The planning process uses inputs from a variety of people at all levels throughout the organization.

2.3 The organization analyzes both internal data (e.g. operational performance, quality indicators, etc.) as well as external data (e.g. customer feedback, market intelligence, industry trends, etc) in its planning process.

2.4 The organization's plans are systematically cascaded down to all levels, and corporate goals are translated into departmental and individual objectives.

2.5 The organization regularly evaluates its planning process, and refinements are made to improve planning cycle time, planning accuracy and plan deployment.

2.6 The long-term and short-term goals are comprehensive, covering all key aspects of the business, and well-defined in measurable terms.

2.7 Targets set are challenging and achievable.

2.8 The planning process produces an overall business plan, not just a financial or budget plan.

2.9 The organization has appropriate indicators and data which are regularly monitored to track the achievement of its plans and targets.

3. Information

3.1 Data and information are carefully selected to help in management decision-making, and to track the organization's performance vis-à-vis its corporate objectives.

3.2 Data/information used for performance measurement and planning cover a broad spectrum of areas including financial, sales and marketing, production, product and service quality, supplier quality and customer satisfaction.

3.3 The organization integrates data on various aspects of performance into a few key indicators (e.g. a balanced scorecard) to track overall performance.

3.4 The organization has an effective and integrated system to collect and manage data and information which are used in day-to-day management and to drive performance improvements.

3.5 All data/information are assigned owners who reveal and ensure the accuracy, reliability and accessibility of the data/information.

3.6 The organization regularly obtains new knowledge required to create value for stakeholders.

3.7 The organization has created systems to capture and disseminate knowledge (e.g. overseas visits to result in presentation or trip report).

3.8 The organization has a systematic approach to analyze data and information to support organizational planning and review.

3.9 The organization regularly evaluates and improves its management of data and information.

3.1 The organization uses comparative data/information and/or competitive analysis to set "stretch" or challenging goals.

3.11 The organization has a systematic process to collect and analyze comparative data and information to drive performance improvements.

3.12 The organization has a systematic approach to benchmark its processes against best-in-class organizations and adopt best practices to improve operational performance.

4. People

4.1 HR is involved in the strategic planning process, providing its inputs as well as developing appropriate plans to support the organization's short and long-term goals.

4.2 HR planning is proactive rather than reactive, covering all key issues including recruitment, retention, training and development, leadership succession, employee participation, recognition and reward, management-labour relations and employee satisfaction.

4.3 The organization has a wide variety of mechanisms to encourage employee participation at all levels, promote team work and tap on the innovative potential of its employees.

4.4 The organization has a systematic approach to identify training and development needs for all levels of employees, taking into account skills requirements and current skills inventory.

4.5 The organization has a systematic approach to assess the effectiveness of training and development undergone by employees.

4.6 The organization has a systematic approach to measure employee satisfaction, obtain feedback from employees, and act on issues arising from such feedback.

4.7 The organization has a fair and effective system to measure employee performance.

4.8 The organization has a wide variety of reward and recognition schemes that support high performance, innovative and creative behaviour, and are linked to the corporate objectives and values.

4.9 The organization regularly evaluates and improves on its HR planning process, employee participation, training and development process, employee satisfaction approach, and recognition and reward systems.

5. Processes (100 pts)

5.1 The organization has a systematic process to acquire, evaluate and implement creative ideas from all sources.

5.2 The organization has a systematic process (e.g. quality function deployment) to translate customer requirements and expectations into product or service design, production and delivery.

5.3 External parties (customers, suppliers, business partners) are involved in key aspects of the design process (e.g. giving inputs, design reviews, product/service reviews).

5.4 The innovation and design processes are evaluated and improvements are made to shorten cycle time, improve design quality and reduce costs.

5.5 The organization's key processes have clear objectives and targets (e.g. cycle time, quality level) which are linked to business and quality goals.

5.6 The key processes are systematically measured and regularly reviewed to ensure conformance to performance standards or targets set.

5.7 The organization has a system to analyze root causes, take prompt corrective action and prevent future reoccurrence when a process fails to meet specified standards or targets set.

5.8 There are a wide variety of methods (e.g. internal assessment, third-party audit, customer audit) to regularly assess the quality and performance of the organization's key business processes and supporting processes.

5.9 The organization has a systematic approach to act on the results of the various assessments conducted on its key processes as well as supporting processes.

5.10 The organization identifies and selects its suppliers and partners who support the overall organization strategy.

5.11 The organization has methods to communicate and proactively ensure that suppliers have the capability and capacity to meet its requirements (e.g. supplier audits, supplier rating and certification system).

5.12 The organization has plans and actions to help key suppliers improve their abilities to meet key quality and response time requirements (e.g. training, joint planning, long-term agreements, incentives and recognition).

6. Customers

6.1 There is a logical method for segmenting the customer base, which contributes to improving business performance.

6.2 The organization has a wide variety of "listening posts" (e.g. focus groups, frontline employees, surveys, feedback forms, etc.) to determine both current and future customer requirements and expectations by customer segment.

6.3 The organization has a systematic approach to collate, analyze and summarize various sources of customer feedback (e.g. complaints, customer interviews, focus groups, surveys, etc.) into actionable information. There is continual scanning of the marketplace to anticipate potential opportunities to exploit competitive advantage.

6.4 There is demonstration that customers' requirements and expectations are systematically used as inputs in the planning process, and incorporated into the strategic business and improvement plans.

6.5 Several methods are used to ensure ease of customer contact (e.g. toll-free lines, pagers for contact personnel, internet emails, account managers, etc.).

6.6 Service standards are set for various interfaces with the customer (e.g. answering calls within 3 rings, responding to complaints within 24 hours, etc.).

6.7 Customer-contact employees are adequately trained and empowered (within limits) to manage customer relationships and delight customers.

6.8 There is a system to ensure prompt and effective resolution of all customer complaints.

6.9 Customer complaint data are systematically tracked and used to initiate prompt corrective action to prevent future re-occurrence.

6.10 The organization has different methods and indicators to measure customer satisfaction (e.g. customer survey, complaints/compliments, repeat business, feedback forms, warranty claims, customer interviews, etc.), and these are regularly and systematically monitored.

6.11 The organization's ability to satisfy customers has been recognized in the form of customer awards, or other forms of recognition schemes.

6.12 The organization regularly evaluates and improves on its processes and methods for determining customer requirements and expectations, managing customer relationships and measuring customer satisfaction.

6.13 There is progression beyond customer satisfaction to customer loyalty and retention.

7. Results

7.1 There is a clear link between the strategy of the organization and what it measures.

7.2 The organization has key indicators of customer, financial and market, people, supplier and partner, and operational and financial performance results.

7.3 All results have targets and trends which are three years or more.

7.4 Absolute results are high relative to competitors or industry standards.

7.5 Results consistently meet or exceed targets.

7.6 There is clear linkage of results to approach and deployment.

7.7 Adverse trends are explained and corrective action, already taken or planned, can be demonstrated.

7.8 There are comparisons done with benchmarks within the industry and across industries, as the organization search to learn from the best.

7.9 The organization demonstrates best-in-class results in some or most of its key indicators.

12.8 The SQA Scoring System

i) Introduction

The SQA evaluation process is a structured, analytical method for evaluating an organization's performance system. A three-dimensional scoring system is used to look at the approach taken by an organization to improve performance, the deployment of that approach through all operations and the results achieved both within the organization and with its customers.

ii) Scoring Guidelines

The definitions of the three evaluation dimensions and the requirements associated with them are given below:

o Approach

"Approach" refers to how an organization addresses the criteria requirements (the method(s) used). The factors used to evaluate approach include the following:

- Extend to which methods, tools and techniques are appropriate for the requirements.
- Extend to which methods, tools and techniques are effective.
- Degree to which the approach is systematic, integrated and consistently applied and based upon information that is objective and reliable.
- Evidence of innovation, including significant and effective adaptations of approaches used in other applications or types of business.

o Deployment

"Deployment" refers to the extent to which the organization's approach is applied to all requirements of the award criteria. The factors used to evaluate deployment include the following:

- Appropriate and effective use of the approach in key operational areas.

- Appropriate and effective use of the approach in interactions with customers, employees, suppliers/partners of goods and services and the public.

o Results

"Results" refers to the outcomes in achieving the purposes given in the award criteria. The factors used to evaluate results include the following:

- Current performance levels.
- Performance levels relative to appropriate comparisons and/or benchmarks.
- Rate, breath and importance of performance improvements.
- Linkages of result measures to key performance requirements identified in the Organization Profile and Approach/Deployment criteria items.

SCORE	EVALUATION DIMENSION		
	APPROACH	DEPLOYMENT	RESULTS
0-19%	♦ Some form of approach exists but it is reactive and not systematic	♦ Approach is deployed to few functional/operational areas of the organization	♦ Poor results ♦ Improvement trends and/or good performance level in few areas of importance to the organization ♦ Results not reported for most areas of importance to the organization
20-39%	♦ Direction for approach is defined ♦ Beginning of a planned and prevention based approach	♦ Approach is deployed to some major functional/ operational areas of the organization	♦ Improvement trends and/or good performance level in some major areas of importance to the organization ♦ Early stages of obtaining comparative information ♦ Results reported for most areas of importance to the organization
40-59%	♦ A sound, effective approach is in place with evidence of prevention activities ♦ Approach is aligned with basic organizational needs identified in other criteria categories	♦ Approach is deployed to most major functional/ operational areas of the organization	♦ Improvement trends and/or current performance level are good in most major areas of importance to the organization ♦ Favourable comparisons with external organization and/or benchmarks in some areas ♦ Results address most key customer, market and process requirements

SCORE	EVALUATION DIMENSION		
	APPROACH	DEPLOYMENT	RESULTS
60-79%	◆ A proven and well-defined approach which is prevention based with evidence of refinement through learning and improvement ◆ Approach is well-integrated with organizational needs identified in other criteria categories	◆ Approach is deployed to all major functional/operational areas of the organization ◆ Practised consistently by all levels	◆ Current performance levels are good to excellence in all major areas of importance to the organization ◆ Improvement trends are sustained in most areas ◆ Favourable comparisons with external organization and/or benchmarks in key areas ◆ Results address key customer, market and process requirements
80-100%	◆ Exceptionally well defined, innovative approach ◆ Approach is accepted as best practice in the field ◆ Approach is fully integrated with organizational needs identified in other criteria categories	◆ Approach is deployed to all functional/operational areas within and outside the organization ◆ Practised consistently by all levels	◆ Current performance levels are excellent in most areas of importance to the organization ◆ Excellent improvement trends and/or excellent sustained ◆ Excellent comparisons with external organization and/or benchmarks in most areas ◆ Results fully address all customer, market and process requirements

12.9 The 2017 Business Excellence Framework

The Singapore Business Excellence Framework (BEF) is reviewed and enhanced biannually to reflect the dynamic operating environment and changing management priorities. The enhancements include placing customers at the core of the business strategy, a stronger call for leadership with vision and integrity, a greater emphasis on harnessing innovative and productive capabilities across the organisation, and anticipating the future for sustained growth.

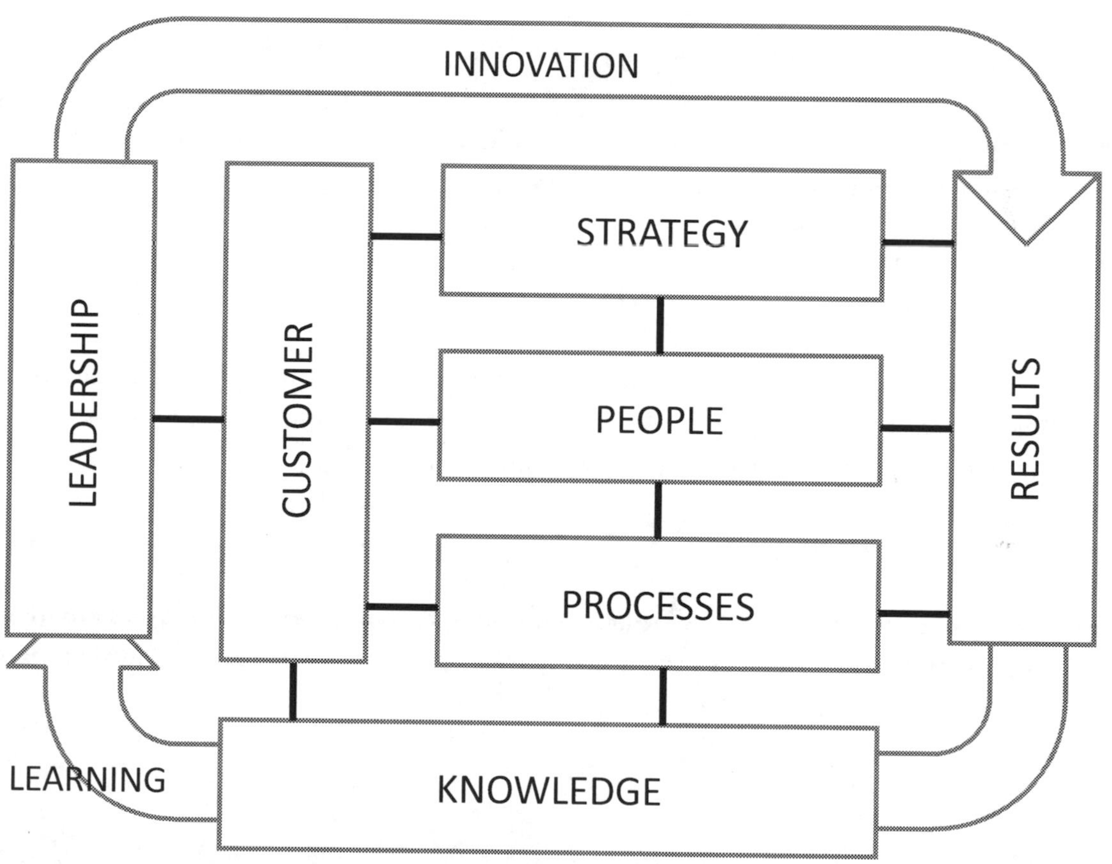

i) Attributes of Excellence

a) Leading with Vision and Integrity

Leaders inspire with their vision and values. They are steadfast in their principles but flexible in the details. They co-create the future with stakeholders and set the direction for achieving excellence.

b) Creating Value for Customers

Value is created when organisations know their customers intimately. They understand the complexity of their evolving needs and expectations and enhance the customer experience through quality offerings.

c) Driving Innovation and Productivity

Innovative organisations succeed not by imitation but by re-invention. Employees are passionate about innovation, committed to improvements and processes are highly effective and efficient.

d) Developing Organisational Capability

Future-ready organisations embrace new knowledge and technologies to keep abreast of global trends. They strengthen internal capabilities and knowledge sharing to identify opportunities for growth and improve decision-making.

e) Valuing People and Partners

Valuing people and partners creates a culture of empowerment. Employees are highly skilled and deliver high performance. Organisations build strong partnerships for shared ownership and achievement of goals.

f) Managing with Agility

Competition demands organisations to execute with consistency and respond to changes with agility. This requires flexibility in their operations to manage change and skills in assessing rewards and risks.

g) Sustaining Outstanding Results

High performing organisations are poised for market leadership and growth. They achieve outstanding financial and customer results while meeting the interests of employees and other stakeholders. They balance short-term gains and long-term returns.

h) Adopting an Integrated Perspective

An integrated perspective promotes a culture of alignment internally and with external partners. It reaps synergies from optimising linkages among core functions.

Anticipating the Future

High performing organisations anticipate and invest for the future. Leaders are committed to responsible and sustainable business practices. Understanding and balancing these priorities provide key stakeholders and customers with confidence in the organisations' sustainability.

ii) Key characteristics of the framework criteria

a) The criteria are non-prescriptive

The criteria are made up of performance-oriented requirements which are non-prescriptive. They do not describe how an organisation is to be managed or organised. Instead, the focus is on outcomes derived by adopting appropriate methods, tools or techniques, the selection of which may depend on many factors such as the organisation's size, type, stage of development and capabilities.

b) The criteria are comprehensive

The criteria address all internal and external requirements of an organisation, including how all processes are managed with internal and external stakeholders, customers, employees and partners. Existing and new or evolving strategies may be described when addressing the same set of criteria requirements.

c) The criteria emphasise learning cycles

The criteria encourage learning and improvement cycles in all parts of an organisation. The cycles generally include four stages: strategising or planning, execution of plans, assessment of progress and improvements based on assessment findings.

d) The criteria emphasise alignment

The criteria support a systems perspective to maintain alignment of goals within the organisation. This is achieved through understanding the cause-effect linkages among the criteria, and connecting strategies and measures that reinforce overall organisational goals. These strategies and measures drive overall performance.

e) The criteria support goal-based diagnosis

The criteria and the scoring guidelines form a two-part diagnostic (assessment) system. The criteria are a set of performance oriented requirements and the scoring guidelines spell out the dimensions (approach, deployment and results) used to assess an organisation. An assessment thus provides the organisation with a profile of the strengths and areas for improvement relative to the criteria requirements. This diagnostic assessment is a useful management tool that goes beyond most performance reviews.

iii) The Holistic Business Excellence Standard

It provides organisations with a holistic model for business management and it examines seven categories, i.e. Leadership, Customers, Strategy, People, Processes, Knowledge and Results with their respective criteria.

Criteria

1. LEADERSHIP (120 points)

The Leadership category focuses on the organisation's leadership, mission, vision and values, governance system as well as responsibility to the community and the environment

Excellence Indicators

Senior leaders have developed a clear vision, mission and set of values which drive excellence and they personally exemplify the values

- Senior leaders have developed a clear vision, mission and set of values which drive excellence and they personally exemplify the values.
- Senior leaders are personally involved in communicating the organisation's directions to key stakeholders and in engaging them for regular feedback
- Senior leaders drive the organisation's performance and engage key stakeholders to contribute to such efforts
- Senior leaders advocate an organisational culture which embraces organisational change, and employees are empowered to innovate and take responsible risks
- Senior leaders role model desired behaviours and are committed to grooming future leaders for organisational sustainability
- Employees are committed to the organisation's mission and vision, and demonstrate the values in their work
- The organisation has a well-defined corporate governance system to ensure business continuity and risk management, as well as accountability and transparency that is consistent with statutory and regulatory requirements or guidelines
- The organisation has well-defined policies and programmes to contribute to the sustainable development of the community and environment which it operates

1.1 Senior Leadership (50 points)

How senior leaders guide the organisation to achieve and sustain excellence

Describe how the organisation's senior management:

a) Develops the organisation's mission, vision and values, and communicates them to key stakeholders
b) Engages key stakeholders to drive the organisation's performance
c) Acts as role models and grooms future leaders

1.2 Organisation Culture (40 points)

How the organisation develops a culture that is consistent with its values, and encourages learning, innovation as well as the achievement of strategic goals

Describe how the organisation:

a) Develops a culture that supports the organisation's mission, vision and values to drive growth
b) Translates values into desired employee behaviours to enable innovation, learning and achieve the organisation's goals learning, innovation and the achievement of strategic goals
c) Embraces organisational change for sustainability

1.3 Corporate Governance and Social Responsibility (30 points)

How the organisation maintains a governance system that practises good corporate citizenship, protects the interests of stakeholders and fulfils its responsibility to the community and the environment it operates in

Describe how the organisation:

a) Establishes a governance system to ensure accountability and transparency
b) Implements policies and involves stakeholders to contribute to the community and the environment

2. CUSTOMERS (100 points)

The Customers category focuses on how the organisation understands market and customer requirements, and future trends to build relationships with customers and create superior customer experiences

Excellence Indicators

- The organisation places customers at the core of its business model and culture
- The organisation uses various channels (e.g. market intelligence, focus groups, frontline employees, surveys) to identify opportunities and enhance its value proposition

- Markets and customers are segmented to determine and address specific requirements to differentiate customer offerings and enhance customer satisfaction
- Customer requirements and expectations are incorporated into the strategic development and implementation processes
- The organisation engages customers to co-create and improve the customer experience
- Customer-contact employees are well-trained and able to answer customers' queries or resolve their issues effectively to ensure a positive customer experience. Issues and feedback from customers are tracked and used to prompt improvement plans
- Customer satisfaction is monitored through different channels (e.g. customer surveys, feedback forms, complaints and compliments) to increase customer loyalty

2.1 Customer Requirements (30 points)

How current market and customer requirements are determined and future needs are anticipated.

Describe how the organisation:

a) Segments markets and customers and understands their current and future requirements
b) Incorporates market and customer requirements into the strategic plans

2.2 Customer Experience (40 points)

How the organisation engages customers to co-create products, services or experience, improve customer loyalty and enhance customer experience

Describe how the organisation:

a) Incorporates customer expectations in designing touch points, products, processes and services
b) Ensures customer feedback is resolved and analysed

c) Provides ease of access for customers to seek assistance and information to enhance the customer experience
d) Sets performance standards at customer touch points to ensure consistent service delivery

2.3 Customer Satisfaction (30 points)

How the organisation determines and improves customer satisfaction

Describe how the organisation:

a) Determines and improves customer satisfaction for various customer segments
b) Determines current and future drivers of customer satisfaction
c) Incorporates customer insight and feedback into the strategic improvement plans

3. STRATEGY (80 points)

The Strategy category focuses on the development and implementation of strategic plans based on the organisation's external environment and internal capabilities. The plans should address current and future challenges as well as the organisation's mission and vision

Excellence Indicators

- The strategy is systematically developed based on the external environment (e.g. customer feedback, market intelligence, industry trends), internal capabilities (e.g. data on operational performance, quality indicators) and with inputs from stakeholders
- The long- and short-term goals and plans are comprehensive, quantifiable and forward-looking
- The strategy development process produces an overall business plan, and goes beyond a financial or budget plan. The process is robust and responsive to changing needs
- The strategy implementation process involves cascading plans to all levels, and translating corporate goals into department and individual goals. Relevant and well-defined indicators are identified to track the achievement of the plans and goals

3.1 Strategy Development (40 points)

How the organisation develops a strategy and determines strategic goals

Describe how the organisation:

a) Determines organisational challenges and anticipates external changes and risks
b) Develops long and short-term strategies to achieve organisational goals
c) Engages key stakeholders in the strategy development process

3.2 Strategy Implementation (40 points)

How strategies are translated into long- and short-term action plans

Describe how the organisation:

a) Develops and implements long- and short-term action plans
b) Manages organisational risks associated with plans
c) Allocates resources in a timely manner to achieve strategic goals
d) Engages key stakeholders in the strategy implementation process
e) Measures performance against plans and targets

4. PEOPLE (90 points)

The People category focuses on how the potential of employees is effectively harnessed to achieve excellence

Excellence Indicators

- Human Resource (HR) plans support the organisation's strategic goals. The plans cover areas such as talent management and retention as well as employee recruitment, engagement, satisfaction and development
- There are talent management plans and programmes to groom future leaders at all levels
- The learning and development needs of employees are identified and effectively addressed to drive organisational productivity and personal growth

- The organisation understands the contribution of the employees to the organisation's success, their needs and expectations, and how best to care for them
- The organisation encourages and measures employee participation and engagement to ensure high levels of satisfaction
- There is a performance management system that effectively measures, recognises and rewards high performance and innovative behaviours

4.1 Human Resource Planning (30 points)

How the organisation develops HR plans to achieve strategic goals and ensures high performance of employees

Describe how the organisation:

a) Anticipates HR needs and develops HR plans and policies which are aligned to strategic goals and organisational values
b) Establishes a recruitment and selection process to meet organisational needs
c) Identifies and grooms employees for high performance

4.2 Employee Learning and Development (20 points)

How the learning and development of employees result in higher productivity and personal growth

Describe how the organisation:

a) Engages employees to identify current and new competencies required to achieve strategic goals
b) Provides learning and development opportunities to employees to achieve organisational and personal growth

4.3 Employee Engagement and Well-Being (20 points)

How the organisation engages employees, and enhances their well-being and satisfaction to improve organisational health and performance

Describe how the organisation:

a) Supports individual and team participation to achieve organisational goals
b) Develops a work environment that enhances employee health and well-being
c) Measures employee satisfaction, engagement and well-being

4.4 Employee Performance and Recognition (20 points)

How the employee performance management and recognition systems encourage employees to achieve high performance and productivity as well as cultivate work behaviours that support innovation

Describe how the organisation:

a) Supports high performance, productive and innovative behaviours to achieve organisational goals
b) Reinforces desired behaviours and organisational values
c) Rewards and recognises employees to achieve organisational goals

5. PROCESSES (90 points)

The Processes category focuses on the management of key and support processes to achieve the organisation's strategic goals

Excellence Indicators

- The organisation has a systematic process to acquire, evaluate and implement creative ideas from all sources. Innovative ideas are evaluated and implemented to create value
- Improvements are made to the innovation and design processes to shorten cycle time, improve design quality and reduce costs
- The organisation's key processes have clear objectives and targets (e.g. cycle time, quality level) which are linked to organisational goals. They are regularly reviewed to ensure they meet performance standards or targets
- External parties (e.g. customers, suppliers, business partners) are involved in key aspects of the design process (e.g. giving inputs, design review, product/ service reviews)

- There is a system to analyse root causes, take prompt corrective action and prevent future re-occurrence when a process fails to meet specified standards or targets
- The organisation identifies and selects its suppliers and partners who support the organisation's strategy
- The organisation proactively ensures that suppliers have the capability and capacity to meet its requirements (e.g. supplier audits, supplier rating and certification system)

5.1 Innovation Capabilities (30 points)

How the organisation harnesses innovation to design new products and services as well as their related production and delivery systems

Describe how the organisation:

a) Develops and implements innovative ideas to create value
b) Involves key stakeholders in generating and implementing innovative ideas and solutions

5.2 Process Management (30 points)

How production, delivery and support processes for products and services are managed

Describe how the organisation:

a) Manages key and support processes to meet customer and operational requirements
b) Drives process improvement to enhance productivity and achieve higher organisational performance
c) Sustains key processes in times of emergencies to ensure business continuity

5.3 Supplier and Partner Management (30 points)

How key suppliers and partners for the production and delivery of products and services are managed

Describe how the organisation:

a) Identifies and manages key suppliers and partners to achieve organisational goals
b) Engages key suppliers and partners to co-create products and services

6. KNOWLEDGE (70 points)

The Knowledge category focuses on how the organisation harnesses information for learning, planning and decision-making, which includes competitive analysis and benchmarking. This helps the organisation to determine performance and drive improvement and innovation for superior performance

Excellence Indicators

- Relevant information is selected and used to support planning, decision-making, and track performance relative to the strategic goals
- There is an effective approach for collecting and managing information (e.g. business development and financial growth) for strategy development and performance improvement
- There are systems to capture information and knowledge, which are shared with stakeholders and are used for organisational learning and value creation
- There are robust systems to ensure the accuracy, reliability and accessibility of information
- There is a systematic process to analyse comparative data and information to drive performance improvement
- Information and knowledge used for performance measurement and planning cover all result areas including customer results, financial and market results, people results and operational results
- Competitive analysis and benchmarking of best practices are used to set "stretch" goals and drive superior performance

6.1 Knowledge Management (35 points)

How knowledge is generated from information collected, and used to create value for the organisation

Describe how the organisation:

a) Collects and manages information for strategy development, decision-making and organisational learning
b) Ensures the accuracy, accessibility and security of information

6.2 Analytics for Performance Management (35 points)

How the organisation leverages on analytics for decision-making, performance management, organisational learning and improvement

Describe how the organisation:

a) Leverages on knowledge and information to create new value
b) Uses comparative and benchmarking knowledge to improve performance

7. RESULTS (450 points)

The Results category focuses on the organisation's performance in key areas. This includes qualitative and quantitative results, as well as comparative data and competitive analysis. The indicators should go beyond current levels to include relevant indicators of future success

Excellence Indicators

- There are key performance indicators which track customer, financial and market, people and operational results
- The indicators are linked to the organisation's strategic goals. They include both actual results and projections to demonstrate organisational sustainability
- There are trends which show that the organisation consistently meets or exceeds targets
- Comparisons are carried out within the industry and across industries, and the results indicate high performance relative to competitors or industry standards
- There are reasons provided for adverse trends and improvement actions have been taken or planned for

7.1 Customer Results (110 points)

Area to address:

a) Customer satisfaction and experience
b) Product and service performance

Different market and customer segments should be addressed

Examples (may be quantitative and qualitative):

- Customer satisfaction, loyalty and overall experience
- Customer feedback
- Customer's overall assessment of products/ services
- Customer awards
- Net promoter score/mystery audit results
- Other relevant indicators on customer relationships

Related sub-category: 2.1-2.3

7.2 Financial and Market Results (120 points)

Area to address:

a) Financial performance, including financial results and economic value
b) Marketplace performance, including growth and market share, position and acceptance

Competitors and industry standards should be considered

Examples (may be quantitative and qualitative):

Aggregate measures such as revenue growth, net income and profitability, value-added, liquidity, debt-to-equity ratio, return on investment, asset utilisation, surplus, and market share

Other relevant indicators on marketplace challenges and opportunities as well as financial and market sustainability

7.3 People Results (110 points)

Area to address:

a) Human Resource Planning
b) Employee learning and development
c) Employee engagement and well-being
d) Employee performance and recognition

Different categories of employees should be addressed

Examples (may be quantitative and qualitative):

- o Employer Branding Activities
- o Recruitment Programme (e.g. cost per hire, revenue per employee)
- o Engagement levels
- o Training and development levels and expenditure
- o Talent development programmes and retention rates
- o Leadership grooming programmes
- o Coaching and Mentoring programmes
- o Workplace Diversity (e.g. employee awareness, multicultural investments,
- o Employee survey and feedback, perception of practices/policies)
- o Generic factors such as safety, absenteeism, turnover, recruitment and overall satisfaction

Related sub-category: 4.1-4.4

7.4 Operational Results (110 points)

Area to address:

a) Process performance
b) Supplier's and partner's performance
c) Governance system and contribution to the community, society and the environment

Results not addressed in sub-categories 7.1, 7.2, and 7.3 which relate to the organisation's key performance requirements should be considered

Examples (may be quantitative and qualitative):

- o Relevant indicators on productivity, efficiency and innovation such as inventory turns and delivery time
- o Specific indicators on process performance
- o Compliance, audit findings
- o Contributions to environmental sustainability such as waste reduction and participation in community outreach efforts

Related sub-category: 1.3, 5.1-5.3

12.10 Case Study

i) Project Title

- A Practical Approach to Moving Towards Business Excellence

ii) Implementation Approach

- Localized and customized
- Three-phase strategic and four-step execution plans

<table>
<tr><th>TOTAL SERVICE</th><th>PHASE</th><th>STEPS</th><th>INITIATIVE</th><th>TOOLS</th></tr>
<tr><td>CONSULT</td><td rowspan="3">FIRST PHASE</td><td>FIRST STEP</td><td>To win a war, the best option is to use strategy, and the best strategic thrust is to win their heart.</td><td>HIMS®
SDMS®
HIMS-IRS™</td></tr>
<tr><td>DEVELOP</td><td rowspan="2">SECOND STEP</td><td rowspan="2">Know yourself as well as the enemy, fight a hundred battles, win a hundred victories</td><td rowspan="2">HIMS®
SDMS-PC®
HIMS-ERP™
HIMS-CRM™
HIMS-OPS™</td></tr>
<tr><td>IMPLEMENT</td></tr>
<tr><td>TRAIN</td><td>SECOND PHASE</td><td>THIRD STEP</td><td>Continuous Improvement, Sustainable Development</td><td>HOCI®
KOFK®
HIMS-QMS™
HIMS-EMS™</td></tr>
<tr><td>SUSTAIN</td><td>THIRD PHASE</td><td>SUCCESS STEP</td><td>Inculcate core values, Build Business Excellence Culture</td><td>HIMS-BEST™</td></tr>
</table>

iii) Total Service to ensure Total Customer Satisfaction

TOTAL SERVICE	IMPLEMEMTATION SCHEDULE
CONSULT	Customized service
DEVELOP	Proprietary software
IMPLEMENT	Hands-on implementation
TRAIN	Continuous improvement
SUSTAIN	Sustainable development

iv) Standard Requirements

- World Class Business Excellence Criteria

SQA Category	Weightage	Number of Indicators	Indicators covered by HIMS-BEST™
Leadership	12%	10	7.5
Planning	7%	9	8.5
Information	7%	11	11
People	10%	9	7.5
Processes	9%	10	8.5
Customers	10%	12	10
Results	45%	9	7.5
TOTAL	100%	70	60.5 (87%)

- Balance 13% Qualitative Measurement also covered by HIMS-BEST™

v) Implementation Schedule (Month)

	Activity	1	2	3	4	5	6	7	8	9	TOOLS
1	Interview all management and supervisory staff										HIMS®
2	Develop strategic deployment structure										SDMS®
3	Develop Performance Cards for all employees										SDMS-PC®
4	Review existing computer software solutions										SDMS-OPS™
5	Design integration format for data collection										SDMS-OPS™
6	Implement HIMS and SDMS modules										HIMS® SDMS®
7	Implement HOCI continuous improvement module										HOCI®
8	Implement KOFK key of the keys module										KOFK®
9	Implement HIMS-ISO Quality Management System module										HIMS-ISO™
10	Implement HIMS-IRS Incentive & Rewarding System module										HIMS-IRS™
11	HIMS-BEST implementation, user testing & feedback										HIMS-BEST™
12	Finetune and final HIMS-BEST implementation										HIMS-BEST™

- The implementation schedule shows the average time required for an organization with 100-200 employees.
- It covers the 1st phase and steps 1 and 2 of the execution plan illustrated in point ii).

vi) Estimated Benefits

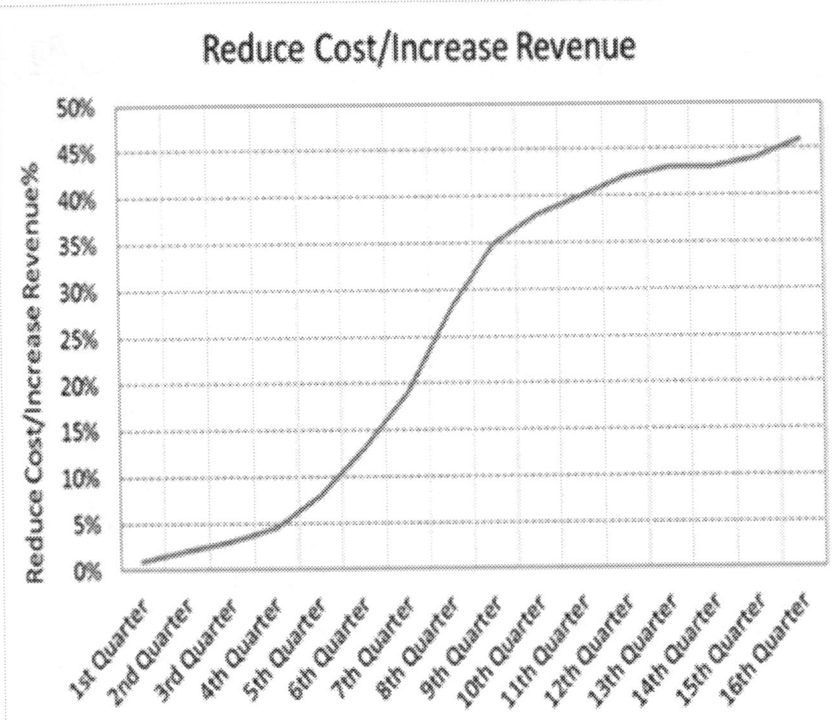

- The benefits of cost reduction and revenue increase are mainly accrued from the harnessing of the Total Factor Productivity (TFP) of the organization.
- Please refer to the case studies in chapter 2.9 which illustrate how TFP are used to enhance productivity, reduce cost and generate synergic benefits.

ACKNOWLEDGEMENT

I would like to thank the following organizations for granting me the permission to use their resources for writing some of the contents of this book.

1. Enterprise Singapore (ESG) for using Singapore Quality Award Model, and 2017 Singapore Business Excellence Framework as examples in the chapter "World Class Organization Standards". Please note that "All right reserved to ESG".

2. International Standards Organization (ISO) for using ISO9001:2015 Quality Management System and ISO14000:2015 Environmental Management System as the international standards in the chapters "ISO9000 Quality Management System" and "ISO14000 Environmental Management System. Please note that "All right reserved to ISO".

3. European Foundation of Quality Management (EFQM) for using EFQM Excellence Model as a reference to a world class organization standard. Please refer to EFQM for more details and note that "All right reserved to EFQM".

4. Union of Japanese Scientists and Engineers (JUSE) for using Japanese Deming Prize Model as a reference to a world class organization standard. Please refer to JUSE for more details and note that "All right reserved to JUSE".

5. Motorola Singapore for facilitating QC Projects from 1989 to 2013.

I would also like to thank the American Society of Quality (ASQ) for using the American Malcolm Baldridge National Quality Award as a reference to a world class organization standard. Please refer to ASQ for more details and note that "All right reserved to ASQ".

Printed in the United States
By Bookmasters